Using

Your PC

Clayton Walnum

Gerald R. Routledge

Using Your PC

Library of Congress Catalog Number: 94-69631

ISBN: 0-7897-0093-X

97 96 95   6 5 4 3 2 1

Interpretation of the printing code: The rightmost double-digit number is the year of the book's printing; the rightmost single-digit number, the number of the book's printing. For example, a printing code of 95-1 shows that the first printing of the book occurred in 1995.

Publisher: *David P. Ewing*

Associate Publisher: *Joseph B. Wikert*

Publishing Manager: *Charles O. Stewart III*

Managing Editor: *Kelli Widdifield*

Credits

Acquisitions Editor
Lori A. Angelillo

Product Director
Robin Drake

Product Development Specialists
Lisa D. Wagner
C. Kazim Haidri
Lorna Gentry
Bryan Gambrel

Production Editor
Lori Cates

Editors
Patrick Kanouse
Maureen Schneeberger
Heather Kaufman
Lisa M. Gebken
Jeff Riley
Nancy E. Sixsmith

Technical Editors
Todd Brown
Michael Watson

Novice Reviewers
Kelli Widdifield
Richard Thomas

Editorial Assistant
Michelle Williams

Acquisitions Assistants
Patricia J. Brooks
Angela Kozlowski

Book Designers
Amy Peppler-Adams
Sandra Schroeder

Cover Designer
Jay Corpus

Production Team
Claudia Bell
Chad Dressler
Aren Howell
Daryl Kessler
Elizabeth Lewis
Malinda Lowder
Steph Mineart
Kaylene Riemen
Caroline Roop
Clair Schweinler
Donna Winter
Jody York

Indexer
Kathy Venable

Composed in *ITC Century*, *ITC Highlander*, and *MCPdigital* by Que Corporation.

About the Authors

 **Clayton Walnum** has been writing about computers for a decade and has published more than 300 articles in major computer publications. He is the author of 18 books, covering such diverse topics as programming, computer gaming, and application programs. His most recent book is *Borland C++ Tips, Tricks, and Traps*, also published by Que. His earlier titles include *Creating Turbo C++ Games*, *Borland C++ Object-Oriented Programming*, *Borland C++ Power Programming*, and *QBasic for Rookies* (Que); *PC Picasso: A Child's Computer Drawing Kit* and *The First Book of Microsoft Works for Windows* (Sams); *PowerMonger: The Official Strategy Guide* (Prima); and *C-manship Complete* (Taylor Ridge Books). Mr. Walnum is a full-time freelance writer and lives in Connecticut with his wife and their three children.

Gerald R. Routledge is a Canadian consultant who specializes in computer training, course development, and technical writing. He is a consulting trainer for Data-Tech Institute, where he teaches courses in Windows and upgrading, repairing, and troubleshooting PCs. He is the owner of Routledge Computer Services in Dollard des Ormeaux, Quebec.

Acknowledgments

The authors and Que Corporation would like to thank the following people for their hard work, creativity, grace under pressure, and dedication during the genesis of this book:

Keith Aleshire, Lisa Bucki, Bill Eager, Brad Koch, Mike Miller, Joe Wikert, and Steve Schafer, for providing important technical assistance. Your expertise helped ensure this book's usefulness and broad appeal.

The outstanding and tireless development team of Robin Drake, Lisa Wagner, Chris Haidri, Lorna Gentry, and Bryan Gambrel, for ensuring that this book would measure up to the high standards set for the *Using* series. Special thanks to the rest of the Product Development group, who pitched in on other projects to free up development staff for this one.

Production Editor *nonpareil* Lori Cates, for doing an incredible job of keeping the project on track, pulling it all together, and making sure the text was consistent, accurate, and readable. Thanks also to editors Patrick Kanouse, Maureen Schneeberger, Lisa Gebken, Jeff Riley, and Heather Kaufman.

The acquisitions team of Jenny Watson, Lori Angelillo, and Fred Slone, for working closely with the authors and making sure we had a constant flow of text. Thanks also to coordinators Patty Brooks and Angela Kozlowski for keeping this project running smoothly.

The technical editing team of Todd Brown and Michael Watson, for ensuring the book's technical accuracy. Thanks also to Kelli Widdifield and Richard Thomas for a "novice review" that enabled us to fine-tune the approach and content accordingly.

For help with the book's design, thanks go to Mireles/Ross, Inc., Mike Zender of Zender & Associates, Professor Elizabeth Keyes of Rensselaer Polytechnic Institute, and Amy Peppler-Adams of designLab.

Product Series Director Charles O. Stewart III, for developing the concept of the *Using* series, and Nancy Sixsmith, who helped coordinate the rollout of the first books in the series.

The production staff, who turned the final draft on disk into this printed copy in record time—a monumental task.

Trademarks

All terms mentioned in this book that are known to be trademarks or service marks have been appropriately capitalized. Que cannot attest to the accuracy of this information. Use of a term in this book should not be regarded as affecting the validity of any trademark or service mark.

Screen reproductions in this book were created using Collage Complete from Inner Media, Inc., Hollis, New Hampshire.

We'd Like to Hear from You!

As part of our continuing effort to produce books of the highest possible quality, Que would like to hear your comments. To stay competitive, we *really* want you, as a computer book reader and user, to let us know what you like or dislike most about this book or other Que products.

You can mail comments, ideas, or suggestions for improving future editions to the address below, or send us a fax at (317) 581-4663. For the on-line-inclined, Macmillan Computer Publishing has a forum on CompuServe (type **GO QUEBOOKS** at any prompt) through which our staff and authors are available for questions and comments. In addition to exploring our forum, please feel free to contact me personally on CompuServe at 72002,2515 to discuss your opinions of this book.

Thanks in advance—your comments will help us to continue publishing the best books available on computer topics in today's market.

Robin Drake
Product Development Specialist
Que Corporation
201 W. 103rd Street
Indianapolis, Indiana 46290
USA

Contents at a Glance

{ Table of Contents }

*How can
fun be edu-
cational?*

see page 14

Chapter 3: The First Day at Home: How to Hook It All Up

The PC's comfy—now what about me?

see page 34

Chapter 4: Inside and Outside the Box

*Parts of the System Unit
see page 47*

Chapter 5: What Exactly Is a CPU?

*Pentium?
I was just
getting used
to numbers!*

see page 64

Chapter 6: Understanding Memory

Chapter 7: What You Need to Know about Monitors

Chapter 8: Disks and Disk Drives

How much can they hold?

see page 96

Chapter 9: Of Mice and Keyboards

Chapter 10: Putting Data in Its Place Using DOS

Chapter 11: Doing Stuff with Files (DOS)

Chapter 12: Doing Stuff with Disks (DOS)

It says "Bad command or file name"!

see page 128

Uh, oh. I think I just reformatted the wrong disk.

see page 148

Chapter 13: Doing Stuff with the System (DOS)

Chapter 14: How Do I Do Windows?

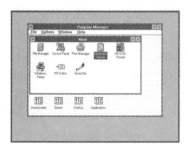

Help! I can't find that file I need!

see page 197

These screens are boring. Can I change them?

see page 210

Chapter 19: My Written Work Has to Look Good—Tell Me about Word Processors

*Making Documents
Exciting with Formatting
see page 222*

Chapter 20: I Crunch Numbers—Tell Me about Spreadsheets

Chapter 21: I Manage Lists—Tell Me about Databases

Chapter 22: I Do Slide Shows—Tell Me about Presentation Graphics Programs

If you've ever used an address book, you're already an expert at using databases.

I'm not an artist; how do I design a slide?

see page 260

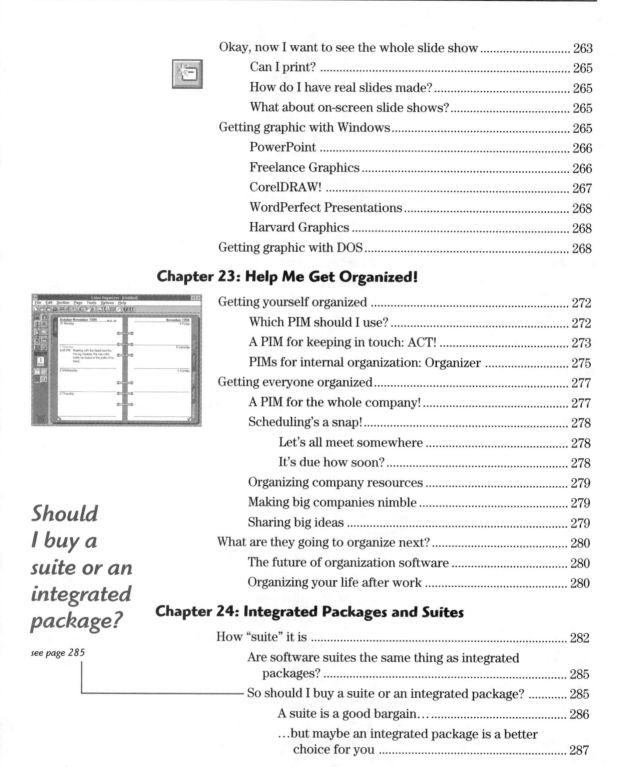

Chapter 23: Help Me Get Organized!

Chapter 24: Integrated Packages and Suites

*Should
I buy a
suite or an
integrated
package?*

see page 285

Chapter 25: CD-ROM Software, Games, and Family Software

Chapter 26: Printers and Scanners

What do I look for in a multimedia system?

see page 329

Chapter 27: Multimedia Mayhem: CD-ROMs and Sound Cards

Chapter 28: Hooking Up to the Information Superhighway with a Modem

How to download a file.

see page 339

Chapter 29: Networks: Getting Connected

Chapter 30: What Is E-Mail?

What are all those little smileys and things?

see page 360

Chapter 33: The Internet

Chapter 34: Taking Care of Your Disks and Files

*Defrag-
menting
your hard
drive.*

see page 401

Introduction

Computers used to be run by scientists or people who worked for the government. These folks wore white lab coats and didn't seem to speak English. In those days, a computer was something to respect—and even fear. In general, you just avoided computers then. You didn't have to use them, and you didn't have to care about how they worked.

Times have changed. These days, computers are on your desk, in the ATM where you get cash, even in your *car*. You can't avoid them. In fact, you probably already know more about computers than you ever thought you would. And you need to know more.

That's why we put together this book. It's for people just like you, people who use computers and need someplace to go—quickly—when a question pops up. This book assumes that you've already mastered the *really* hard things in life, like raising kids, running a business, killing crabgrass, cooking a soufflé, and maybe even programming a VCR. You're an experienced computer user but not a computer expert—nor do you want to be.

What makes this book different?

You don't need an advanced degree in engineering or computer science to read this book. In the pages that follow, every topic from the parts of a computer to finding out about the so-called information superhighway is covered in plain English. We tell you just what you need to know without all the technical mumbo-jumbo, the zillion ways to do the same thing, the mass of nonessential details. After all, you're not studying for a degree in computer science—you're trying to get some work done! You can think of this volume as the ultimate "quick-answer" book for anyone who uses a computer—at work, at home, or at school.

How do I use this book?

This isn't a textbook. You don't have to start at page 1 and read all the way to the end. It's not a mystery novel either, so if you want to skip to the last chapter first, help yourself.

You'll probably be surprised at some of the things that you can do with a computer. That's why, if you have the time, it's worth flipping through the chapters, looking at the headings, and searching out the references to the things you do at work. The people who published this book went to a lot of trouble to make sure that those interesting ideas would leap off the page and catch your attention as you browse. (And it shouldn't take that long—after all, this isn't one of those 1200-page monster books that helps you build up your biceps every time you lift it.)

This book will come in especially handy when you have a big job to do or need to know something and you're not sure where to begin.

How this book is put together

For easy reference, the text is divided into eight major parts that run the gamut from what's in your system to what kind of software is available to what the heck a BBS is. These parts are listed below with a brief summary of their contents.

Part I: Why Do You Need a Computer?

Chapter 1 explores various home and office uses for a computer. Your PC is a hard working machine, but it can also provide you with entertainment, help you communicate with the rest of the world, and even squeeze in a little fun!

Part II: What Is All This Stuff?

Chapters 2 through 9 give you a more detailed look into what makes up a computer. Illustrations show which piece of your computer is which, and what plugs in where. We explain how a CPU works, what a disk drive is for, and why you should care about any of this stuff. You even get a crash course on how to set up your computer.

Part III: How to Work and Play with DOS

You've probably heard for years about how complicated DOS is. You may even believe you're too dumb to use it. Well, Chapters 10 through 13 show you that you *can* use DOS, and you'll probably be surprised at how really easy it is. We teach you some important DOS basics, and help you to understand exactly what you're doing. Chapter 13 even shows you some *fun* things you can do with DOS!

Part IV: How to Work and Play with Windows

You probably have Windows on your computer. You may even like it already. After you read Chapters 14 through 18, though, you'll probably like Windows a *lot*—and you'll be able to do more than just play Solitaire. Step-by-step explanations of common Windows activities show you that Windows is actually intended to be *useful*, not just decorative.

Part V: What Do You Want to Do with Your PC? You'll Need Software!

Computers aren't really very useful without a good collection of software, so Chapters 19 through 25 provide a fast introduction to some of the major programs. Do you crunch numbers? Read Chapter 20 to learn about popular spreadsheet programs. Is your address book a mess? Explore the world of the Personal Information Manager in Chapter 23. Other chapters in this section provide details on word processing, databases, graphics—even educational programs and games!

Part VI: Other Cool Stuff to Buy for Your PC

Printer. CD-ROM. Scanner. Multimedia. Modem. Do you know what all this stuff is? It's the cool equipment you can add to your computer to make it more productive, or just more fun. Chapters 26 through 28 provide the details on what each of these items is good for. If you're interested, you'll even find out what to look for when you go shopping.

Part VII: Network? Internet? On-Line? More Choices

There's a wealth of information you can access with your computer just by connecting it up to some sort of network. And it doesn't have to be expensive or even very complicated. Chapters 29 through 33 give you your options, discussing everything from e-mail and CompuServe to the Internet and the information superhighway.

Part VIII: Care and Feeding of Your PC

Your computer is not unlike your car. If you don't do a little maintenance now and then, you'll eventually have problems. Chapter 34 lists some things you can do easily and quickly to keep your computer in tip-top shape.

Information that's easy to understand

This book contains a number of special elements and conventions to help you find information quickly—or skip stuff you don't want to read right now.

(Tip)

Tips either point out information often overlooked in the documentation or help you use your PC more efficiently. Some tips help you solve or avoid problems.

 **{Note}** — Notes contain additional information or "reminders" of important information you should know.

⊗<Caution> — Cautions alert you to potentially troublesome situations or activities. In general, the text will warn you of things you need to avoid doing.

②Q&A — **What are Q&A notes?**

Cast in the form of questions and answers, these notes provide you with advice on ways to avoid or solve common problems.

 Plain English, please!

These notes explain the meanings of technical **terms** or computer **jargon.** 🙶

Watch for different typefaces. Things in a `special typeface` indicate what you see on your screen. **Bold** indicates new terms that you need to know or stuff that you type. Every once in a while, you'll see <u>underlined</u> letters in Windows commands; pressing these letters is a faster way to use the commands.

Sidebars are interesting nuggets of information

Sidebars provide interesting, nonessential reading, side-alley trips you can take when you're not at the computer or when you just want some relief from "doing stuff." Here you may find more technical details, funny stories, personal anecdotes, or interesting background information.

Need more information? Try these other books

This book gives you a lot of information about how your PC works and how you can use it. As you become more comfortable with your computer, you may need a more complete reference book on DOS, Windows, or other subjects. Que has books on a large variety of subjects and in a wide range of series for different users. These are a few you may find interesting and useful:

- *Computers Illustrated*
- *Upgrading Your PC Illustrated*
- *MS-DOS 6.2 QuickStart*
- *Using MS-DOS 6.2*, Special Edition
- *Using the Internet*
- *Windows QuickStart*, 3.11 Edition
- *Windows VisiRef*, 3.11 Edition
- *Using Windows*, 3.11 Edition, Special Edition
- *Que's Computer User's Dictionary*, 5th Edition

Que also publishes multiple books on most major software products, including Microsoft Office, WordPerfect, NetWare, Lotus 1-2-3, etc. For more information on purchasing Que books, call toll-free 1-800-428-5331.

1

What Good Is a PC?

Personal computers have come a long way. What was once a novelty and status symbol is now pretty much a part of mainstream life.

In this chapter:

- What can a computer do for me?
- How can I use a computer at work?
- Is it a good idea to have a computer at home?
- What about the kids and the computer?

A **personal computer** (**PC**) can make your life easier and more enjoyable. The more you use your computer, the easier it gets— and the easier using your computer gets, the more you can do with it.

The fact is that a PC can do just about anything you can imagine. They're so popular because everybody can find at least one good use for one. My neighbor uses his as a paperweight. The rest of us probably manage to accomplish more *productive* objectives, such as writing letters or plotting a hostile financial takeover. Just spending some time playing a good computer game tends to fill more than a few lunch hours, too. A PC is a versatile machine, indeed.

Fig. 1.1
What good is your PC?
You can do productive
work or fool around
with games. You might
even find that error in
your tax form before
the IRS does.

I just want to get some work done!

This section shows you some of the many ways you can use a computer.
You'll discover word processors, spreadsheets, computer communications,
and lots of other programs to make you more productive and make your job
easier. If you don't use a computer at work, well, read this section anyway.
Most of the things people do in an office can be done at home, too.

Write it. Print it. Sell it.

A computer being used for word processing is a lot like a typewriter on
steroids. Sure, it still has a keyboard, but no typewriter ever worked like this!
A typewriter's text appears permanently on paper. Corrections are made by
tearing the paper out of the machine in frustration and throwing it across the
room. A computer's text appears on the screen; you can change it all around
by pressing a few keys. Need to change the prices on that quote? Go ahead!
Move sentences or entire paragraphs. Delete words. Change margins.

When you're sure the words are perfect, print them and sell them to a publisher. They say everyone has at least one Great American Novel in them.

We discuss the most popular word processing programs in Chapter 19, "My
Written Work Has to Look Good—Tell Me about Word Processors."

Fig. 1.2
You can't do this with a normal typewriter, but with a computer, this type of document is easy to create. Of course, if you insist, you can still type regular letters and memos!

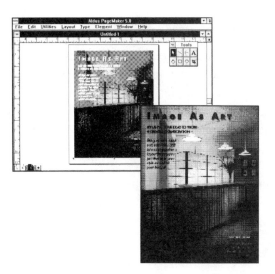

Do I need different PCs to do different things?

Not at all. Think of the PC as an eager job trainee willing to do anything you can dream up. You teach the computer to do things by loading **programs** that contain the instructions the computer will use.

These programs can help you write memos, calculate your financial standing, draw a masterful piece of artwork, or communicate with people around the world. There is a different type of program for just about any activity you can imagine.

You probably wonder why some programs tell you "for IBM PCs and compatibles only," and others say "for the Macintosh." That's because programs designed for use on IBM-compatible PCs are slightly different than programs designed to be used on Apple Macintoshes. Many popular types of programs are designed to be used on both kinds of computers. In fact, some programs like Microsoft Word or Microsoft Excel look and act identically on either the Macintosh or the PC. They just talk to the computer in a slightly different way.

You can work with any kind of program anytime you like. It only takes a second or so to switch from writing words to drawing pictures. This versatility is why so many people use a PC in some way everyday. This book shows you which type of program to use for which kind of activities, and even recommends some specific programs as the best of their type.

Calculating and crunching numbers

When it comes to numbers, computers have always been Number One. In about one second, a **spreadsheet program** can calculate hundreds of formulas and numbers representing all your business's sales projections for the next ten years. Want to see what the bottom line would be if another salesperson was hired? Change one number and wait another second while the PC calculates it for you.

We do a comparative analysis of the most popular brands in Chapter 20, "I Crunch Numbers—Tell Me about Spreadsheets."

Fig. 1.3

Spreadsheet programs make the average calculator look like something from the stone age.

Presentations with power and pizzazz

Being in business usually means communicating your ideas to other people. Whether you're sending a memo, presenting a proposal to your boss, or motivating a sales force, you need to convince people to see things your way. The faster you can do this, the more efficient and professional you appear.

When you use a computer to create a presentation, you suddenly have access to a complete graphic arts department. Combine graphs from your spreadsheets with text from your word processor. Add a dash of color, some photos, and a few fancy arrows. Before you know it, you have a professional presentation that practically sells itself.

To do all this, you use a **presentation program**. Chapter 22, "I Do Slide Shows—Tell Me about Presentation Graphics Programs," will convince you of the value of these programs.

Fig. 1.4
Presentation programs
get your point across
without putting your
audience to sleep.

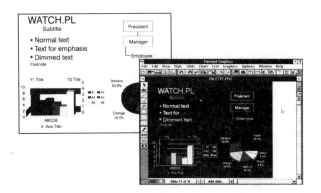

Use your computer to communicate

Most people do the majority of their work over the phone—it only makes
sense to let your computer do some of that work for you. Luckily, computers
are experts at communication, so the rest of the business world can be as
close as the phone plug in the wall.

Up-to-the-minute stock market quotes, news of the day, and even computer
technical support are all available to the PC that's plugged in, turned on, and
tuned in. You can make airline reservations, get the latest software update
from a software company, or start a trace on that missing courier package.
Your computer can even send and receive **faxes**, usually with better quality
than an "old-fashioned" fax machine. Your computer can't do all of this stuff
without a **modem,** though. Chapter 28 tells you everything you need to know
about modems.

66 *Plain English, please!*

> A **modem** is an electronic device that translates computer information so that
> it can be sent and received over phone lines. If you want to talk
> to other computers by phone, you have to have a modem. 99

If your computer is part of a **network**, you can send documents almost
instantly to anyone else in your building. Is the Vice President of Sales out to
lunch? Send him electronic mail, and he can read it as soon as he gets back to
the office. You can even send him messages late at night and on weekends so
he'll know you're a dedicated worker. (Of course, the VP may also think you
work too slow and lead a boring life.)

66 *Plain English, please!*

A **network** is just a group of computers connected together so that they can exchange information easily and also share printers and other expensive equipment. About one-third of all computers in the world today are connected to other computers by some sort of network. 99

Fig. 1.5
A computer network is just a bunch of inter-connected computers. Not so mysterious, after all.

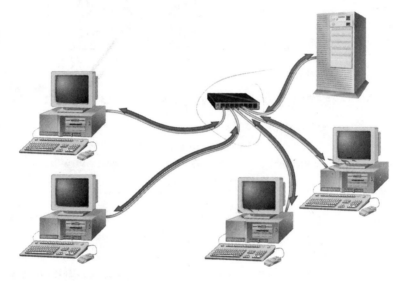

The PC at home

Sure, computers are essential at work, but they can be great at home, too. Kids *really* love 'em. There's nothing like exploring an ancient dungeon or learning to fly a plane after a long day at school.

A little added benefit to these recreational activities is that the kids become **computer-literate** and actually start using the machine for homework assignments. Never tell them this.

Adults in the house can write letters, balance the budget, track the family's roots, and more. You might even be able to fly the plane when the kids aren't looking.

Fig. 1.6
Where does all the money go? A home computer can tell you.

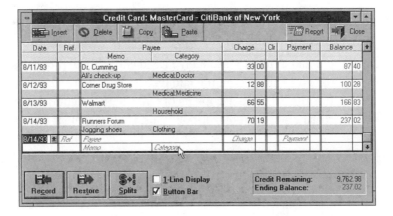

Interested in joining an on-line service? Read this.

If all that stuff about using your computer to get stock quotes and reserve airline tickets grabbed your attention, you should subscribe to something called an **on-line service**, which is a gigantic network that connects computers from all over the world. Some popular on-line services are **CompuServe**, **GEnie**, **America Online**, **Prodigy**, and **Delphi**.

To get started with an on-line service, go down to your local software store and buy a modem (the fastest you can afford). Next, pick out an on-line service startup package. The store's sales rep should be able to give you pointers on which to buy. You can also find ads for various on-line services in major computer magazines. Some services even send you free software to get you started.

Note that many modems include special membership offers from different on-line services. If the special offer is from a service you want to subscribe to, great! In any case, read the fine print! Many "free" offers end up costing you money every month unless you call and cancel your membership.

But although the software may be free, keep in mind that the service isn't. Most on-line services charge a basic monthly fee (around $10) for a certain amount of on-line time. If you go over the time or use features that cost extra, you can end up spending a lot of money. In spite of the cash outlay, though, joining an on-line service is a great way to expand your computer's usefulness.

How can fun be educational?

A computer can be a veritable school in a box. Your local computer store is crammed full of reasonably priced educational programs. There's something for every member of the family, from the toddler right up to the adults. My favorite is the encyclopedia of dinosaurs. It's got detailed color pictures, roaring sounds—the works! (Plus, it's less violent than *Jurassic Park*.)

- Little kids can have fun with computer games that teach reading, math, and problem-solving skills.

- Older kids can use the computer to dig through an electronic encyclopedia, write up their homework, or run their own computerized city. A note to parents: If the high cost of home encyclopedias has kept you from buying, check out the rock-bottom price for a 20-volume set that comes on one compact disc!

Fig. 1.7

Kids can sharpen many skills by using educational programs on a home computer.

- What about you? Interested in learning a new language? Maybe you'd rather study up on classic art and literature, explore the far reaches of the universe, or learn to solve quadratic equations. A home computer puts all this information at your fingertips.

Games, games, games!

Most computer people hate to admit it, but recreational computing is as popular as business or educational computing. If you need proof, just walk into a software store and count the number of games on the shelf. Sure, computers are sophisticated machines that can handle Herculean calculations, but what happens when this tremendous power is harnessed for *fun*? You get a heck of a LOT of fun.

A computer can take you to worlds filled with exciting challenges, fearsome creatures, and mind-numbing puzzles. Adventure and role-playing games, for example, plunge you into computerized fiction where you control the story through your on-screen character. Strategy games, on the other hand, sharpen your wits as you plan a military campaign or defend a castle from attack. Monopoly was never like this.

Fig. 1.8
Got your sword ready? You'll need it as you make your way through strange and dangerous fantasy worlds.

Let's not forget hobbies

Hobbyists of all types are discovering the computer as a valuable tool that adds a new dimension to their work. You can keep records of baseball cards or stamp collections, compose music, organize a bowling league, play chess with someone in another country, or get involved in a fantasy football league. Some people have even been known to computerize the record-keeping in professional football pools.

Whether you're into cooking, home design, landscaping, or model railroading, hobbies can become even more enjoyable when the home computer gets in on the action.

The Pieces and How They Fit

This chapter explains how the parts of your PC work and why you have them. It's much easier than taking one apart (and potentially less expensive).

A few years ago, I showed an older lady how to take a PC apart and put it back together again. As each part came out of the box, we discussed its purpose and set it aside. Then she put it all back together again. She did this to overcome a fear of PCs. She had been a typist for 25 years and her typewriter had just been replaced with a computer. Being an overly sensitive man, her boss had said to learn it or retire.

I don't recommend that anybody start taking their PC apart. Margaret was a special case who couldn't learn about it until she knew it wouldn't bite her. Instead, just read this chapter. When you know the pieces of the puzzle, all other PC concepts in this book will be easier to understand.

That big box is where the action is

You might want to think of your PC's main box, or **system unit**, as an orchestra pit filled with different musical instruments. Here's the best part of this analogy: *You* get to be the conductor. All the instruments in your orchestra work together to convert your directions (called **input**) into a new musical masterpiece (called **output**). No one part is more important than another. They all depend on each other in some way. Here's the list of instruments you'll generally find in the PC orchestra:

- A floppy drive (sometimes an *ensemble* of two)
- A hard drive
- Expansion slots
- A power supply
- A motherboard
- Memory
- A CPU

 Plain English, please!

Input is information, or data, that flows into your computer. **Output** is information that flows out of the computer after the computer has done something to it in some way. If you ask a computer to add two and two, the twos are input. Whatever answer comes out is output. The whole point of having a computer is to turn input into output.

Inside the box

Expansion slots
Expansion slots allow you to add adapter cards that add capabilities to your computer. Speakers, CD–ROM drives, and telephone wires all plug into devices that sit in these slots.

Memory chips
These computer chips hold programs and data while you're using them. Since they turn off when the PC is turned off, we use the disk drives as permanent storage.

Power supply
The power supply converts electricity from the wall into lower voltages that are more suitable for the computer. It also has a fan that helps keep all the parts cool.

Motherboard
Every computer has a motherboard, which holds most of the electronics that make a computer work.

CPU
The letters stand for Central Processing Unit. This is a computer chip that lives on the motherboard and controls what goes on inside the computer.

Floppy drives
This is where floppy disks are shuttled in and out. The drives record and play back information from the floppy disks, using them as a storage location.

Hard drive
Contains a non–removable disk that stores information you use a lot. The hard drive is faster and holds more information than a floppy disk, so it serves as the main storage facility.

The floppy disk drive: Where all the disks go

The floppy drive (see fig. 2.1) works like a tape recorder except that you use a magnetic floppy disk instead of magnetic tape. Any work that you do can be **saved** onto a **floppy disk** (often just called a **disk**). Later, it can be **read** or played back into the computer so you can work on it some more.

Floppy disks are most often used to carry information from computer to computer. They are also pretty handy for making **backup copies** of information stored on the hard disk.

Fig. 2.1

Disk drives hold floppy disks, which carry information from computer to computer.

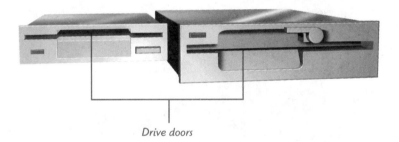

Drive doors

The hard disk is for permanent storage

The hard drive contains a **hard disk** that is mounted permanently inside the computer. Think of the hard disk as a really big floppy that you can never misplace. You need a hard disk because it is a *permanent* place to store your work. Any letters you type are held in computer memory while you work on them, but that just fades away (taking your work with it) every time the PC is turned off. By saving your work to disk, you can always get it back again. All the information that you need on floppy drives and hard disks is stored in Chapter 8, "Disks and Disk Drives."

Now you'll finally know what a "motherboard" is!

Your computer's motherboard is simply the "Mother of all Boards" in the PC. It is the biggest circuit board in the box and everything else connects into it in some way. On the motherboard is your computer's memory (sort of an electronic scratch pad) where most of the work gets done. The CPU chip

(Central Processing Unit) also plugs in there. It performs calculations and directs traffic as information flows from component to component. Chapter 5, "What Exactly Is a CPU?," and Chapter 6, "Understanding Memory," will demystify CPUs and computer memory.

Why do I need expansion slots?

Your computer's expansion slots are designed to accept special plug-in **adapter cards** that add to the PC's features. Almost anything that you can attach to a PC must connect to an **adapter card** that plugs into one of the expansion slots. For example, your computer probably has adapter cards that provide connections for the printer, the monitor, or the mouse. Without the **video adapter** sitting in an expansion slot, there'd be no place to plug your monitor into the PC! Collectively, the expansion slots are usually called the **bus**, and we take it for a ride in Chapter 4, "Inside and Outside the Box."

The monitor: A window into your computer

Besides being the most obvious part of a PC, the monitor is also your main source of output information from the computer. If you type something wrong, you can see the mistake on the screen. You can correct it, too—and make any other editorial or layout changes before finally sending a job to the printer.

Messages that appear on the screen give you feedback about whether or not a command was successful. The PC will even use the screen to tell you when it's not feeling well. See Chapter 7, "What You Need to Know about Monitors," for details on picking the best monitor.

You can guess what the keyboard is for

Just as the monitor is the PC's standard output device, the keyboard is your usual input device. Obviously, you type with it—using about 26 of the hundred-odd keys that are found there. The rest of the keys are used for giving commands, editing work, or moving around on the screen.

The far right of the keyboard consists of a **numeric keypad** where people who like calculators can enter numbers. The numbers across the top of the keyboard will do the same thing if you are more comfortable typing numbers like a typist. Maybe we don't need all these keys after all. We typed up the whole story on keyboards in Chapter 9, "Of Mice and Keyboards."

Think of the mouse as an electronic hand

Using a mouse is like using a remote-control hand to move things around inside your screen. If you stuck your real hand in there, you'd probably get electrocuted. As you push the mouse around on your desktop, the pointer on your screen duplicates those movements. Pressing the buttons on the mouse makes the pointer press buttons on the screen. You can use it to select from **menus** of commands—and to draw pictures, too.

The printer takes your stuff from computer to paper

Every year, someone says that the paperless office is coming. But every year, the sales of printers skyrocket as we strive to produce fancier, bigger reports in less time than before. There's just something very reassuring about holding a printed report in your hand. You can pay anywhere from $100 to $10,000 for a computer printer today, and the choices are constantly increasing. Thankfully, the costs are decreasing as well. Chapter 26, "Printers and Scanners," explains the different models and capabilities.

Speakers, modems, and other luxuries

I went to a car dealership last month and was overwhelmed by all the expensive options that were available. Quadraphonic sound, electric seats, cruise control, a compact disc player, and a built-in cellular phone nearly tempted me—until I saw the price tag. I settled for the standard model.

Computer stores will work the same magic on you if you're not careful. They display shelf after shelf of colorful packages that scream out, "Buy me!" Granted, some of these options that you can add to your system are pretty useful. Others are just plain fun. If you feel compelled to go shopping, bring your bank card. Remember that your PC worked just fine before you fell prey to the bells and whistles. My car still gets me around even if it doesn't have mag wheels.

Add a little sound to your system

Speakers and a sound card, for example, allow your computer to play digital sound effects and music. If you're going to go "hi-fi," you better get a CD-ROM player, too. Besides using it to read through that digital encyclopedia, you can play your favorite stereo CD at the same time. These are called **multimedia devices**, and we tell all in Chapter 27.

And you might want a modem

If you're stranded on the shoulder of the information superhighway, get into the fast lane with a high-speed modem that connects your computer to the phone lines. Modems let your computer chat with (or scream at!) other computers that are equipped with modems. With the right programs and about three months of experience, you'll be burning up the wires. Modems and communication are explained in Chapters 28 to 33.

Protect your equipment, your data, and yourself

As long as we're talking about burning up the wires, are you protected against lightning strikes and power surges? Buy your computer a surge suppressor (see Chapter 3). Since you're protecting your hardware, how about a tape backup unit to protect your data? Since you're protecting your data, how about an ergonomic chair to protect your back (see Chapter 3)?

The soft side of computing

All the stuff we've talked about so far is called **hardware**, the computer equipment that you can actually touch, drop, and break. **Software**, on the other hand, consists of the programs that you load into your computer, and this is a primary concept for all users to understand. Software can't be seen or touched by humans because it is simply a set of instructions for the computer to follow.

Wait a minute, here. A disk would be software then, right? Sorry. A disk is strictly storage. It's a way to store software—just like a CD stores music. Instructions on the CD tell the CD player what sounds to make through the speakers. Software on a disk tells the computer what to show on the screen or print on the printer.

There are two kinds of software: **system software** and **application software**. System software performs your computer's housekeeping chores and keeps everything running smoothly. Application software is the stuff you use to get real work done. **DOS** is an example of system software, while a word processor like WordPerfect is an example of application software.

 **{Note}** In this book, and elsewhere in the world, *application software* is generally just called a *program*.

Software that works with the hardware

Without *some* kind of software, your computer would be little more than an expensive paperweight. Fortunately, something called an **operating system** (also called **system software**) keeps tabs on your computer hardware and makes all the components work in unison. When you first turn on your computer, it's the operating system that makes all those panel lights blink and gets everything going.

Unlike most programs that you deal with, you don't have to give any commands to load the operating system (probably DOS) into the computer. This is done automatically whenever the machine is turned on. Once DOS is on the screen, you can start using whatever program you want to work with that day.

GUIs are like operating systems, but with a pretty face

GUIs (graphical user interfaces) make an operating system easier to understand and use. The two most common PC GUIs are Windows and OS/2. Of the two, Windows is currently the more popular. It pretties up DOS with a lot of graphics, push-buttons, and pop-up messages. It's sort of an operating system with lipstick, matching pumps, and a handbag. Like most GUIs, Windows is at its best when you use a mouse. In either case, the GUI makes it easier to take advantage of the underlying power of the operating system.

To give you some idea of how helpful software like Windows can be, take a look at figure 2.2, which shows a normal PC's screen after turning on the computer. Not much to look at. No hints about what to do, either. Now, look at figure 2.3, which shows the same computer with Windows. Now we're getting somewhere!

What operating system do you have?

Operating systems vary from computer to computer, depending on the type of computer and the type of application the user wants to run. Different operating systems have different abilities.

Most IBM-compatible computers these days run DOS as their operating system. DOS stands for **Disk Operating System**. DOS systems can only support one user and one application at a time. However, adding Windows to DOS allows DOS to use more than one application at a time.

There's also a good possibility that your computer runs a type of operating system called a **graphical user interface**. (Don't ever actually say this. Say **GUI** instead but pronounce it *gooey*.) A GUI operating system replaces all the text you see on a DOS screen with lots of little pictures. You give commands to the operating system by clicking buttons and choosing menu commands with your mouse. Windows is considered a GUI, although it is not *really* an operating system because DOS is still hidden back there somewhere. The operating system **OS/2**, which is also a GUI, works much like Windows, except it doesn't need DOS to do its thing.

Because this is a book about IBM-compatibles, you'll be learning about DOS and Windows, which are the most popular systems for IBM-compatibles. Parts III and IV of this book will show you how they work.

Fig. 2.2
This *is* how DOS looks. Kinda boring and gives few clues on what to do next.

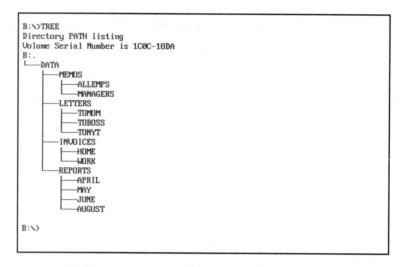

```
B:\>TREE
Directory PATH listing
Volume Serial Number is 1C0C-18DA
B:.
└───DATA
    ├───MEMOS
    │   ├───ALLEMPS
    │   └───MANAGERS
    ├───LETTERS
    │   ├───TOMOM
    │   ├───TOBOSS
    │   └───TONYT
    ├───INVOICES
    │   ├───HOME
    │   └───WORK
    └───REPORTS
        ├───APRIL
        ├───MAY
        ├───JUNE
        └───AUGUST

B:\>
```

Fig. 2.3
GUIs are easier and more fun to use than DOS and certainly easier to look at.

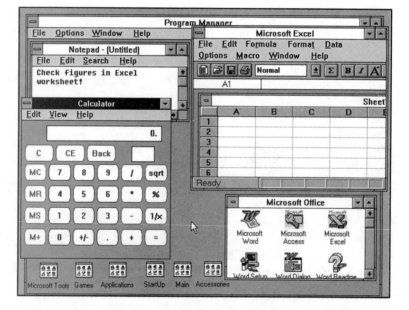

Software that works with you

If your computer had nothing more than system software, it would be about as useful as a horse with two legs. Sure, you could make the disk drives spin or the monitor light up, but that's not exactly useful work. Luckily, the world has programmers who create programs—such as word processors, spread-sheets, and games—which let you do interesting things with your computer.

You might say that you talk to the program and it talks to the operating system for you.

Here are some typical programs you may already know about:

- WordPerfect—a word processor
- Lotus 1-2-3—a spreadsheet program
- ProComm Plus—a communications program
- PC Paintbrush—a graphics program
- Wing Commander—a game
- Math Blaster—an educational game
- Quicken—a home-finance program

So where do I store all this stuff?

A computer disk is not unlike a tiny filing cabinet that stores programs and data and organizes the information so that you can get it back anytime (see fig. 2.4). What's really cool is how much information they can hold. A floppy disk can easily hold the equivalent of 1,000 typewritten pages. A hard disk can hold 200 times that or more!

Fig. 2.4
Think of the computer disk as a filing cabinet that stores and organizes information.

Later in this book, you'll learn the details of how disks work. But, for now, be aware that there are several kinds of disks, including floppy disks, hard disks, and CD-ROMs. All of them perform the same function: They provide a safe place for you to keep information until you need to use it.

Memory that forgets faster than you do

Just having a disk full of software isn't really enough to start using a computer. To use the software, you have to load it into your computer's memory. What's computer memory? Technically, it's a row of microchips on your computer's motherboard (see fig. 2.5). But from a practical viewpoint, it's more like an electronic desktop where you do your work. Just as you have to open a filing cabinet and spread your files out on your desk to start working, you get copies of your software, letters, and memos from your disk and put them into memory. That's when you can see them on the screen and start working with them. For complete information about your computer's memory, see Chapter 6.

Fig. 2.5
Your computer's memory is made up of microchips.

Now you understand why a computer needs memory. Disks, however, have a big advantage over memory: The information on a disk stays there until you erase it. The computer's memory gets blanked out the instant you turn off your computer. Good thing your brain doesn't work that way! You'd sure learn to hate mornings.

Types of computers

In this book, we talk mostly about desktop computers, which are, of course, the kind of computer that you usually see sitting on a desk. But other types of computers work similarly:

- **Laptop computers** weigh only around 10 pounds. In spite of their light weight, they include a full (although sometimes smaller) keyboard, hard drive, floppy drive, and built-in screen.

- **Notebook computers** (see fig. 2.6) are a lot like laptop computers, but are even smaller, weighing only about six or seven pounds. Still, like a laptop, a notebook computer comes with a full keyboard, floppy drive, screen, and hard drive.

Fig. 2.6

Notebook computers are light and easy to carry around.

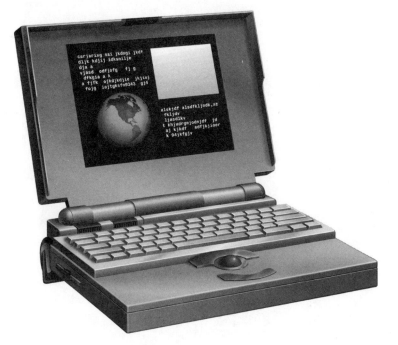

- **Palmtop computers** are the smallest of the lot but, surprisingly, often feature built-in applications like simple word processors, databases, and spreadsheets. Their tiny keyboards, however, make typing about as easy as building a ship in a bottle.

The First Day at Home: How to Hook It All Up

You're just itching to rip open the boxes and see what's inside. Be careful! There are right and wrong ways to set up a computer.

Congratulations! You're the proud owner of a brand-new, bouncing baby PC! Like any new parent, you probably took extra care bringing your bundle (or more likely, bundles) of joy home. You started up slowly at every intersection, and you went around manhole covers so the PC wouldn't get bumped and bruised. Don't feel silly—everybody does it!

Choosing a good place for your PC to live

It's important to make sure that your PC gets settled in someplace appropriate (see fig. 3.1). You can add years to your computer's life by setting the system up carefully, or subtract years by setting it up poorly.

Fig. 3.1
Careful planning of the system's location makes your work more productive and also protects the PC.

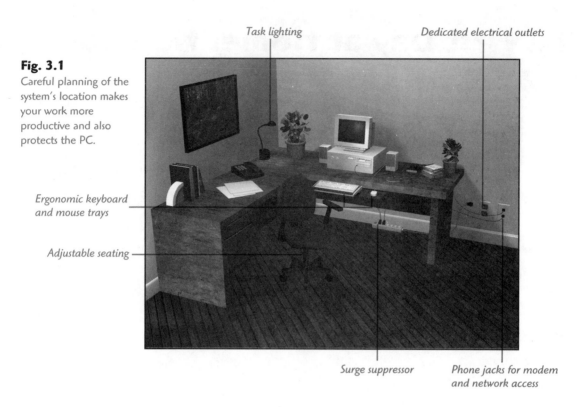

Task lighting

Dedicated electrical outlets

Ergonomic keyboard and mouse trays

Adjustable seating

Surge suppressor

Phone jacks for modem and network access

A good place to live doesn't sit on a fault line

Choose a table or desk that is sturdy and won't break under the weight of the PC, monitor, pizza crusts, and all the other things that tend to accumulate in work areas.

 **<Caution>** | Never place your computer on one of those little wheeled tables. You'll be too tempted to roll it around the room now and then, looking for the ideal spot. Assuming that the PC doesn't fall apart completely, the vibration could loosen components, or even severely damage them. For the same reason, avoid placing the PC on a filing cabinet. The shock created when you slide heavy drawers open and closed can be rough on the PC's internal components.

If you bought a printer with your system, it's wise to keep it on a different surface than the computer. Many printers shake around more than Charo does. Invest a few extra dollars and buy a separate printer stand.

A good place to live has lots of fresh air!

Your PC needs air, and lots of it. Be sure that you leave at least three inches of space all around the main box. A tiny little fan in there has the enormous task of sucking cool air through all the slots and vents to keep the machine from burning up, but the fan needs access to air outside the box.

 (Tip)

> Check periodically to make sure the fan is running and not blocked with dust. If the machine is ever quieter than usual, make sure the fan is still running. If it isn't, save your work immediately, shut down your computer, and seek help from a computer professional.

The **monitor** needs as much fresh air as the computer itself. There are little slots along the top and back of most monitors to aid in cooling the electronics.

 Plain English, please!

The **monitor** is the part of your computer system that looks like a TV.

 Q&A

> *Since ventilation is so important, would it be good to put the whole PC near a window?*
>
> No. Sunshine causes heat problems, too. I know of an office that had three PCs which locked up and died every afternoon at 2:00, but always worked fine the next morning. When Daylight Savings Time arrived, the three PCs began stopping at 3:00. As soon as the company bought window blinds, the problem went away.

A good place to live is set back from the highway!

Try to place the PC away from main traffic lanes, because people carelessly knock plugs out of outlets, loosen cables, spill drinks, and lean on keyboards.

After you locate a spot with less traffic, it's time to plan how you'll route the **cables** for your system. You have at least two power cords, as well as a cable from the computer to the printer. If your system includes a modem (see Chapter 28 to find out what to do with your modem), you have telephone wires running around, too. All the cables and wires should be placed behind the desk or wherever they won't be kicked, tripped over, or pulled.

The electronics in your PC are pretty sensitive—even the slightest loss of power or power surge can render your system useless! For less than ten bucks you can buy a power strip with surge protection, an on/off switch (so you don't have to flip a bunch of switches every time you turn your system on/off), and several outlets. When you're ready to hook everything up, be sure that the power strip isn't anyplace where you can kick it.

Rather than just pushing an armload of wires over the back of the desk, coil the extra-long cables into neat loops, then secure the loops with twist ties to keep the cables neat.

The PC's comfy—now what about me?

Ergonomics is a field concerned with the study of human characteristics in order to design things that will be more useful to humans. An ergonomic work environment is one that lets you work fast, work smart, and stay comfortable and avoid injury while doing it.

The most common problem affecting people who use computers for a living is a disorder called **repetitive strain injury**. The most common repetitive strain injury is **carpal tunnel syndrome**, which is a painful nerve disorder caused by a buildup of tissue in the nerve channels of the hand and wrist.

The following table might help you to fend off computer-related pain:

Problem	Prescription
Most desktops are not the right height for comfortable typing.	A sliding keyboard tray that pulls out from under the desk.
Back pain can be caused by marathon typing sessions.	Spend some money on a good chair that is fully adjustable.
Your high school typing teacher lied to you. You're allowed to rest your wrists on something.	Office supply stores sell special pads that help keep your wrists at a proper angle.
The early design of the desktop computer was wrong and nobody has bothered to fix it.	Place the monitor on the desk so that you can angle your head and neck to avoid back pain.
Too much time spent sitting still causes problems.	Take breaks every hour or so and move around to circulate the blood. Don't forget to flex your fingers and twiddle your thumbs.

Emptying the cartons

You're standing in the middle of the floor with a collection of different-sized boxes around your feet. Where do you start? First, identify as many things as possible by the markings on the cartons. Monitors and printers come in large boxes and usually are clearly marked by the manufacturer. Another big box (which also may be clearly marked if you bought a "name-brand" PC) contains the computer's system unit.

 Plain English, please!

The main part of the computer, where all of the "thinking" occurs, is called the **system unit**. This usually looks like a flat, rectangular box.

As long as you're examining the boxes, look around for the packing slip. It should contain a complete list of the items shipped to you—use this as a checklist to make sure you got everything you paid for.

Always start by unpacking the system unit since it's the central point of the system.

⓵ (Tip) ___

> A small knife will come in handy now, but make sure you cut the tape on the boxes and not the cardboard. If there's something wrong with the system and you have to send it back, you may find that the warranty insists on "original packaging." Consider saving the original boxes in a storage closet or garage for the next time you move.

Once the box is open, lift out the system unit and place it on the desk, the floor, or wherever you plan to use it.

Don't put the system unit in its final resting place just yet. You still have lots of wires to connect to the back, so turn the back to face you, and leave yourself room to work. If there's a plastic bag around the system unit, remove it now.

Take the monitor out of its box and place the monitor beside the system unit. Again, if there's a plastic bag, take it off.

✱ {Note} ___

Some monitors come with a separate swivel base that snaps onto the bottom of the monitor. If you have one of these, turn the monitor over and snap the base on now. There may be a diagram in the box that explains how all the little tabs and slots go together.

Dealing with Styrofoam

The easiest way to get a bulky item out of the box might affectionately be called the *Newton method*. Open the top flaps all the way and gently roll the carton over so that the opening is facing the floor. The box can be lifted off easily, as gravity keeps the contents of the box pressed down against the floor.

The other advantage to this method is that you get a good look at all the Styrofoam. Be sure to check for hidden holes stuffed with goodies, because power cords and manuals are sometimes hidden in slots in the foam.

The keyboard might have been packed with the system unit, or might be in its own flat box. Either way, remove the packaging and place it wherever you intend to use it, in front of the system unit or the monitor.

If you bought a printer, open its box now, and place the printer wherever you like. Leave any other boxes aside for now. They contain cables and manuals that you'll use in a minute. Now that you're ready to connect all the pieces, take a moment to set the system unit, monitor, keyboard, and mouse in a useful relationship to each other (see fig. 3.2).

Fig. 3.2
Everything's out of the boxes now! As soon as you connect a few plugs and turn a few screws, you'll have a fully connected, working system.

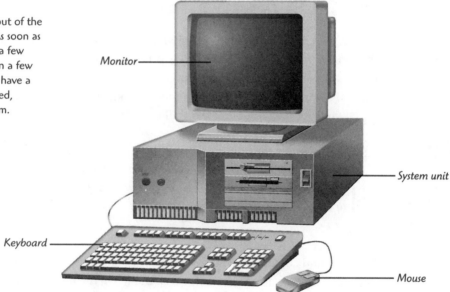

Monitor

System unit

Keyboard

Mouse

Wrestling with cables

There are two ways to hook up a computer. You can wade right in, plug things together wherever the plugs will fit, close your eyes, and flip the big switch. Or you can read this section carefully.

Tiny tool time

Start by arming yourself with a few useful tools:

- A small Phillips screwdriver (the kind with the cross-shaped head)

- A small standard screwdriver (the kind with the flat head)

- A pair of long-nosed pliers (optional, but handy when you need to hold something)

Plugging in

Now is a good time to open any remaining boxes and bags. You'll probably find power wires, a mouse, and a few other cables used to connect the printer or the modem. Your computer and monitor probably have power wires that are not attached to the units. It's okay to plug these into the back of the units now, but not into the wall!

 Don't turn on the power until everything is connected properly. Since it's often difficult to tell by looking at a power switch whether it is on or off, don't allow any power into the unit until you're ready. Let the wires dangle, or unplug the power strip if you have one.

Monitors and computers usually use the same kind of power cord, so it doesn't matter if you accidentally swap them. On the back of the monitor, there's a male three-prong plug that one end of the cord fits onto. A similar power supply plug is on the back of the PC.

You should have one leftover wire coming out of the monitor. This is the cable that connects the monitor to the PC. We'll find a place for that one later.

Attaching the printer

The printer is pretty easy to figure out, so you can attach the cable for this right away if you want. One benefit of hooking up the printer cable first is that it reduces the possibilities of connecting something to the wrong spot on the system unit later on.

 **{Note}** This section describes how to hook up a dot-matrix printer. A laser printer is more complicated; consult the manual and/or get help from your equipment dealer.

The printer cable is probably heavy, gray, and about six feet long. One end has a D-shaped connector with 25 pins. This will go to the PC's **parallel port**. The other end has a strange-looking connector that could be male or female depending on your outlook (see fig. 3.3). This end attaches to the printer, and instead of being held by screws, is secured by two clips that snap into place.

Fig. 3.3
The printer cable is the easiest to connect because there usually is only one possible combination of plugs.

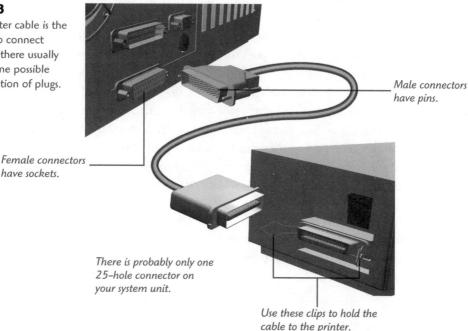

Male connectors have pins.

Female connectors have sockets.

There is probably only one 25–hole connector on your system unit.

Use these clips to hold the cable to the printer.

 Plain English, please!

The 25-pin female connector on the PC is called a **parallel port**. This port is sometimes referred to as **LPT1** (you have to pronounce each letter in LPT1, because trying to say it as a word really makes you spit like a camel). **"**

Since the plugs are D-shaped, there is only one way that they will fit. The end that connects to the PC may have little twisty knobs that screw onto the plug, or it may have tiny screws. If it has knobs, turn them by hand. If it has screws, use the screwdriver to screw them in, but not too tightly. Someday you may need to remove them.

What are all the other connection sites for?

The remaining connection locations on the back of your system unit are for the keyboard, monitor, mouse, and other things you might want to buy in the future. We'll do the simplest things first and then see what's left over.

The keyboard is pretty easy to figure out. The only thing to watch for is that some PCs have a mouse port that looks identical to the keyboard port. A little sign over each port should show a picture of a mouse or a keyboard or should be labeled with the word "mouse" or "keyboard." If your computer doesn't have these two plugs side-by-side, your job is even easier—look for the only round hole in the back. Once you've located the keyboard port, hold the keyboard connector against it while rotating slowly. The connector is round, but only goes in at one spot (sometimes this is found by lining up arrows like those on an aspirin bottle). Push it in gently until it's snug.

The monitor is the last major part to connect. Look on the back of the PC for a small D-shaped connector with 15 holes in three rows (see fig. 3.4). This is called the **video port**.

Fig. 3.4
The video port often is located off by itself at one end of the computer.

The video cable plugs in here

 Don't get confused. Besides the video port, your PC may have a port with 15 holes in two rows, which is where you could plug in a joystick if you bought one to play games with.

Remember the monitor cable we left hanging a while ago? Now it's time to connect that cable to the PC. Attach the monitor's cable to the port shown in figure 3.4. Secure the cable to the PC by turning the little screws. Remember not to screw them in too tightly.

You may see a black plug on the back of the PC that looks like the power plug, but is female. This is typically used to provide power to a monochrome monitor from the PC, but few companies use it. Your monitor probably doesn't have the right type of connector. (Of course, if the monitor's cable *does* fit, then by all means, plug it in.)

These wires are too short

The unfortunate truth about tower PCs is that they look great on the floor, but the wires for the mouse, keyboard, and monitor usually are designed for desktop systems. They are rarely the right length to reach behind a box that's sitting four feet away on the floor. This throws your ergonomic planning out the window as you bend over double across the desk to reach the keyboard.

Luckily, most computer stores and business centers sell extension cords for common computer devices, including the keyboard, mouse, monitor, and printer. For a complete set, expect to pay about $30 or $40.

 Keep one thing in mind when buying a printer extension: Never allow the cable to exceed 20 feet. That's a reliable cable length for error-free printing. After 20 feet, the signals from the PC start to get mixed up and fade away before they reach the printer.

Finishing up

As I mentioned before, some computers have a special mouse port that resembles the keyboard connector. They are always marked to distinguish one from the other, so if you have that kind of connector, just attach it the same way you did the keyboard—use a gentle twisting motion until you feel it slip into place. Then push gently.

If your PC doesn't have any round ports left and you do have a mouse, then it's probably a **serial mouse** that connects to a **serial port**. Look for a 9-pin male connector on the PC that matches the 9-pin female connector at the end of the mouse's "tail" (see fig. 3.5). If your PC only has a 25-pin male connection on the back, you may need a 9-to-25-pin adapter. This adapter is often included with your mouse.

Fig. 3.5
A 9-pin serial port is very common for the mouse connector.

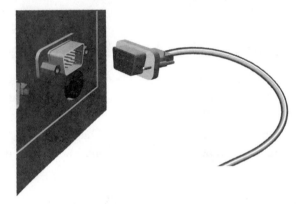

I bought a modem—I think

If you decided that your computer should talk to other computers in the outside world, you probably got a modem. Modems come in two styles and therefore may have either of two types of connections. They can be **internal** (inside the case of the PC) or **external**, where they sit on the desktop (see Chapter 28 for more information on modems).

Internal modems are the easiest to hook up because they're already a part of the PC. Look for two telephone plugs in the back of the PC, near the other connectors. Now, look around on the floor for a telephone wire that has one of those clear plastic telephone plugs at each end. One end goes into the wall telephone outlet and the other goes into the hole on the back of the PC, marked "Line." Still have one telephone jack in the back of your PC? Plug your phone into it so you can talk, too.

If you don't have two jacks on your PC, you can buy an adapter (called a **line splitter**) so that you can switch between using your modem and your phone without having to plug and unplug them each time you want to switch.

External modems have a couple of extra connections to make. If you have one of these, you still hook it to the wall with a telephone wire and attach a regular phone, so make those connections first. The next two connections you must make, however, are to connect the modem to the computer, and then to provide electricity to the modem.

To connect the modem to the PC, look around for a gray cable that resembles the printer cable. It should be a **serial cable** with a 25-pin male connector at one end and a 25-hole female connector at the other. The male connector goes into the modem and the female connector goes into the remaining 25-pin port on the PC.

❋ {Note}

Serial ports on PCs come in two sizes (9-pin and 25-pin) for no apparent reason. Most manufacturers cover all the bases by providing one plug of each type. If you're stuck at the end of all your connections with one large plug and one small hole, you can buy an adapter in most computer stores for less than $5.

Your last modem connection brings electricity from the wall. You can't have too many power cables left, so look around. Many modems use a little black transformer. Plug 'er in and you're set.

Looking for cardboard

As a final step, look into the slots on the front of the PC to see if any little cardboard tabs are sticking out. These are often used to protect the disk drives from damage during transit, and must be removed before use. If you don't see anything poking out of the front of the PC, you're okay.

 Never attempt to pull the cardboard disk drive protectors out without releasing them from the drive. After you flip open the latch or push the button on the drive to release them, they should come out easily, or with at most a little wiggling.

4

Inside and Outside the Box

With a few simple tools and some basic instruction, novices can open the computer case and noodle around, even if they've never changed the oil in a car.

Most people have a stereo system somewhere at home. And most stereos have several components—a receiver, tape deck, CD player, and speakers—connected with a bunch of wires. Your computer system is a lot like that stereo setup, with different components and wires going everywhere. Just as a receiver is the central part of a stereo system, the **system unit** (that big gray box) is the central part of a computer system. Everything that goes in and out of your computer goes in and out of the system unit.

 **{Note}** People call the main computer box the **system unit** because it contains all the key components of the computer system. You may hear it also referred to as the **CPU**, which stands for central processing unit. The CPU contains the electronic chip, called the **microprocessor**, that does the bulk of the actual "computing" for the PC.

So, tell me about the system unit

Like the front of your stereo receiver, the front of your system unit has buttons and switches that you use to control the computer. If you can run your stereo, you sure won't have any trouble running your computer. Look over the illustration on the next page to see what all the stuff on the front of the system unit does.

{Note} Computers aren't all alike. Your system unit may not have all the bells and whistles or may have something extra. Check the documentation that came with your computer if you have any trouble identifying what's on your system unit.

Working on a computer is like brain surgery—not!

Some kinds of repair work require highly specialized skills. Brain surgery is a good example. Radio repair is another (remember the "no user-serviceable parts" sticker?) Repairing your system or adding circuit boards doesn't take the special training of a brain surgeon or radio repair person. With a few simple tools and some basic instruction, novices can open the computer case and noodle around, even if they've never changed the oil in a car.

Look at the back of your system unit (see fig. 4.1). See those slots filled with little metal plates? Those are the cover plates for the expansion slots where you can add expansion cards to your computer to make it do cool stuff like produce digitized sound effects and talk to other computers over phone lines.

Know your system unit

Here's an introduction to the buttons and lights found on the typical system unit. Being familiar with these can help you identify when the system unit's working correctly.

No, the **key switch** isn't an ignition that you turn to start the PC's engine, though you wouldn't be the first person to try. It's actually a lock to keep people from using your computer. (Most people rarely utilize this lock.)

Press the **reset button** when you want to restart your computer without turning it off.

The **turbo light** comes on when the turbo button is on (pressed in) to show that your computer is running at its fastest speed.

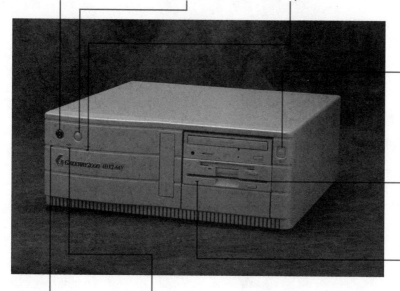

Press the **power switch** to turn on the system unit, but don't expect components like your monitor and printer to come on, too. They each have their own power switch.

From the front, a **floppy disk drive** looks like a slot with some sort of button or lever.

A **floppy disk light** indicates when the floppy disk drive is reading or writing information.

Of course, the **power light** shows that your computer is on.

The **hard disk light** comes on when your hard disk is busy reading or writing data.

Your system may also have a **turbo button**, which changes your computer's speed. When the button is pressed in, your computer runs fastest. Hint: Leave it in all the time, unless you're the type who would always opt for the stairs over the elevator in the Empire State Building!

66 *Plain English, please!*

A basic PC comes with limited capabilities. Usually it can send information to a monitor and a printer and can deal with a mouse. To add more features to your computer, you have to add **circuit boards** to slots in the motherboard, so that the sockets for the card show at the back of the system unit. The circuit boards you add are called **expansion cards**. Examples include sound cards and internal modems (to learn more about sound cards and modems, respectively, see Chapter 27, "Multimedia Mayhem: CD–ROMs and Sound Cards," and Chapter 28, "Hooking Up to the Information Superhighway with a Modem"). 99

Fig. 4.1

Your computer's expansion slots are definitely user-serviceable. The circuit boards you put in these slots give your computer extra abilities.

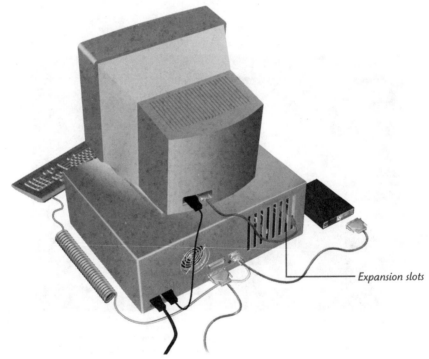

————— *Expansion slots*

To get at those slots, you have to take the cover off your system unit. To do so on the typical system unit, you unscrew a half-dozen screws around the back of the computer and slide the cover toward the front of the computer. When you've slid the cover all the way forward, lift it vertically off the system. Then you can add an expansion card simply by pressing the card gently into one of the slot receptacles (see fig. 4.2) on the motherboard. You can find more specific instructions for installing cards into expansion slots by reviewing the instructions that come with the card.

Fig. 4.2

Your PC can get new power from expansion cards that you place in the PC's expansion slots.

What else do I need to know about adding stuff to my computer?

You should give some thought to expansion slots when you buy your computer. If you're buying a basic system unit with only a hard drive and a floppy drive but think you'll add other components like a CD-ROM drive later, make sure you buy a system unit with five to seven expansion slots to give yourself ample room to grow.

You also need to give some thought to your

warranty before you open your computer to upgrade it. For some systems, especially laptop units, opening the case voids the warranty, which is something you never want to do. To avoid the void, postpone your upgrade until the warranty expires. Or check with the manufacturer to see if the upgrade can be performed by a licensed dealer (this'll cost you, depending on what you're having done).

 **Electrostatic discharge (ESD)** is one of the biggest killers of electronic
components. There is enough ESD in the human body to destroy not only
a circuit board, but all of the components that you touch while you are inside
the system unit. Your local computer retailer probably sells a variety of devices
you can use to ground yourself to prevent ESD damage. Be sure to use a
grounding device before touching anything inside your computer.

Spinning a disk

Cassettes and compact discs (CDs) store the music that you play with your
stereo. Without a tape or CD, your cassette deck or CD player remains silent.
Every computer has to have at least one floppy disk drive so you can copy
information between computers, as well as install new software. Within the
system unit, there's also a hard disk drive. This drive stores the operating
system software that lets you control your computer. It also stores the
different programs that you use to perform computing tasks. Let's take a
closer look at drives.

Disk drives from the outside in

Like a cartoon character's face, the outside of a floppy disk drive has only
a few distinguishing features: the disk slot, the floppy disk light, and the
disk door button or latch. The disk slot is, of course, where you insert the
disk. On a 5 1/4-inch floppy drive (see fig. 4.3), you have to turn the disk-
door latch in order to insert or remove disks. For a 3 1/2-inch floppy drive
(see fig. 4.4), you simply insert the disk and press it gently to place it in the
drive; you press the drive button to eject the disk.

 Never remove a disk from a drive while the drive's light is on. If you do,
information on the disk might be damaged.

Fig. 4.3
A 5 1/4-inch disk drive
has a disk-door latch
and a very wide slot for
the disk.

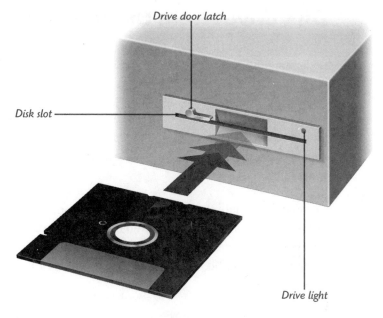

Drive door latch

Disk slot

Drive light

Fig. 4.4
A 3 1/2-inch disk drive
is the most popular
type of drive these
days. When you get a
new computer, make
sure it has one of
these!

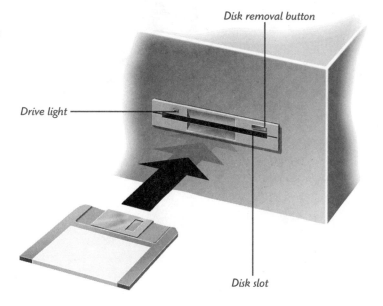

Disk removal button

Drive light

Disk slot

The hard disk drive lives within your computer. It has a light that tells you when it's reading and writing information. Observing this light tells you when your computer is trying to do its job.

Disk drives from the inside out

If you understand the way a cassette recorder works, you have a jump on understanding disk drives.

A cassette recorder reads and writes information (usually music) by running a magnetic tape over the recorder's record and play heads. A disk drive reads and writes information in a similar way, but instead of using record and play heads, a disk drive has read and write heads—different names for almost the same thing.

Because a computer needs to rapidly read information stored in many different locations (that is, in different files), disk drives record information on a spinning magnetic disk. The read and write heads float above the spinning disk (see fig. 4.5), rapidly reading and writing information as needed.

Fig. 4.5
A floppy disk drive works somewhat like a cassette recorder, recording information on a magnetic disk.

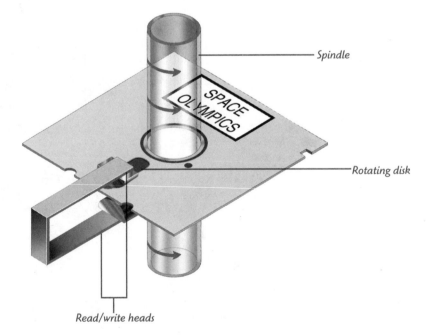

Spindle

SPACE OLYMPICS

Rotating disk

Read/write heads

Floppy disks contain a single, flexible magnetic disk **platter** (a round, flexible plastic disk) enclosed within a plastic case. Hard disk drives, whether external or built-in, contain several rigid disk platters, providing plenty of storage room.

To CD-ROM, or not to CD-ROM

More and more often, software comes on **CD-ROMs** (see fig. 4.6) rather than on floppy disks. This is because a single CD-ROM can hold more information than 500 floppy disks and more than many hard disk drives. If you consider that some software packages (especially games) come packed with 20 or more floppy disks, you know why software publishers are anxious to switch to CD-ROMs.

 Plain English, please!

> CD-ROM stands for **compact disc, read-only memory**. CD-ROMs are small, silvery disks that are read by the CD-ROM drive using a laser. They are called "read-only" because you can't change the data on them—your computer can only read and copy the data on them.

Although most software can still be purchased on floppy disks, it won't be long before CD-ROMs dominate. For this reason, you should consider adding a CD-ROM drive to your computer as soon as possible. Otherwise, you may not be able to install all the software you want to. See Chapters 25 and 27, respectively, for more information about CD-ROM software and CD-ROM drives.

Fig. 4.6
CD-ROMs can store more information than a 1/2 gigabyte hard drive. CD-ROMs are ideal for multimedia information because fancy graphics, digital video, and sound take lots of storage space.

All roads lead to the motherboard

Your entire computer boils down to one circuit board called the **motherboard**. All the components of your computer—disk drives, modems, sound cards, and printers—end up attached to the motherboard in one way or another. Just like the expression "all roads lead to Rome," all roads in your computer lead to the motherboard.

The motherboard is the largest green circuit board inside the system unit, usually lying flat in the bottom of the case. The motherboard holds the brains and memory of your computer and, via slots on the board, connects with all peripheral equipment (such as a printer) that's part of your system.

Finding the CPU

If all roads lead to Rome, they also lead to Rome's Senate. And, as surely as the Senate ruled Rome, your **CPU** rules your computer. Nothing happens until the CPU decrees it should happen.

The CPU (central processing unit), also known as the **processor** or **micro-processor**, determines the speed and capabilities of your computer and is the most important part on the motherboard. If you look at a motherboard (see fig. 4.7), you'll discover that the CPU is usually the biggest chip on the board. The CPU processes and computes data (you can learn all about CPUs by reading Chapter 5).

Fig. 4.7
Your computer's motherboard holds the CPU, where your computer makes most of its decisions.

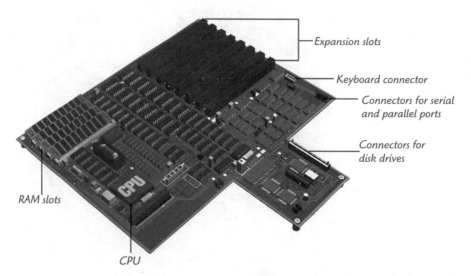

Expansion slots

Keyboard connector

Connectors for serial and parallel ports

Connectors for disk drives

RAM slots

CPU

Oops! I forgot where I put the memory

Your computer's memory, too, is on the motherboard. The **RAM** is easy to find because it's a bunch of small chips on little circuit boards that plug into the motherboard (see fig. 4.8).

 Plain English, please!

Random-Access Memory (RAM) temporarily holds data and program instructions that the CPU is currently working with. Using RAM makes your PC faster because it doesn't continually have to say, "Excuse me, what program was I executing?" or "I'm sorry. Where is that file located? I need it again." The more RAM your PC has, the more tasks it can juggle for you.

Fig. 4.8
Your computer's memory comes on little circuit boards that plug into the motherboard's RAM slots.

 The total memory in your computer depends on the size and number of memory chips you have. To run today's heavy-duty programs, you need a computer with at least 4M of memory, but 8M is better.

A slot machine where you can't lose

The motherboard offers **slots** where you insert cards, including expansion cards for adding new components to your PC. Figure 4.2 shows what a slot looks like. Most PCs come with some slots already filled. For example, your monitor attaches to a video card that's plugged into one slot. The remaining slots are for adding sound cards and other types of cards, as described earlier in this chapter.

Lots of other things that nobody cares about

Ancient Rome was a big city, with lots of buildings where the city's business was conducted. Your PC's motherboard is also like a small city. Instead of buildings, though, it's filled with computer chips and other electronic parts that help conduct the computer's business. Outside of the CPU, memory, and expansion slots, however, there's not much else of interest to anyone except a computer technician. You're off the hook!

Riding the bus

Roads that led to Rome were made of stone. The roads in your PC, called **buses**, are made of thin metal conductors, which are like thin wires. Your PC uses these metal roads to shuttle information between the parts of your PC. You don't need to do anything with your PC's buses. It's just nice to know they're there.

✱ {Note}_____ | All roads have speed limits, and the same is true of your PC's buses, which have a limit to how fast they can transfer information. Obviously, the faster the buses, the faster the PC can work.

The local power company

Your computer has its own power company, called a **power supply**. The power supply isn't, of course, a big building filled with spinning turbines. Instead, it's a large, rectangular box inside your computer's system unit (see fig. 4.9).

Fig. 4.9
Who shut off the lights? Your computer's power supply provides power to the computer and its many components.

Power supply

Power connector leading to the floppy drive

All your computer's internal components connect to the power supply in one way or another, usually by way of a bundle of wires leading from the power supply to each component. These wire bundles end in a plug that is pushed into the component.

Because the power supply just transfers power, it leaves your computer subject to power fluctuations and spikes from your power lines. As you learned in Chapter 3, you need to plug your computer into a surge protector to protect its circuitry; don't forget this cheap piece of protection for your computer.

5

What Exactly Is a CPU?

Most people get really
upset when I tell them a
CPU is not much more
than an adding machine.
Despite rumors to the
contrary, it is not really
a brain.

In this chapter:

- What does the CPU do?

- 8088, 8086, 80286, 80386, 80486—and Pentium

- What's this math coprocessor I keep hearing about?

- SX, DX, SL—which is best?

- What's a Power PC?

- Can I add something to my system to speed it up?

The real workhorse behind any computer is the **CPU**. This is another cryptic acronym that techies throw out all the time to mystify the average person. In reality, CPU stands for Central Processing Unit, which itself is a holdover from the 1950s when computers less powerful than your average PC filled entire buildings.

Obviously, computers are much smaller today and a zillion times more powerful, but the name stuck just the same. The CPU now takes the form of a tiny electronic chip within the system unit, and is often referred to as the **microprocessor** or **processor**.

If you really want to read the gory details, this chapter thrashes the topic around in a little more detail.

What does the CPU do?

The CPU is kind of like a traffic cop with a calculator in his hip pocket. Information is constantly flowing back and forth between the various parts of the PC and the CPU. The CPU stands in the middle, deciding what goes where. One of the CPU's jobs, then, is the *control* of information flow. When you type at the keyboard, the CPU receives every keystroke and redirects it to the right place. When you print a letter, the CPU takes the characters from the screen or the disk and sends them streaming through the cable that connects your computer to your printer.

Every once in a while, the CPU notices that some of the data flowing by is actually a command to perform a mathematical calculation. It stops the traffic for a second, pulls out its calculator, and adds up the next two numbers going by (or divides them, multiplies them—whatever). Then it returns to its traffic control duties.

It's a good thing that CPUs are very fast, because if there was nobody directing the traffic while the cop was off crunching numbers, there would be a heck of a mess! The operating speed of the CPU is the major factor in determining the **power** of the computer.

Fig 5.1
The CPU is the computer chip that controls all the information flowing between the other components, and calculates numbers when required.

CPU

A sort-of-technical discussion of what a CPU does

The traffic cop analogy holds true for every computer in the world, but the story raises a couple of questions:

- Where is this mysterious "right place" where the CPU redirects information?

- What gives the CPU the command to stop controlling and start calculating?

The "right place" is the computer's electronic memory, or **RAM**. (See Chapter 6 for more information about memory.) The "commander" that directs the CPU (and is the real brains behind the outfit) is the software program that's also in memory. (See Chapter 2 for more information about how software controls the hardware.)

The CPU has to work very closely with memory because the most powerful CPU around can only juggle about eight characters at one time (granted, it juggles VERY quickly!). The RAM in your computer constantly cycles through millions of characters that may need the CPU's attention. In order to process the characters stored in RAM, the CPU must move data to and from RAM at an incredible pace. If there is a lull between the CPU needing information and RAM being ready to send it, the computer slows down. Eventually, the CPU will get around to handling all the information waiting to be processed. The faster the CPU, and the more efficiently it moves data to and from RAM, the more processing power in the computer.

The CPU gets its orders from the software program that is loaded into the computer's memory as well. Some of the information being shuttled around by the CPU takes the form of **program commands** that tell the CPU what to do with particular pieces of data. In fact, if the CPU were not constantly being instructed how to do things, it wouldn't do anything at all.

CPUs have not only gotten faster over the years, they have become capable of handling data in bigger chunks, they can work with more memory than ever before, and they now have small amounts of extremely fast memory to help move information to and from RAM.

How CPUs are named, and what that name tells you

The CPUs used in all IBM and IBM-compatible computers have all been invented by Intel Corporation (or copied by those who duplicate, or clone, Intel CPUs). Intel named all but their newest CPU (the new Pentium CPU) with model numbers—boring, but a good way to tell one from another.

 **{Note}**

IBM-compatible computers are computers designed to function identically to actual IBM systems. These systems are largely based on IBM's original design, although many IBM compatibles offer unique features that set them apart from IBM computers.

Intel did have some logic to its numbering system. The first two numbers are always "80"—and since these numbers are always there, most people leave them off when describing a CPU. For example, the 80486 CPU is often referred to as just a "486" (pronounced "four eighty-six").

A good rule of thumb is that the higher the number (i.e. a computer with an 80486 CPU will be faster than a similar computer with an 80386 CPU), the more powerful the CPU.

There's a good chance that this is all you really need to know, but if you want to know more about the capabilities of *your* CPU, read the rest of this section.

The (snicker) 8088

Pronounced "eighty eighty eight," this was Intel Corporation's first commercially successful CPU. It also had a cousin known as the 8086. We avoid talking about them today because they have become downright embarrassing to the "Eight Oh" family. Strictly stone knives and bear skins technology. If you have one, sell it to someone you hate.

Computers that use 286 or 8088 CPUs today don't even have a resale value. You'll be hard-pressed to find someone willing to pay for one. Why not consider donating these old machines to schools or charitable organizations?

80286, getting to the 20th century

Intel and IBM started the computing equivalent to the Industrial Revolution when the 80286 was installed in the first **IBM AT**. Although CPUs have been improved since then, most modern IBM-compatible computers are descendants of this computer. At twice the speed of the 8088 and with a potential of 16 times the allowable memory (see the following note), this was the first power-user machine. Today, though, software programs are too big and require more power than the 286 can dish out. It's sad to see an old champion put out to pasture.

80386, a trial run

If the 286 was the Model T of CPUs, the 386 is a '65 Cadillac. Big, fast, and smooth with lots of goodies under the hood that only an engineer would appreciate. This CPU is the absolute minimum if you want to run modern operating systems (see Chapter 2 if you don't know what an operating system is) like Windows or IBM's OS/2. Even games and educational software have begun to suggest "at least a 386" to make programs run smoothly.

❋ {Note}

The various CPU models have limits on how much memory they can really use. We call this the **maximum addressable memory**. The 8088, for example, only had enough internal circuitry to talk to, or **address**, one million characters of memory. The 286 could address 16 million characters if needed. Later CPUs address much more than that.

Understand that *maximum addressable memory* is not a reference to how much memory is in a PC. It is a technical specification for how much you could put in a PC, which is defined by the model of CPU.

80486, the real thing

Although technically, this chip is really a 386 with a supercharger, it is fast enough to last a few more years on the market. Graphical presentations and large calculations, both of which need a lot of processing power, really barrel along on these systems. Intel would like to aim this CPU at the home market in the future so that it can sell **Pentiums** in the workplace.

Pentium? I was just getting used to numbers!

The Pentium was supposed to be called the 80586, but Intel realized that other manufacturers were copying their designs and selling '86 clone CPUs. They tried to protect themselves behind copyrights, but a judge determined that numbers can't be owned by anybody. So the name was changed to Pentium. Whatever it's called, it's today's top-of-the-line CPU. The Pentium is still fairly expensive (after all, there's no competition!), but the prices are falling fast. If you haven't seen a Pentium machine yet, you will soon.

What's a math coprocessor?

Since day one, Intel has offered a **math coprocessor** chip as an option to anybody who thought they needed one. Its purpose is simple. The CPU must always stop controlling the flow of information whenever it has to crunch some numbers. It stands to reason that having an assistant who specializes in mathematics would make for a pretty efficient team. Essentially, the traffic cop can put away his calculator and direct traffic all the time, because he has a Certified Public Accountant standing beside him.

How do I know how fast my computer is?

You already know that each subsequent improvement in CPUs made the CPU more powerful. Basically, every new model is able to handle more data in a single operation than "last year's" model could. The speed with which the CPU performs those operations is measured in **megahertz**, or millions of cycles per second. CPUs are sold by model and speed. A 486DX-50 runs at 50 megahertz. This is a faster machine than a 486DX-33, but not as fast as a 486DX-66.

Intel uses model numbers that end in a "7" to designate the various math coprocessors it sells. The models are matched to specific CPUs, so an 80286 CPU requires an 80287 math coprocessor. A 386 would require a 387, and so on.

If your CPU is a 80486DX or a Pentium, you got a math coprocessor as standard equipment. These two models have the math coprocessor built right into the chip. You couldn't take it out if you tried.

Do I need one?

You will definitely benefit from the speed enhancements as long as your usual work requires a great deal of mathematics. Applications that rely heavily on calculations are spreadsheets, graphics programs, and computer-aided design (CAD) programs. That last one is **computerese** for drafting. (See Part V for more complete descriptions of software.)

If your work doesn't fall into any of these categories, you probably don't need a coprocessor. If you do, though, your local computer store can probably install one inside the PC in about five minutes.

What do the DX and SX mean?

The 386 and 486 lines of CPUs are sold in two trim levels, just like cars. Think of DX as the deluxe model and SX as a sporty entry-level model. In a nutshell, the DX can move and operate on twice as much information at once as can the SX. (The 386SX, for example, is considered to be too slow for modern Windows-based software.)

Okay, I get the DX and SX. Now what's SL? I've heard of that, too

There is yet another type of 486 chip on the market and it carries the designation *SL*. This is a low-power-consumption version that is intended for laptop computers to extend their battery life. It is used in desktop models sometimes, under the banner "environmentally friendly."

What's a Power PC?

Depending on what happens in the marketplace, it may be your next CPU. For years, consumers have been complaining that Apple and IBM machines cannot communicate or run each other's software because their internal designs are so different. The two companies finally got together, and with the help of Motorola, designed what they hope to be the CPU of the future. Theoretically, if IBM makes a new computer using this chip, and Apple does the same, everybody will be happily sending information back and forth with no worries.

⊛ *{Note}*

The Power PC is actually faster and cheaper than Intel's Pentium at this time. Its biggest problem is that Intel has 15 years' worth of software programs written specifically for its chips. This head start by Intel gives the '86 family a bit of a cushion while Intel goes back to the drawing board and designs a newer, more powerful chip.

Can my PC be upgraded?

This is a common question that can't be answered easily. It depends very much on what you start with and what you want it to be when you're done. For this discussion, we'll assume that you want to upgrade a 486 to a Pentium, and anything else to a 486DX.

Bits and bytes defined

The computer recognizes only two things—0s and 1s. These numbers are arranged in a kind of Morse code, where different combinations represent the various letters of the alphabet. These groups of 0s and 1s are called **bytes** (pronounced *bites*). A byte is therefore one character. The little 0s and 1s in each byte needed to be called something, too, so they were called **bits**. A byte is always made up of 8 bits.

- If you still have an 8088-based PC, the answer is no. Too many parts have to be switched to make it a worthwhile investment.

- 286s and 386SXs can theoretically be upgraded to 486s, but you have to buy a completely new motherboard. Total cost is between $300 and $1000 dollars.

- A 386DX can be upgraded to a 486DX by simply replacing the CPU chip. One company makes this upgrade kit, which sells for about $400. But the performance may not be worth the cost.

- Most 486s can be made better or faster by replacing the CPU chip with a chip that operates at a faster speed. Prices vary by model and the speed desired.

- Many 486 computer manufacturers have advertised their PCs as *Pentium-upgradable*. We have two problems with this. Intel has not yet produced the chip that is supposed to fit in the "upgrade" socket. And design differences between the 486 and the Pentium mean that this chip will have to be a Pentium SX if and when it comes out. Again, the performance may not be cost-effective.

6 Understanding Memory

Ever had to "cram" for a test—only to forget everything the next day? Your computer's memory works the same way.

What is memory, anyway? To understand what memory is, think of your computer's memory as a desktop where you work. Files, letters, and reports can't be read if they are still in a desk drawer or filing cabinet, right? You have to open them on your desk before they can be used. When you're finished with a document, you can put it away again, clearing off your desk for the next project.

If you've just typed a letter to Mom and you can see it on the screen of your word processing application, then both the letter and the word processor are in memory right now. Unless the information you're working on is in memory, along with the application that knows how to do it, you can't do anything with a computer.

 When you finish typing, don't just turn it off! A computer isn't a typewriter. When your letter or whatever is finished, you have to **save** the stuff you typed to disk. If you just turn off the machine, you turned off your letter, too—and it's gone! See the section "You can't trust your memory" for the gory details.

Why does everyone keep harping on memory?

Quite simply, you need it to make the whole system work, and if you want to keep the system working, you should learn about a few of its quirks.

- If you don't have enough memory, the system runs slow or won't run at all.

- If you have too much, you wasted precious dollars you could have spent elsewhere.

- If it's not set up correctly, some programs won't load.

- If you (or the power company) turn off the electricity, it forgets everything you did with it—forever.

There is no doubt that memory issues in a PC can be confusing at first glance. But simple common sense and an understanding of the facts will avoid a lot of frustration down the road.

You can't trust your memory

The computer's memory isn't permanent, any more than yours is. You have to write down important stuff that you need to know later, right? (Was that 555-*1291* or 555-*1921*?) So does your computer. And just like you're going to record your thoughts on paper, tape, or sticky yellow notes, the computer can record the stuff you enter on paper (as a printout), tape, or disk.

Electronic memory is okay to work in for short periods...

Your computer's memory is electronic. It's formed from rows of little micro-chips. Microchips push electrons around, electrons come from electricity, and electricity comes from Niagara Falls. Well, mine does anyway. If something happens to Niagara Falls or to any of the wires between there and the back of your computer—Poof! Instant amnesia. Any work that hasn't been saved to disk is lost forever.

...but magnetic storage is the long-term solution

Because the information in memory is so susceptible to the whims of the power company, disk drives become the place for long-term storage. They store data magnetically, rather than electronically. You're probably familiar with this concept from cassettes or videotapes. You may not understand how it works, but you know that you can record Jay Leno, take the tape out of the machine, and you've got Jay on file forever. Your computer works the same way, but generally you store the stuff you type on magnetic disks instead of tapes.

(Tip)

Don't stick your floppy disks to the sides of filing cabinets with refrigerator magnets; exposure to magnets makes disks "forget" what you've put on them.

Q&A

Where's that file I was working on yesterday?

If you think you've lost a file, and the computer was turned off sometime between then and now, there is a good chance that you forgot to save your work to disk.

To prevent this problem in the future, remember that memory needs electricity to hold information and disks don't. Before you throw the big switch at the end of the day, use the program's command to save the file to disk. For example, in most Windows-based programs, you can just choose the Save command from the File menu.

Even my software programs need memory?

When you buy software programs—for word processing, accounting, design, graphics, and so on—they come on floppy disks or maybe a CD. They may get installed onto your computer's hard disk so you can get to them quickly, but they don't do their work there. Remember, all programs are kept on disk, so they're safe when the computer is turned off. When you're ready to use a program, your computer must copy it into its memory—computer people call this **loading** a program into memory. In this case, **load** and **copy** mean the same thing.

Where is the memory?

If you ever look inside a computer while someone is working on it, you'll see the memory sitting right there in nice straight rows of identical chips. From outside the computer, you can't *see* the memory, but you can see what it *does*.

The next two sections describe the major types of memory on your computer—**RAM** and **ROM**. Later sections describe how memory is subdivided even further—into conventional memory, upper memory, and so on.

What are RAM and ROM?

When computer jocks discuss computer memory, they generally talk about RAM, which is an acronym for **random-access memory**. RAM (pronounce it like the male sheep) actually describes the kind of chips used to make up the computer's memory, but most people just use "RAM" and "memory" interchangeably.

The term *random access* means that the microprocessor doesn't have to search through every character in memory when it needs only a certain piece of information. It goes directly to stuff that it needs and reads it. Computers are so fast because they use this random-access method to push information around inside the memory chips.

ROM stands for **read-only memory**. The term *read-only* means you can't write anything onto that chip. A ROM is a chip that contains a simple program or set of instructions; in a computer's case, the instructions that start your computer when you turn on the power.

Will you or anyone you know ever have to actually do something with ROM? Probably not. It's installed at the factory and just quietly does its job.

What's the difference between RAM and ROM?

Punch in a bunch of numbers on your calculator and then turn the switch off and on again. The numbers disappeared because they were in the calculator's RAM memory. But if you punch in some more and push one of the buttons to add or subtract, you'll get a result. You want the calculator to always know how to do math, right? That knowledge is stored in a program—built into the ROM—and can't be forgotten by the calculator. The numbers that you add or subtract exist only in temporary memory—RAM. After you get the result, you don't care about the numbers anymore, so they're erased from memory.

There is no difference between a calculator and computer when you're discussing memory—except of course for the size (or **capacity**) of that memory. A calculator can hold about eight numbers before it shows you that little "E" on the display. With a computer, you can type pages and pages of meaningful text and will probably run out of things to say long before you run out of memory.

SIMMs are simple

In most recent desktop computers, you can add more memory if you want or need it. If you're thinking about doing this, you need to add a new term to your computer vocabulary: **SIMM**. (It stands for **Single In-Line Memory Module**, but you don't really need to know that.) In a SIMM setup, the memory chips are permanently attached to little circuit boards about three inches long. They just plug right into empty slots on your computer's motherboard. That's really about all you need to know about SIMMs, except what they look like (see fig. 6.1).

Fig. 6.1
SIMMs consist of many chips mounted on a single card. They can be changed and upgraded quickly.

> Don't just go out to the discount office supply warehouse and pick a couple SIMMs off the shelf. You just can't stick any old SIMM in any old computer. Leave this to a qualified person who can tell you what you have and what you need. And NEVER try to install them yourself!

Extended? Expanded?

Like the science-fiction writers of the fifties who dreamed of going to the moon and beyond, programmers and technical support personnel look up to the skies and dream of a day when there will be just plain *memory*. Until that day arrives (it *is* coming), we will have to accept the fact that the memory inside our PCs gets categorized into a confusing mishmash of names that sound alike and describe very little.

Bytes, kilobytes, and megabytes

A byte (pronounced *bite*) is exactly one character in computerese. The word *byte*, for example, is four bytes long. The byte is the basis for all measures dealing with the computer. We also talk in *kilobytes* (each kilobyte is roughly 1,000 bytes) and *megabytes* (roughly 1,000,000 bytes). The abbreviation for kilobytes is *K*. Therefore, 640K is about 640,000 bytes. Megabytes shortens to *meg* or *Mb* or just *M*.

You might see an ad for computers with the phrase, "360K, 1.2M floppies." This computer has one floppy drive that accepts 360,000-byte floppy disks and one that takes 1,200,000-byte floppy disks. Remember to pronounce it right! Say, "Three-sixty K" and "One point two meg" or everyone will think you're a dummy.

Think of memory as being stacked much like the floors in a high-rise building. The first 640 floors (640K) of RAM is **conventional**. The floors between 640 and 1024 (1M) are called **upper memory**, and any floors above 1024 are called **extended memory**. Figure 6.2 helps you figure out all this stuff.

Fig. 6.2
When memory is installed in a new computer, the first 640 kilobytes to go in is called *conventional*. The next 384 kilobytes is called *upper memory,* and anything after that is called *extended.*

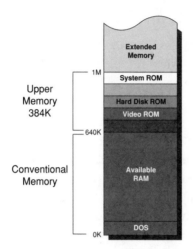

Conventional memory

When DOS was written for machines with 8088 processors, the programmers limited the amount of RAM memory the microprocessor could use to 640K: "Yes, that's right! Our new operating system can take advantage of all your computer's memory, right up to 640,000 bytes! Nobody will EVER need all that, but this baby is built for the future!"

Unfortunately, we outgrew that "infinite limit" two or three years into the PC's childhood, and DOS is still the operating system installed on 99 percent of the PCs ever sold. It's still around because some of the most popular software packages need DOS to work. No matter how many mega-gobs of memory your system really has, if you ask DOS to count up the bytes, it will say you have 640K of conventional memory.

Upper memory

Actually, early computers *could* use a little more memory than 640K—up to one full megabyte of memory. Remember that your computer has more than just RAM for memory—it also has ROM. Years ago, somebody made the arbitrary decision that the megabyte of potential memory for the 8088 processor should be broken down into 640K of conventional memory where it could talk to RAM, and another 384K of **upper memory** for ROM. Add the two numbers together and you get 1024K, or 1 megabyte. (See the preceding sidebar if you don't follow this math.)

Simply put, when the processor is talking to RAM, it's moving things around in conventional memory. When it's reading from ROM, it's working in the 384K upper memory area.

Expanded memory

Expanded memory was invented to work around the 640K limitation of the old 8088/DOS combination. As desktop computing gained in popularity, people began seeing unpleasant messages on their screens like Out of memory. It became obvious that the bottomless 640K was more shallow than anyone had ever imagined. Lotus (the 1-2-3 company) was forced to sit down with Microsoft (the DOS company) and Intel (the chip company). Together, they hammered out a solution using hardware and software. The result actually fooled the processor and DOS into using more memory than either of them thought they could. (It's called **expanded memory**.)

Why does a 360K floppy disk hold 368,640 bytes?

No matter how smart they seem, computers are only capable of seeing things as "on" or "off." Computers represent "on" with a number 1 and "off" with a 0. So how do they get anything done? They just put a bunch of 0s and 1s together into strings that represent any number or character the computer needs.

All this counting by twos forces us humans to make weird adjustments when we deal with computer memory. If you take the number 2 and keep doubling it (2, 4, 8, 16, and so on), you arrive at 1024, which is the closest you can get to 1,000. Somebody years ago decided that this would be a good unit of measurement and called it a kilobyte even though it's not really a *kilo*-anything. So a K is really 1024.

The 360K floppy disk? Get out your calculator and do the math. 360 times 1024 is 368,640.

And, a megabyte is actually 1,048,576 bytes. Don't worry about it. Just keep thinking that *kilo* is a thousand and *mega* is a million.

(Tip)

If you use an XT-type of computer or DOS-based business programs (for example, Lotus 1-2-3 Version 2.3 or WordPerfect 5.1), your system might already have or could benefit from expanded memory. Ask your favorite computer consultant.

If you only use more recent software such as that written for Windows or OS/2, you probably don't need it.

Extended memory

Is your computer an 80286 or an 80386SX? It can talk to 16 megabytes of memory. 80386, 80486, or Pentium? Cool. You get four **gigabytes** (that's billions of bytes). Any memory installed over one megabyte is classified as **extended memory**. This kind of memory is easier and faster for a processor to use than expanded memory. Plus there's a lot less chanting and wand-waving.

{Note}

Windows and OS/2 *love* extended memory. In fact, they can't live without extended memory, and the more the better.

(Tip)

You gotta have enough memory to run today's programs without any problems. The more you have, the more likely it is that you'll be able to do all the things you want, when you want. So aim for eight megabytes or more of RAM.

(Tip)

The highest amount of memory that a CPU can talk to is called **Maximum Addressable Memory**. A 286 chip can handle 16 million different memory addresses. A 386, 486, or Pentium can handle four billion. Now you know what it means when a techno-nerd says, "My CPU can address four gig of RAM. How about yours?"

How much memory do I have on my computer?

There are a few ways to find out this number. The easiest is to watch the screen right after you turn on the main switch. It helps to make sure that the screen is turned on and warmed up before turning on the computer. Most computers go through an internal diagnostic procedure that verifies the memory installed in the system by counting the bytes. (Sometimes this is accompanied by a nifty ticking sound.) The highest number reached before the screen goes blank and the operating system loads is how many kilobytes of memory you have. Just round it off, divide by one thousand, and say "Meg." The computer I'm typing on counts to 8064 then wipes it out and does other stuff. My laptop counts to 3968 and then goes blank. The first is an eight-megabyte machine. The second has four megabytes.

Okay, some computer models don't do it. Nobody knows why. For these machines there is yet another test. If you are using a version of DOS that is 5.0 or higher, you can use the MEM command.

At the DOS prompt (see Chapter 10 for stuff on DOS), follow these steps:

1 Type **mem** and press the Enter key.

A report should appear on the screen. See figure 6.3 for an example of what your screen should look like.

 **{Note}** If you don't have DOS 5 or higher, you'll see the message Bad command or filename. Skip the rest of this procedure.

2 If your version of DOS doesn't show total memory, write down the numbers for Total Conventional Memory and Total Extended Memory (or XMS).

3 Add the two numbers together and round them off to the nearest million. That's how much RAM is installed in your computer. Some versions of DOS make the addition unnecessary. Simply look at the first number next to Total Memory!

Fig. 6.3

The MEM command gives a complete report on memory in your system. The total memory installed in this PC is 4 megabytes.

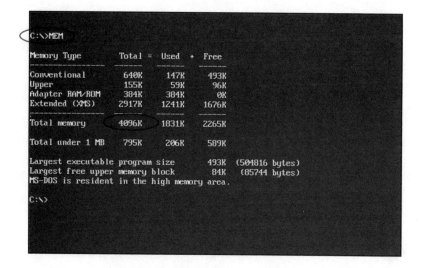

```
C:\>MEM

Memory Type        Total =  Used  +  Free
                   ------   ------   ------
Conventional        640K    147K    493K
Upper               155K     59K     96K
Adapter RAM/ROM     384K    384K      0K
Extended (XMS)     2917K   1241K   1676K
                   ------   ------   ------
Total memory       4096K   1831K   2265K

Total under 1 MB    795K    206K    589K

Largest executable program size      493K   (504816 bytes)
Largest free upper memory block       84K    (85744 bytes)
MS-DOS is resident in the high memory area.

C:\>
```

If you can't use MEM, there are diagnostic software utilities that do the job very well, but they are far outside the scope of this book. Ask around at your office or among your friends. Somewhere, you'll come across someone with the know-how and the willingness to help.

 (Tip)

> The MEM command can also be used to find out how much memory is available to your programs. (A portion of the total memory is used up by DOS and other programs after the computer has been started, so you never get to use all that's there.) Simply look at the Largest Executable Program Size. Using a memory manager can often improve these numbers.

How much memory do I need?

The type of work that you do and the kinds of software that you do it with determine your memory needs. If you only work with DOS and a few software applications that were written for it, you might be quite happy with 640K. Lotus 1-2-3 Version 2.3, Harvard Graphics Version 3, WordPerfect 5.1, and MS-Word 5.0 are all examples of DOS applications that are quite content sitting in that little space we call conventional memory. You *might* want to look into obtaining some expanded memory (see the preceding section), but this depends entirely on how big your documents and spreadsheets are. If everything seems to be running smoothly, don't worry about it.

Windows is a memory hog

If your computer runs Windows 3.1 or if you are thinking about getting it, buy as much memory as you can reasonably afford without going into bankruptcy. First of all, Windows has lots of pretty colors and lots of little pictures that you can grab with your mouse and drag around the screen. This stuff takes a lot of memory just to display, and you're not even doing any work yet.

Remember how you're supposed to think of your computer's memory as a desktop? Windows puts so many nifty gadgets and tools on your desk that you don't have any room left for your work unless you get a larger desk.

The box that Windows comes in says, "You need two megabytes of memory to run this software." Don't believe them for a minute. Sure, it'll run, but so does a Yugo. Windows only runs efficiently with 4M or more of RAM. Trust me.

The programs that you buy to run with Windows generally need more memory than their DOS cousins. How many programs you use at the same time also has an influence on how much memory you should have. If you use just a word processor or a spreadsheet most of the time, and if your documents are not the size of *War and Peace*, the four meg is probably okay. If you use both of them at the same time and cut and paste numbers between them, you probably need eight megabytes to hold both programs and all their data.

If you are doing any work with computer graphics (that's pictures, page layouts, and so on), you may need 16M of RAM. This is particularly true if you have a scanner attached to your system and you are scanning photographs (see Chapter 26, "Printers and Scanners," for information about scanners).

Managing your memory

The various types of memory, how they relate to each other, and how they get massaged by different kinds of software is called **memory management**. Only in the world of DOS could such a thing even be possible. Remember that we're discussing an operating system that was written around 1980, then added to and patched up here and there over the years.

The concept behind memory management is to try and get as much conventional memory free as possible by moving smaller programs out and putting them into other types of memory such as upper or extended. You know already that having lots of memory is a good thing (the bigger the desk, the more work you can do). But since DOS can't work with more than 640K of memory, the size of the desk is fixed from the start. The only thing you can do is clean it off a bit.

What does it mean, Out of memory?!

You probably just have too much information in there for the memory to hold. Save your work, exit the software, and restart the computer. If it happens again while working on the same job, you probably do need more memory. Work with smaller documents until you can get someone to install it for you. This might also be a symptom of needing to get your memory managed a bit.

Windows keeps giving me a General Protection Fault

Although it sounds like some kind of electrical short circuit, it's really only a memory management problem most of the time. Write down what you were doing when you saw the message, exit the software, and try again. If it happens again, especially with the same window open, call the paramedics.

Uh oh—I got a parity error

The parity error happens when a special parity chip tattles on RAM and tells the CPU that memory is not giving it the right information. If you've never seen one, it's because memory chips are pretty dependable. If you do get one, panic right away and run around the office waving your arms in the air. Just kidding. Try turning the PC off, waiting thirty seconds, and turning it on again. You lost all your work anyway, so turning it off won't hurt. (Humming a funeral dirge at this point is appropriate.) If the error occurs again, or if the system won't start at all, you've got a serious problem that needs under-the-hood servicing.

If parity errors only occur once in a while, then the problem might be something *external* to the PC that you can fix yourself. The following table might help pinpoint the problem. If not, you've got a hardware problem and you need to take the PC in for service.

Possible Cause	Try This
Static electricity	Raise the humidity or buy a special static mat from the computer store.
Power surges and spikes	Invest in a good-quality surge suppression outlet (see Chapter 3).
Other devices on the same circuit	Take the Mr. Coffee, the electric fan, and the laser printer off the same extension cord and plug them in somewhere else.

If none of these solutions help, it's off to the service depot. You've got some kind of a hardware problem.

7
What You Need to Know about Monitors

In this chapter:

- What are my choices?
- What are graphics modes and graphics adapter cards?
- What types of graphics can my computer display?
- What does "resolution" and memory have to do with graphics?
- How many colors can my computer show?
- Can I make my screen work faster?
- What's a "screen saver"?

It may look like a TV, but you can't get Cinemax, Showtime, or HBO on your computer's monitor. But without it, you and your computer won't have much to say to each other.

A waggish friend and former office mate once put an old pair of TV antennas on top of her computer's monitor to make it look, as she put it, "really retro"—like one of those funky black and white TV sets from the 1950s. Your computer's **monitor** (also known as the **screen** or **display**) looks a *lot* like a TV and functions in much the same way, although don't try channel surfing on it!

Besides being the most obvious part of a PC, the monitor is also your main source of output information from the computer. If you type something wrong, you can see the mistake on the screen. You can correct it, too—and make any other editorial or layout changes before finally sending a job to the printer. Or if you'd like to try your hand at playing a computer game, the monitor can show you all the really *cool* graphics in the latest versions of, say, DOOM, Myst, or Return to Zork.

Messages that appear on the screen give you feedback about whether or not a command was successful. The PC will even use the screen to tell you when it's not feeling well. Because so much of your time is spent staring at your monitor, it pays to have one that won't make you go blind.

What are my choices?

When you're ready to buy a monitor for your PC, you have lots of choices. Everything from old-fashioned black and white to photographic-quality color. Because the picture on the monitor also depends on your computer's graphics abilities, you need to know what kind of graphics adapter your computer uses. The **graphics adapter** is a board that plugs into one of the expansion slots. It must be the same type as the monitor you select.

- The minimum you should settle for is called **VGA**, or in technospeak, Video Graphics Array. If you settle for less and get **EGA** (**Enhanced Graphics Adapter**) or the really horrible **CGA** (**Color Graphics Adapter**), you'll have a hard time with much of the modern software that likes brilliant colors and fine resolution.

- If you plan to use your PC for graphic design, photographic work, or drafting, you want a state-of-the-art display. Go with a **SuperVGA** (**SVGA**) system, which has higher resolution and can show even more colors (up to 16.7 million!) than VGA.

We'll tell you a lot more about this stuff in the sections that follow.

What the heck do "graphics modes" have to do with my monitor?

Here's the low-down: personal computers display information in various **graphics modes**. *What*? Just think of a graphics mode as a way of drawing information on the screen. The simplest graphics mode is text-only (see fig. 7.1) and allows only two colors, black and white.

Fig. 7.1
The simplest displays show only text, which can get real boring real fast.

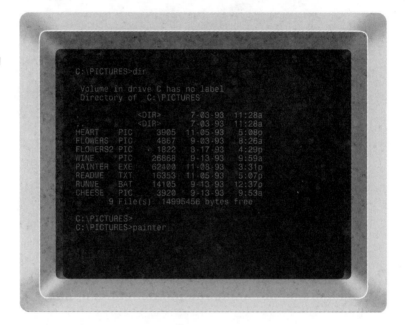

```
C:\PICTURES>dir

 Volume in drive C has no label
 Directory of  C:\PICTURES

.              <DIR>        7-03-93  11:28a
..             <DIR>        7-03-93  11:28a
HEART    PIC    3905      11-05-93   5:08p
FLOWERS  PIC    4867       9-03-93   8:26a
FLOWERS2 PIC    1822       8-17-93   4:29p
WINE     PIC   26868       9-13-93   9:59a
PAINTER  EXE   62400      11-08-93   3:31p
READNE   TXT   16353      11-05-93   5:07p
RUNME    BAT   14105       9-13-93  12:37p
CHEESE   PIC    3920       9-13-93   9:53a
         9 File(s)   14995456 bytes free

C:\PICTURES>
C:\PICTURES>painter
```

The most sophisticated graphics modes can display everything from two-color text to photographic-quality pictures containing hundreds (or even millions) of colors (see fig. 7.2).

Fig. 7.2
The best monitors can
show pictures with
almost as much detail
as a photograph.

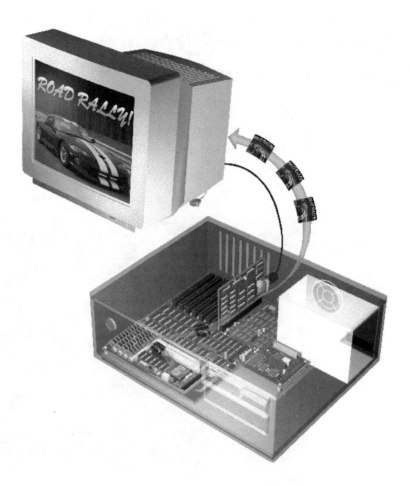

①(Tip)

Monitors can be real energy hogs, especially if they're left on all the time. One
way of treating the environment nicely is to conserve energy, which is what so-
called green monitors do. Also called Energy Star monitors, these displays know
when they're not being used and, even while still on, can cut their power
consumption considerably.

Monitors and adapter cards: A matching game

For your computer to be able to display a specific graphics mode, both the computer and the monitor have to be able to handle it.

The computer's end of things is handled by something called a **video adapter card**, which plugs into the motherboard. In order for everything to work right, the monitor and the video adapter card have to match. If you have a terrific monitor but only a so-so adapter card, you're going to get a so-so picture. The reverse is true, too.

 **{Note}**

When you buy a new computer system, it comes configured with a matching video adapter card and monitor. Most today can operate in VGA and SVGA (see table 7.1). You mainly need to be aware of what's covered in this chapter if you have an older computer and want to upgrade the video or if you're considering buying a specialized or oversized monitor with your new system.

Table 7.1 Graphics Adapters from A to Z

Acronym	Meaning	Type	Comments
MDA	Monochrome Display Adapter	Black and white	Mostly limited to displaying text. Cheap.
CGA	Color Graphics Adapter	Color	Allows "chunky" (ugly, that is) graphics in only four colors. This display standard has all but disappeared. Don't bother.
HGC	Hercules Graphics Card	Black and white	Allows both text and graphics that are a lot less "chunky" than CGA.
EGA	Enhanced Graphics Adapter	Color	Can show 16 colors at a time with less "chunky" lines. A little better than CGA but also obsolete. Again, don't bother.

continues

Table 7.1 Continued

Acronym	Meaning	Type	Comments
MCGA	Multi-Color Graphics Array	Color	A lot like EGA, but with the ability to show 256 colors at a time. Never caught on, though, and is mostly dead.
VGA	Video Graphics Array	Color	The reigning king, although it's losing ground to SVGA. This adapter gives detailed graphics with up to 256 colors. A nice choice for most folks.
SVGA	Super Video Graphics Array	Color	The current cutting edge, allowing even more detailed graphics than VGA with *tons* more colors. If you're going to play video games or plan to use your PC for graphic design, photographic work, or drafting, you'll want this kind of adapter.

❋ **{Note}** In most cases, the better adapter cards can handle all graphics modes from text-only up to the maximum ability of the card. For example, a VGA card can show MDA, CGA, EGA, and VGA images. For that reason, an SVGA adapter card can handle just about any graphics mode in existence. This capability ensures that the adapter can display older software that displays in a particular mode.

What makes for a good picture on my screen?

A lot of things work together to determine how great the picture on your monitor looks. You know now that the two pieces of important hardware are the monitor itself and the video adapter card. But what, specifically, are the important characteristics of these two pieces of hardware? Here's a list:

- Resolution
- Number of colors
- Memory
- Speed

What is meant by "screen resolution"?

The image on a monitor is made of rows of tiny dots. The number of dots that a monitor or adapter card can display horizontally and vertically on the screen is called *resolution*.

On a VGA display, for example, the best resolution is 640×480, which means the picture can have at most 640 dots across and 480 dots down. Obviously, the smaller the dots, the more that fit on the screen. And, the more dots that fit on the screen, the more detailed on-screen text and graphics can be (see fig. 7.3).

Fig. 7.3
The upper left half of this screen shows an image using 320x200 resolution. The other half of the screen has a screen resolution of 640x480. See how the lower half of the image has smoother, more detailed lines?

⊛ {Note}_____ These days, your system should handle resolutions of no less than 640x480. Any less, and your computer won't be able to display current software programs.

Q&A

My monitor's documentation talks about "pitch"; is this a baseball thing?

No, you can put away your cleats. Another way monitor manufacturers describe resolution is using something called **dot pitch**. This fancy term means nothing more than the distance between the dots on the screen. The closer the dots, the better the picture. Some of the best monitors have a dot pitch of .28mm (millimeters) or less, which is great for SVGA displays. For regular VGA, you can probably get by with a dot pitch of .31mm. If you're buying a new computer system or monitor, make sure the dot pitch isn't over .31mm.

How many colors are enough?

Another factor that controls how rich a screen display looks is the number of colors that can be shown at one time on the screen. When a display can use lots of colors, the pictures look more realistic. Imagine a Monet or another of the French Impressionists trying to paint a landscape scene with only a few colors in his palette. The minimum number of colors needed to show detailed graphics these days is 256. So if you have an older graphics adapter that can't display 256 colors, consider upgrading your video.

How much video memory do I need?

Your graphics adapter card has its own memory, so it has room to construct graphical images without hogging the memory used by the system and your programs. Generally, the greater the resolution and the more colors displayed, the more memory needed to construct an image.

A good adapter card carries at least 1M of memory on board. Any less, and you may not be able to display quality images with your computer. Of course, if all you do is write fan mail to Claudia Schiffer or Fabio, you don't need fancy graphics.

Do I need a fast adapter card?

Adapter cards are a lot like little computers whose specialty is graphics. As such, different adapter cards work at different speeds. A slow adapter card limits what your computer can do because it takes so long to draw and display a screen. (Yawn.) Fast adapter cards, on the other hand, generate images...well...faster. If you're using a graphical operating system like Windows or OS/2, a speedy adapter card is a *must*. Fast adapters for this type of work are often called **video accelerators**.

 Beware of monitors that use **interlacing** to generate their displays. Because of the way interlaced monitors generate images, they flicker a little, which can bother your eyes.

 Plain English, please!

An **interlaced** monitor displays every other line of the screen image in one pass, then displays the remaining lines in a second pass. These displays flicker, and that flicker can really bug you after a while. That's why we recommend that you avoid or replace interlaced monitors with **non-interlaced** monitors whenever possible.

How can I soup up my display?

The more you have to wait for your computer to draw all those little pictures and windows, the less work you're going to get done. Even if you upgraded your system to have a really fast processor, a slow adapter card would still limit how fast you could get anything done.

 Another way some PCs get faster graphics displays is by using something called a **local bus**. It's a special part of the motherboard that gives a computer's CPU direct access to the graphics hardware. This special connection zaps graphics information through the computer faster than TV networks cancel fall shows. You have to buy your PC equipped with a local bus, though. If your system doesn't already have one, buying an accelerator board is the best way to improve graphics performance.

One way to speed up your computer's graphics is to purchase a video accelerator. These are really more than accelerators; they're a complete video-card replacement. Accelerator boards, which are used mostly with graphical operating systems like Windows, are fine-tuned for graphics tasks and make your system sizzle when it comes to redrawing the display.

❶ (Tip)

> Accelerator boards can be very expensive, as much as $1,000. The good news is that you don't need to plunk down that much cash to improve your Windows graphics speed. A typical graphics accelerator board costs about $100 to $200. Buy the best board that you can afford, but don't go *over*board.

You don't need to buy a top-of-the-line board unless you'll be doing a lot of sophisticated graphics work or want top-quality multimedia capabilities.

Hanging a virtual "out to lunch" sign on your monitor

In the old days, if you left your monitor on and idle too long, the image got burned into the screen. From that point on, whenever you used the monitor, you could see this ghost-like phosphor image in the background. Next time you visit your local ATM, look closely at its screen; you will see what I mean. To avoid the burn-in problem, clever programmers created screen savers, which blacked out the screen whenever the computer was not being used.

Flat-screen monitors

Not all monitors have the same type of screen. A regular monitor has a slightly rounded screen that kind of bulges out at you, as if someone inflated it with a bit too much air. This shape causes some image distortion.

For the last few years, though, manufacturers have been making flat-screen monitors, which are more expensive but produce much less distortion. If you're going to be doing a lot of page-layout work or other types of detailed graphics work, you may find that a flat-screen monitor is well worth the extra money.

Today's monitors are not as subject to the burn-in malady, but screen savers are as popular as ever. That's because screen savers no longer just turn off the screen; now they do all sorts of clever things like showing cartoons or drawing fantastic designs. You can even get screen savers based on a favorite movie (see fig. 7.4) or computer game.

Fig. 7.4

This screen saver comes from the T2 collection, based on the famous Arnold Schwarzenegger film, Terminator 2.

Commercial screen savers cost money, of course. You can expect to pay between $20 and $40 for such graphics extravaganzas. However, there are lots of free screen savers floating around, many of which are clever enough to warrant a look. The Windows operating system comes with its own built-in screen savers. You can find other free screen savers on BBSs or on-line services. (If you don't know about this on-line stuff, check out Chapter 32.)

Disks and Disk Drives

In this chapter:

- I have two different slots for disks in my computer. What's the difference?

- What does the HD mark on this disk mean?

- I'm trying to copy stuff on a disk, but it won't let me.

- A hard disk can hold as much as 500 floppy disks— or more!

If you've ever seen a 5 1/4-inch disk, you'll know why they call them "floppies."

Believe it or not, the whole point of using a computer is *not* to impress your friends with how far you can get in DOOM or some other popular computer game. The boring truth is that you use a computer simply to move information into memory, change it somehow, and move it out again. Regardless of the type of information, it's as simple as that.

The information moves to and from a disk in a disk drive. Chapter 4, "Inside and Outside the Box," explained some basics about disk drives. This chapter gives you more details about floppy disks, disk drives, and hard drives so you can use your drives effectively.

What's the difference, and why should I care?

You could say that floppy drives are your computer's shipping and receiving department. The disks you stick into the drive are like packages that deliver information to the computer and carry information out from your computer. Without floppy-disk drives, you'd have a hard time transferring information from one computer to another (unless you are connected to a network, but we'll talk about that in Chapter 29).

Remember when wooden baseball bats were the only thing going? Wooden bats work great most of the time; but they weaken with age and, if you hit a ball just right, the bat can crack or splinter. So, a couple of decades ago, someone invented the aluminum bat. Aluminum bats quickly became very popular because they're lighter and more reliable—they're nearly impossible to destroy.

Well, as computer technology continues to improve, so do the tools we use to work with them. Floppy disks are no exception. What was once the standard is now the exception.

You may run into several varieties of disks and drives. Luckily, only two characteristics determine the type of drive you have:

- The physical size of the disk that the drive can accommodate

- How much information can be stored on the disk

Sizing up a floppy

The physical size of a floppy disk is either 3 1/2 inches square or 5 1/4 inches square. The larger 5 1/4-inch disks have been around a lot longer, but they don't work as well. They're easier to damage, they don't hold as much information, and they're bulkier to carry around. Since they're so much better, 3 1/2-inch disks took over the floppy disk market as fast as aluminum bats became popular. Today, 5 1/4-inch disks are being phased out fast; a lot of new computers don't even have a 5 1/4-inch drive.

How much can they hold?

Like most other computer size-related stuff, the amount of information a disk can store (its **capacity**) is measured in kilobytes (K) or megabytes (M). (If you don't understand these terms, go back and read Chapter 6,

"Understanding Memory.") And to be sure that you're really perplexed, a disk's capacity is controlled by the disk's **density**, which is how much information can be packed into one place on the disk.

Does this density stuff make sense? If not, think about it like luggage. There's a big difference between soft-side and hard-shell suitcases. Even if they're about the same size, you can always get a lot more in a soft-sider. Disks are like that, too. Some disks—high-density disks—are better at cramming more information into the same amount of space.

For quick reference, table 8.1 lists the various types of disks and their capacities.

Table 8.1   Disks and Their Capacities

Disk Size	Type	Capacity
5 1/4–inch	Double density	360K
5 1/4–inch	High density	1.2M
3 1/2–inch	Double density	720K
3 1/2–inch	High density	1.44M

Yeah, okay...so which kind do I need?

Which disks you can use depends on your drive. A high-density drive can handle any disk. A double-density drive cannot handle high-density disks. If you have a double-density, 5 1/4-inch drive, my suggestion is to replace it with a 3 1/2-inch, high density disk drive.

(Tip)

If you have a lot of information stored on 5 1/4-inch disks, you should transfer that information onto 3 1/2-inch disks as soon as you can.

Since 5 1/4-inch disks are becoming obsolete, you won't be able to get to that information if you get a new computer that doesn't have a 5 1/4–inch drive.

Although it's easy to tell the size of a drive by the width of the slot and by whether it has a lever (5 1/4-inch) or button (3 1/2-inch), drives aren't labeled with their densities. If you don't know what density your drive is, check the documentation that came with your drive or computer.

Which disk is which?

Now that you know which disks you can use, how can you tell the disks apart? With 3 1/2-inch disks, telling a double-density disk from a high-density disk is as easy as separating roses from mushrooms.

Here's the trick: Look at the disk's upper left corner. (Make sure you're looking at the *front* of the disk.) If there's a hole there, you have a high-density disk (see fig. 8.1). If not, it's a double-density disk. Many high-density disks also have an HD stamped in one corner.

This hole means it's a high-density disk

Fig. 8.1
This little disk packs a lot of whallop! It holds over 1.44M.

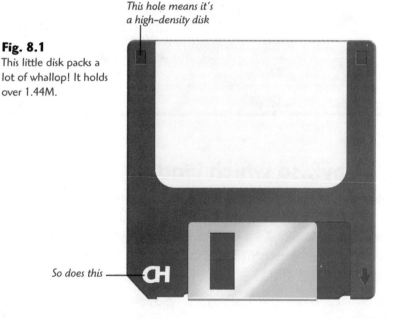

So does this

Figuring out 5 1/4-inch disks is a lot tougher. One way to tell a double-density 5 1/4-inch disk from a high-density disk is to read the label. If there is no label, try looking at the hole in the middle of the disk. If there's a narrow metal ring around the hole like the one in figure 8.2, it's a double-density disk.

Fig. 8.2
A double-density
5 1/4-inch disk has
a narrow band in the
middle of the hole.
High-density disks
don't.

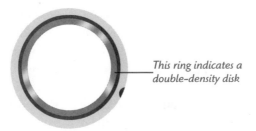

*This ring indicates a
double-density disk*

Getting a disk ready to use

Before you can use a new disk, you have to format it. **Formatting** prepares
the disk's surface to hold information. When you format a disk, the disk drive
marks off tracks on the disk—tracks that are a lot like the grooves on a
record, except grooves on a record hold music and the tracks on a disk hold
computer information. Until you create these tracks, you can't use the disk.

Whether you're using DOS or Windows, formatting a disk is easy to do. If
you're in DOS, read Chapter 12, "Doing Stuff with Disks (DOS)," to learn
about formatting a floppy disk. If you use Windows, see Chapter 17, "Doing
Stuff with Disks (Windows)."

If you're about to do something that requires a lot of disks, such as backing up
your system, buy preformatted disks. The time savings is well worth the small
extra cost.

What is write-protection?

How does your VCR know that it can tape over your recording of last week's
"Seinfeld," but it can't tape over that copy of "Pinocchio" you bought for
the kids? Prerecorded movie tapes are usually **write-protected**. Write-
protection makes it impossible to erase what's already there or write over
it with something new. On video tapes, there's a plastic tab you can knock
out to create a hole. This tells the VCR's "feelers" that it can't use this tape
to record. Of course, it's not really permanent—if you want to tape over it
later, you can fool the VCR by putting a piece of Scotch tape over the hole.

On 3 1/2-inch computer disks, it works nearly the same. If the hole in the disk is covered, the computer knows it's okay to write to the disk. If it feels a hole, it knows it can't. With 5 1/4-inch disks, it's just the opposite; a covered hole means don't write, an open hole means it's okay to write.

Most software programs you buy will come on write-protected disks. You can protect both 3 1/2-inch and 5 1/4-inch disks (see fig. 8.3).

Just like a protected VCR tape, you can still read from a protected floppy disk. You can copy files or run programs from the disk. You just can't change anything that's already on it.

How do I know if my disk is write-protected?

To check the write-protection of a 3 1/2-inch disk, turn it over so you can see the round, silver thing on the back. Look for the notch in the upper left corner (like you see in fig. 8.3). If the little black switch is pushed up, the hole below it is exposed. This means that protection is on. If the black switch is pushed down to cover the hole, the write-protection is off.

To check a 5 1/4-inch disk, face the disk toward you and look for a square notch on the right side. If you can see the notch, the disk is not write-protected. To turn protection on, cover the notch with a sticker or piece of tape, like the figure shows. To turn protection back off, carefully remove the sticker.

Like any other kind of switch, you can a turn disk's write-protection on and off as many times as you want.

Usually, a box of new 5 1/4-inch disks includes several small stickers you can use to write-protect the disks.

Disk is not write-protected.   *Disk is write-protected.*

Fig. 8.3
Write-protect a floppy
disk to keep from
accidentally formatting
it or changing the
information it contains.

Taking care of disks

Now that you know a little about floppy disks
and how they work, you may be wondering how
safe your data is on a floppy disk. The truth is that
3 1/2-inch disks are fairly robust, thanks to their
stiff, plastic shells. Still, there are many ways disks
can be damaged. Here are some ways you can
keep your disks out of harm's way:

- Keep disks away from all magnetic fields,
  including paper clip dispensers and
  electronic equipment like speakers, TVs,
  amplifiers, and telephones (yes, even
  telephones contain magnets).

- The metal detector in airport security gates
  can affect floppy disks. It is better to hand
  the disks to the security attendant for
  manual inspection than to have them
  scanned by the device.

- Store your disks in some sort of disk file box
  that protects them from dust.

- Never get a disk wet, expose it to direct
  sunlight, or toss it on a heater vent.

- Never insert or remove a disk from a drive
  when the drive's "busy" light is on.

In Chapters 12 and 17, you learn some other tips
for keeping your disks happy and healthy.

?Q&A___

Why do I have trouble with other people's disks?

Just like a stereo cassette player, disk drives have heads that must be aligned for the drive to work properly. When a drive's heads become misaligned, you'll suddenly find that disks formatted on another machine or your older disks don't work anymore. Unfortunately, this isn't a problem that you can fix yourself. A trip to the repair shop is a solution. Often, it is cheaper to replace the drive.

What about the hard disk?

If a floppy-disk drive is your computer's shipping and receiving department, then the hard-disk drive is the information warehouse. You use floppy disks to transfer information into and out of your computer. Sometimes, the information on a floppy disk goes directly into your computer's memory. But usually, the information ends up on your computer's hard-disk drive, which is located inside your computer's system unit.

Since you really don't want to open up your computer to see what the hard-disk drive looks like, you can see a picture of one in figure 8.4. From a technical aspect, a hard-disk drive works about the same as a floppy-disk drive. The main difference is that the hard disk never leaves the inside of the computer (it also isn't floppy).

The big advantage of a hard disk is how much information it can hold, sometimes more than fits on *500* floppy disks! This massive storage makes a hard disk great for storing information you need a lot. Also, hard-disk drives work much faster than floppy-disk drives, so you don't have to wait as long.

Because you can pile so much information onto a hard-disk drive, it's easy to end up with an electronic Fibber McGee's closet—tons of stuff crammed into every nook and cranny of the hard-disk drive and no convenient way to reach in and grab just one item if you need it. See Chapter 10, "Putting Data in Its Place Using DOS," for advice on organizing your hard-disk drive so that you can locate anything you want, whenever you want it.

Fig. 8.4
The hard drive is
hidden out of sight
inside the system unit.

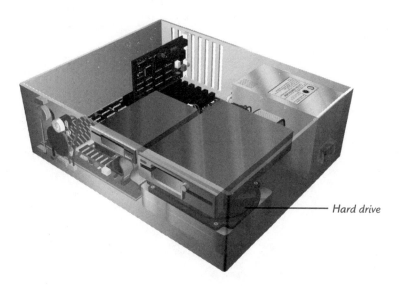

Hard drive

Of Mice and Keyboards

In this chapter:

- What's the difference between my old typewriter and a computer keyboard?

- What are all these weird keys like Ctrl and F10?

- Somebody told me to use the "three-fingered salute" to restart my computer. What's that?

- The mouse does not work like your TV remote control.

About the only thing your computer can't do is teach you how to type. Well, actually, it can even do that if you have the right software!

Until computers learn to read our minds, you need reliable ways to get the information from your head into the computer. Any contraption you use for this purpose is known as an **input device**. The two most common devices are the **keyboard**, which almost anyone would recognize, and the **mouse**, which is newer to the computing world but an invaluable tool nonetheless. If you're not familiar with these devices, this chapter tells you everything you need to know.

A typewriter and then some!

They might look vaguely similar, but don't be fooled! Your computer's keyboard is a lot more than just a typewriter. Not only can you type on a computer keyboard, but you can use it to give your computer commands, complete a whole bunch of boring, tedious tasks in just a few keystrokes, and more. About the only thing it *can't* do is teach you how to type. Well, actually, it can even do *that* if you have the right software!

 **{Note}** — | If you have an older keyboard, you might not have all the keys described in this chapter.

Remember ASDFGHJKL;? That's just the beginning

Even though computers are much more sophisticated than typewriters, the bulk of the keys on your computer's keyboard look and act much like type-writer keys. Most computer keyboards look like the one in figure 9.1.

Fig. 9.1
Look! It's a typewriter!
It's a calculator! No,
wait...it's both!

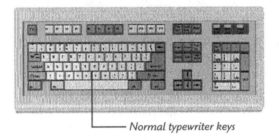

—— *Normal typewriter keys*

And for all you number crunchers out there...

If you work with numbers frequently, you know that typing numbers on a typewriter is a pain in the neck compared to punching them in on a calcula-tor. They're way up there on the top row and out of comfortable reach. Fortunately, keyboard designers realized this and added a **numeric keypad** to the standard set of keys.

The numeric keypad works just like a 10-key calculator, all the way down to the + and – keys. Generally, the only difference is that the multiply key is * instead of ×, and the division key is / instead of ÷. So, if you're a speed demon on a calculator, you should have no problems using the numeric keypad.

Q&A

When I press the keys on my numeric keypad, they're acting like arrow keys. What's going on here?

In the upper left corner of the numeric keypad, look for a key labeled Num Lock. If Num Lock is on (usually indicated by a little light on or above the Num Lock key), the keypad keys work like numbers. When it's off, they work like arrow keys (you'll learn more about arrow keys in a minute).

Here's more about keys

Your computer's keyboard also features a group of keys that are unique to computers. Most of these keys are found sandwiched between the regular keyboard and the numeric keypad. They have strange names like Scroll Lock, Home, End, and Insert. How these keys work often depends on the software you're using. But, table 9.1 shows their most common uses.

Table 9.1 Keys with Words on Them, Part 1

Key	Use
Insert	Switches the between Insert and Overtype modes (see the note after this table).
Delete	Deletes the character to the right of the cursor.
Home	Moves to the beginning of a line.
End	Moves to the end of a line.
Page Up	Moves one page up towards the beginning of the file.
Page Down	Moves one page down towards the end of the file.
Print Screen	Sends the screen image to the printer.
Scroll Lock	Stops screen from scrolling.
Pause/Break	Stops screen from scrolling, or, when used with the Ctrl key, stops a DOS command.
Num Lock	Switches the numeric keypad on and off.
Esc	Usually cancels a command.

Plain English, please!

One of the great things about computers, as opposed to typewriters, is that you can write, rewrite, edit, erase, and otherwise mess around with your files until right before you print them out on paper.

Insert and **Overtype modes** are the greatest thing since sliced bread. When you're in Insert mode, you can start typing in the middle of a line you already wrote, and the existing characters are "pushed" to the right—you don't have to write over what you already have. In Overtype mode, the new characters replace the old characters, just as they would on your typewriter (well, sort of, anyway).

What's with all these arrow keys?

When you type on a typewriter, you have to roll the paper up and down and use the space key to position the carriage wherever you want on a page. Making a minor correction after you've already removed the paper from the machine can be a royal pain.

No more! A computer doesn't have a carriage, so there's no problem with alignment. If you want to make a correction, you just use the arrow keys to position the blinking cursor where you want to make a correction and start typing!

The ones you'll use most of the time

There are two groups of keys on the keyboard that enable you to move the cursor around. The first set is to the bottom right of the regular keys. Each of these keys is marked with an arrow that shows which way the cursor moves when you press that key.

The ones you probably won't use as often

The numeric keypad also has a set of arrow keys that you can use to move the cursor. But to use them, you have to make sure that the Num Lock key is off. (If you press the arrow keys on the number pad and get numbers on the screen, the Num Lock key is still on.)

Q&A

But what about all those other keys that have arrows?

If you look at the keyboard, you'll notice that some other keys (Shift, Backspace, Enter, Tab) have arrows on them, too. Despite the arrow, they don't move the cursor around; they work just as they do on a typewriter.

Ctrl and Alt don't work?

The other keys are pretty straightforward, but two special ones, Ctrl (pronounced "control") and Alt (pronounced just as it looks) aren't so obvious. Ctrl and Alt don't work by themselves. You use them in combination with other keys (usually a letter key) to give commands to programs. Sometimes you even hold down a couple of keys at the same time, like Ctrl and Shift, or Ctrl and Alt.

If you're in Word for Windows, for example, and you hold down the Ctrl key and press *I*, Word makes the words or letters italic.

{Note}

On older computer keyboards, the Ctrl key may be marked "Control," and the Alt key may be marked "Alternate."

(Tip)

You learned earlier that you can restart your computer by pressing the Reset button on the front of the system unit. Here's another way to do it: hold down Ctrl+Alt, and then press the Delete key. Be sure that you are at the DOS prompt when you do this.

Somewhere along the line, this key combination picked up the nickname "three-fingered salute." This is a handy command, but be careful! Just like the Reset button, Ctrl+Alt+Delete wipes out everything in memory and restarts your computer from scratch.

F is for *Function*

There's one more group of keys you haven't seen yet. You'll find these keys either at the top or to the far left of your keyboard, or both. They're easy to find, because they're marked F1, F2, F3, and so on, up to at least F10 and possibly as high as F12.

The F in these keys' names stands for "function," so it's not surprising that these keys are often referred to as **function keys**. How the function keys work depends solely on the program you're running. Usually, they're used for shortcuts or common tasks.

?Q&A

The screen says, `Press any key to continue.` **My keyboard doesn't have an Any key. What should I do?**

Lots of people get confused by this message. It literally means *any* key! DOS just needs to know you're ready to go on; just touch anything on the keyboard (except Shift, Caps Lock, Ctrl, or Alt) when you're ready.

Eeeeeek! A mouse!

These days, having a computer without a mouse is like playing golf without any clubs. You can probably kick or throw the ball along the course and eventually get it in the hole, but it sure is a lot more work!

Your mouse is like an extension to your hand. It lets you select items on the screen—like buttons—almost as if you selected them with your own finger. A mouse is so handy, in fact, that many computer programs (especially Windows programs) rely on it heavily.

Favorite functions

Although the people who create computer programs can make the F keys work any way they like, some uses have become almost standard. For example, in many programs, you can press F1 to get help or F10 to exit the program.

Many Windows programs, especially those that are in a suite of products, use similar key combinations for similar operations. For example, in Microsoft applications, pressing Ctrl+C copies the information that's selected. Look for common functions like this to make programs easy to use (you'll find that many common operations have keyboard shortcuts listed next to them in pull-down menus).

Although you can control Windows from your keyboard, you probably wouldn't want to. It often takes two, three, even four or five keystrokes to accomplish what you can do with one click of the mouse!

Anatomy of a mouse

A mouse is really not much more than a box with a ball sticking out the bottom and a cord sticking out the end (the tail?). When you move the mouse around your desk, the ball (called the **tracking ball**) rolls and sends a signal to the computer. The computer uses this signal to make the on-screen **mouse pointer** move around the screen.

Fig. 9.2
The mouse's "feet" are really a ball that sends signals to the computer. The pointer is then sent scurrying across the screen.

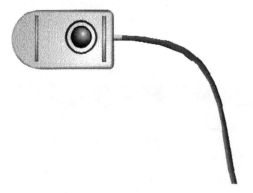

On top of the mouse are buttons. The average, garden-variety mouse has two buttons, but some have three. You use the buttons to activate objects on-screen.

So what do I do with it?

Using a mouse takes some getting used to, but once you master it, you'll never want to be without one.

Here's what you do with a mouse:

These instructions assume you are right-handed. If you're left-handed, reverse all these instructions (but you Southpaws are used to that anyway, right?).

1 Put the mouse on the right side of the computer, near the keyboard. It needs to sit on a flat, clean surface. A **mouse pad** is recommended.

2 Lay your hand loosely on top of the mouse, placing your index finger on the left button and your middle finger on the right button. Don't grip the mouse too hard! Your hand should rest comfortably on the mouse's back.

3 Roll the mouse around on the mouse pad. As you do, watch the screen. The mouse pointer should roll the same way the mouse does.

4 Roll until the pointer is over a piece of text or some other thing on the screen, like an icon or menu name.

5 When you get there, click one of the buttons. Which button you click and how many times you click it depends on the program you're using and what you want to do. Some tasks you can do are listed in table 9.2.

Table 9.2   Push, Pull, Click, Click: Using the Mouse Buttons

Action	How to do it
Point	Roll the mouse until the on-screen mouse pointer is over a screen object.
Click	Press and release the left mouse button.
Double-click	Click twice very quickly.
Drag	Point to an object, press and hold down the left mouse button, and move the mouse.

You may need to practice these actions to get them down, but it won't take long before your mouse is almost as easy to use as your own hand.

 **Plain English, please!**

A **mouse pad** is a little "rug" you put under the mouse to give the tracking ball better traction. It's usually made of soft rubber or rough plastic. A mouse rolls better on the somewhat rough surface of a mouse pad, just like tires work better on dry pavement than on ice.

Mice belong to a family of contraptions known as **pointing devices**. Instead of a mouse, some people use other types of pointing devices, such a **trackball** (which is basically a mouse turned upside down), or a **joystick** (which is common for video games).

?Q&A

Why is my mouse pointer so jumpy?

If you find that your mouse pointer moves erratically even though you're rolling the mouse smoothly, you've probably got dirty rollers (not you, your mouse).

Turn your mouse over and pop off the little door that holds the tracking ball in place. Remove the ball and look inside the mouse. You'll see several rollers that the ball rolls against. To clean the rollers, use alcohol and a Q-Tip. Sometimes it helps to blow a puff of air inside the box, too, to remove any dust. In bad cases, you can try scraping the crud off the rollers with your fingernail.

?Q&A

My mouse is dead! How do I perform CPR?

First, check that the mouse is plugged into the back of your computer. You can't expect to use an unplugged mouse anymore than you can use a car without a battery.

If the mouse is plugged in, try restarting your computer and watching the screen as the various start-up programs run. Usually some sort of mouse-related message appears. If you don't see such a message, your **mouse driver** (the program that makes it run) may not be loading. Finally, make sure that the program you're using takes advantage of a mouse. Many DOS programs don't.

10

Putting Data in Its Place Using DOS

If you're not running a graphical user interface like Windows, DOS is the only choice you have. The good news is that handling disks with DOS is easy.

In this chapter:

- Is it bad to work in DOS?

- How can I see what's on a disk?

- With so much stuff on my computer, how can I find the things I need?

- What's a good way to organize my information?

D o you have a computer guru—someone you can call for help when you're having a problem? Well, when gurus get you out of trouble, they're usually muttering to themselves and typing much too fast for the eye to see. Then they jump up, warn you not to do it again, and walk away quickly before you can ask what you did wrong.

Know this about computer gurus:

- They all act like this.

- They do it on purpose.

- Their knowledge is based on a good understanding of DOS.

Your computer's basic operating system is probably DOS, and DOS is a pain, but ignoring it won't make it go away. Even if you use Windows (covered in Part IV), you still have DOS chugging along under those pretty menus and buttons.

Think of Windows as the glitzy queen of the ball, and DOS as Cinderella before her transformation—underappreciated, hardworking, efficient, and with limitless unrecognized potential. There's no reason to overlook DOS's capabilities just because DOS doesn't look as nice as Windows.

And if you're not running a graphical user interface like Windows, DOS is the only choice you have. So make the best of it. Besides, the good news is that handling disks with DOS is easy. Honestly!

 (Tip)

> Don't be afraid to try out all the commands you learn in this chapter. They can't do any damage.

A guided tour of your disks

Okay, hold your breath. Here's this chapter's big revelation: Everything you store on a disk is placed in something called a **file**. A file is nothing more than a collection of computer information (called **data**) that's related some-how. A file can hold the words in a business letter, the information that draws a picture, the numbers that make up a spreadsheet, or the program-ming code that runs a program—almost anything.

Imagine an office filing cabinet. That filing cabinet has drawers that hold file folders. The file folders hold paper documents or maybe other file folders. As you can tell from figure 10.1, a computer is a lot like that filing cabinet. Instead of drawers, though, the PC uses **disks**. Instead of file folders, each disk contains **directories**, and instead of paper documents, each directory holds **files**.

When you get lots of files on a disk, it's hard to find what you're looking for. To help you find information quickly, you can organize your files into direc-tories. Just as you might keep all your tax records in one drawer of a file cabinet and your correspondence in another drawer, you might choose to store your computer graphics in one directory and your word processor documents in another directory.

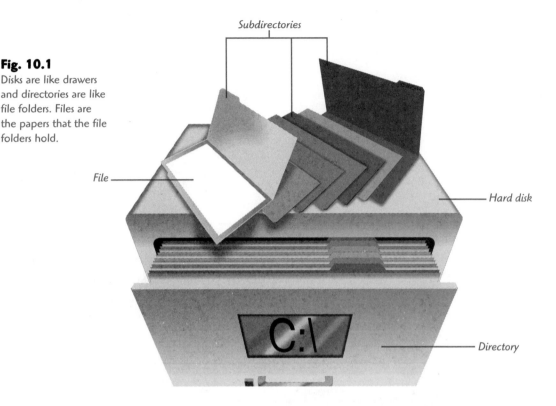

Subdirectories

Fig. 10.1
Disks are like drawers
and directories are like
file folders. Files are
the papers that the file
folders hold.

File

Hard disk

Directory

Of course, if you have a lot of file cabinets in your office, you have to put labels on the drawers so you can tell what's what. The same is true of directories and files, which must all have unique names. (It wouldn't be much help to have 30 drawers all labeled simply "Letters," now would it?) Usually, it's you who decides what a file's or directory's name should be. But, sometimes, software packages create files and directories for you and name them automatically.

Want to see the files and directories on a disk? Try DOS's DIR (DIRectory) command. You might want to turn the PC on first. When you do, your monitor will display something like figure 10.2, the cold and unfriendly DOS prompt (shudder). The prompt is the C:\> with the flashing cursor beside it. Supposedly, it's telling you that DOS is waiting for commands.

Fig. 10.2

When you first turn on your computer, you usually end up at the ever-unpopular DOS prompt.

All set? Type **DIR** and press Enter to *send* your command to DOS. When you do, you see a bunch of information fly up onto your screen (resembling fig. 10.3) like movie credits on fast forward. This information is all the files and directories currently on your hard disk. It may be a few, or it may be hundreds, depending what you have on your hard drive.

Fig. 10.3

The DIR command tells the computer to show you the names of the files on the current disk drive.

```
C:\>DIR

 Volume in drive C is HARDDISK
 Volume Serial Number is 1CAF-AAF9
 Directory of C:\

DOS          <DIR>      06-05-93    2:17p
WINWORD      <DIR>      01-30-94    2:48p
INFO         <DIR>      07-22-93    2:57p
UTILS        <DIR>      06-05-93    3:08p
WORD         <DIR>      06-05-93    3:09p
WINDOWS      <DIR>      06-05-93    3:18p
AMOUSE       <DIR>      03-22-94    2:52p
COMMAND  COM     52925  03-10-93    6:00a
MOUSE    SYS     34581  10-04-90    3:09p
WINA20   386      9349  03-10-93    6:00a
CONFIG   SYS       239  05-15-94    9:23p
AUTOEXEC BAT       270  05-15-94    9:39p
        12 file(s)       97364 bytes
                      22415360 bytes free

C:\>
```

Entries in the list that have the word <DIR> after them are directories. Remember that directories are like file folders because they contain files. After each directory's name, you can see the date and time the directory was created.

Anything in the list that doesn't have <DIR> after it *must be a file*. (Files and directories are the only things you can ever have on a disk.) After each file's name is the size of the file measured in bytes and the date and time the file was created. After the list, DOS displays the number of files (including directories) included in the list, as well as how much space those files consume. DOS also displays the amount of space left on the drive.

❓Q&A

How can I stop the file list from running off the top of the screen?

Usually, there are too many files and directories on a disk to fit all their names on the screen. To stop the list from scrolling out of view, enter the command as **DIR /P**. This forces the display to pause after the screen fills. To see the next screenful of information, press your keyboard's Enter key. Adding something like /P to a command is called adding a **command switch**; you add a switch whenever you want a variation of a basic command.

Isn't it a bad thing to default?

If you ever defaulted on a loan payment, you probably got a nasty phone call from the creditor. As you'll soon discover though, in computer lingo, the word **default** isn't a bad thing at all. It simply means active or "the one the computer turns to first."

When you first start your computer, the default (or active) drive is usually C:, which is your hard drive. You can get the name of the default drive by looking at the DOS prompt. For example, in the following DOS prompt, C: is the default drive:

```
C:\>
```

 **{Note}**

DOS assigns letter-names to each of the drives on your system so you can tell it which drive to work with. The first hard disk is always C:, the first floppy drive is always A:, and a second floppy is B:.

To look at files on a different disk, you can change the default drive. Just type the drive's letter followed by a colon, and press Enter. For example, to change to drive A, type **A:** at the DOS prompt and press Enter. If you get the message Bad command or file name, don't panic. You probably forgot to put the colon right after the drive letter. When you do it right, your computer switches to drive A, and the DOS prompt looks something like this:

    A:\>

You can now type **DIR** to see the files and directories on your floppy drive (see fig. 10.4). Hint: The **/P** switch works here, too, in case the list is too long for one screen.

Fig. 10.4

In this illustration, the user has made drive A the active drive, then used the DIR command to see what's on the disk in drive A.

```
C:\>a:

A:\>dir

 Volume in drive A has no label
 Directory of A:\

LETTERS      <DIR>         10-05-94    3:14a
REPORTS      <DIR>         10-05-94    3:14a
ARTICLES     <DIR>         10-05-94    3:15a
          3 file(s)              0 bytes
                        727,040 bytes free

A:\>
```

⊛ *{Note}*

When you give your computer a DOS command that has something to do with files or directories, DOS applies that command to the default drive (the one that is shown in the prompt). The exception to this rule is if you include a different drive name as part of the command. For example, the DOS command **DIR A:** shows you the directory of drive A, regardless of what the default drive is.

DOS is telling me my drive is not ready. Now what?

If you try to switch to drive A (or any other drive) when it contains no disk, you'll see this:

```
Not ready error reading drive A
Abort, Retry, Fail?
```

To make your computer happy again, put a disk in the drive and press R for retry. Or press F to allow the command to fail, and you'll get this message:

```
Current drive is no longer valid>
```

Although that sounds horrible, it isn't. Simply switch to your hard drive or to a floppy drive that does contain a disk, by typing the drive's letter followed by a colon, and pressing Enter. There you go—you're valid again!

Peeking into directories

In order to get at files stored inside a directory, you have to open the directory, just as you'd open a file folder. DOS's command for opening directories is CD (short for Change Directory). To open any directory, just type CD followed by the directory's name.

Need an example? Suppose you just used the DIR command on drive A (refer to fig. 10.4). Now, you know you have a directory named LETTERS. To open the LETTERS directory, type **CD LETTERS**. Your DOS prompt changes to this:

```
A:\LETTERS>
```

⚡Q&A

I didn't get any kind of error message, but my DOS prompt doesn't show the name of the directory, like you said it would.

No problem. If you're sure you typed the command properly, you probably did change to the new directory, but your prompt isn't set up to show directory names. To add directory names to your prompt, type the mystical DOS command **PROMPT pg** and press Enter. If this makes the directory name appear as part of your prompt, ask your local computer guru to set your computer to do this automatically from now on.

You can now type the DIR command to see the files stored inside the LETTERS directory. You'll see something like figure 10.5.

Fig. 10.5

In this illustration, we've opened the LETTERS directory and then typed DIR to see inside that directory.

```
A:\>cd letters

A:\LETTERS>dir

 Volume in drive A has no label
 Directory of A:\LETTERS

.              <DIR>         10-05-94   3:14a
..             <DIR>         10-05-94   3:14a
OLDLETS        <DIR>         10-05-94   3:16a
LETTER3  DOC   11,264 10-05-94   3:18a
LETTER2  DOC   11,776 10-05-94   3:18a
LETTER1  DOC   10,240 10-05-94   3:18a
        6 file(s)       33,280 bytes
                       692,224 bytes free

A:\LETTERS>
```

As you can see, the LETTERS directory contains not only a few files, but also another directory called OLDLETS. If you open the second directory by typing **CD OLDLETS**, your DOS prompt changes to

    A:\LETTERS\OLDLETS>

The above DOS prompt shows that drive A is the default drive and that you are inside the OLDLETS directory, which itself is inside the LETTERS directory. You might want to think of the OLDLETS directory as being a file folder that's stuffed inside another file folder called LETTERS. The LETTERS file folder is stuffed into the file cabinet drawer named A. What a concept—being inside a file folder! Hope you're not claustrophobic.

Q&A — ***How do I deal with the message*** `Invalid directory?`

You get this message when DOS can't find the directory you typed, either because it doesn't exist or because it's not visible from the active directory. (You can't change to LETTERS if you're not on A, and you can't change to OLDLETS if you're not in LETTERS.) Check your typing and try again.

Q&A — ***I'm a failure! DOS wrote*** `General failure reading drive A` ***on my screen.***

Relax. You have an unformatted disk in the drive. Press F (for Fail) and then switch to a valid drive. You can't use that disk until it's formatted (you can learn what formatting is—and how to do it—in Chapter 12).

I've fallen into a directory and I can't get out!

If you start using the CD command to move around within the directory structure of a disk, you might want to know how to get back out and close all those open folders. Although you might have typed four or five DOS commands to get into a certain directory, it takes one command to get back to the root.

66 *Plain English, please!*

Most people call the top directory on any disk **the root directory**, or just **the root**, because all other directories on that disk branch out from it.

Type **CD ** and press Enter.

The \ character is called the **backslash** and might be located anywhere on your keyboard, based on the manufacturer's whim. Look around, but never confuse it with the **forward slash** (which is on the same key as the question mark). The forward slash is for DOS command switches (remember /P from the DIR command?).

(Tip) _____

Sometimes you just want to go back one level, instead of going all the way to the root. To do this, use a double period instead of a backslash. In other words, type **CD ..** and press Enter.

?Q&A _____

How do I know what directories are on my disk?

There are two ways. First, you can go exploring, which is kind of fun. Type DIR to see what's available in each directory, and then use the CD command to change to any of the other directories you see on the screen. Once there, type DIR again to see what kind of goodies you've stumbled across. If you see another directory, change to it and type DIR again. If you ever get lost, CD \ will always scoot you right back up to the top again.

The second way is with another DOS command, TREE. Make sure that the disk you want to find out about is the default drive. Type **TREE**, press Enter, and stand back. If the list is too long (it probably is), you can make the result of this command come out on your printer. Make sure your printer is turned on, and then type **TREE >PRN**. Something wonderful should happen.

File it your way!

When you first got your office filing cabinet, it was little more than an empty box with drawers. It was up to you to put little labels on the outside of the drawers and to organize your file folders inside them.

Your PC's disks work almost exactly the same way. When you put an unused disk in a disk drive, the disk is as empty as that new filing cabinet. Similarly, when you get a new PC, its hard disk drive is mostly empty, too. (There may be a few things on the hard drive that were loaded there for you by the computer's manufacturer.) To use a disk in an organized way, you should create directories that you can organize your files into.

Go ahead...make my directory

DOS provides the MD command (short for Make Directory) for creating directories. For example, to create a directory called MYSTUFF, type **MD MYSTUFF**. After you enter the above command, you have your own computerized file folder (that is, a directory) into which you can place any files you like.

Directory names follow the same conventions that file names do; up to eight characters, letters, and numbers, avoid special characters, and all those other creative constraints. Don't worry, the MD command will be sure to tell you if you give it a directory name it doesn't like!

?Q&A

What does `Directory already exists` **mean?**

Exactly what it says (for a change). This means that you already have a directory with the same name as the one you're trying to create. To solve this problem, come up with another name and use the MD command again.

Organizing files that go with certain programs

Suppose you have the program Word for Windows (WinWord) as your word processor. When WinWord was installed on your computer, the installation program created a directory named WINWORD on your hard drive. It then placed all of WinWord's program files into the WINWORD directory.

You could use WinWord just the way it's set up, saving the documents you create into the WINWORD directory. But it might be better to make your own directory inside WINWORD. Then you can put all your own WinWord files in that directory, so the documents don't get mixed up with WinWord's program files. (The directory listings will stay short and easy to read, too.)

Am I stuck with all my directories?

If DOS provides a way to make new directories, it must also provide a way to get rid of some, right? Of course. The command to use is RD (short for Remove Directory). If you want to get rid of a directory called MYSTUFF, for example, type **RD MYSTUFF**.

⊛ {Note}

DOS won't let you remove a directory if it still contains files. This feature has prevented many unexpected accidents over the years. In Chapter 11, you'll learn about deleting files.

❓Q&A

When I tried to remove a directory, I got the message `Invalid path, not directory, or directory not empty.`

This means that you're trying to remove a directory that doesn't exist, or one that still has files in it. Double-check the directory name and then try again, or empty out the directory and then try again.

11

Doing Stuff with Files (DOS)

In this chapter:

- How can I tell what's in a file?

- How do I copy a file?

- This file doesn't go here. How can I move it?

- Delete old files, rename others

- I think I lost a file! How can I find it?

- How to work with groups of files—using wild cards

If you want to find things when you need them, you've got to keep the files on your hard disk organized. Just like the files in your office!

At this point, you might feel a little cocky. After all, you've managed to look at a disk's contents and move around from one directory to another—all without anyone holding your hand. You've probably even created a directory or two and maybe even deleted them again. The computer's still working, right? Great! You're familiar with the basic commands for creating a filing system. Now it's time to learn commands that affect the files.

How to peek into a file

You know how to see what files are on a disk by using the DIR command. But what if you want to see the information stored *in* the file? DOS will show it to you when you use the TYPE command, followed by the name of the file you want to see.

For this example, you need to find a suitable file. Most hard disks have a directory named DOS, and most DOS directories contain a file named APPNOTES.TXT. If this file is missing, use any file that ends with .TXT, such as README.TXT.

Make sure that C: is your current drive and type these commands:

CD \DOS *(This puts you into the DOS directory so that the next command will work.)*

TYPE APPNOTES.TXT *(Remember to leave a space after TYPE.)*

When you do, the entire file will go ripping across your screen. Once the scrolling stops, you see a screen that looks something like figure 11.1.

Fig. 11.1

When you first display the APPNOTES.TXT file with the TYPE command, only part of the file can fit on the screen at a time.

```
-------------------------
If you can't start Ventura Publisher, make sure your Ventura
Publisher directory is within the first 70 characters of the PATH
command in your AUTOEXEC.BAT file.

1.23 WordPerfect WPINFO.EXE 5.1
-------------------------------
Some versions of WordPerfect WPINFO.EXE are incompatible with
MS-DOS 5.0. Contact your vendor for more information.

1.24 WordPerfect Office 3.0
---------------------------
Some versions of WordPerfect Office 3.0 are incompatible with
MS-DOS 5.0. Contact your vendor for more information.

1.25 XTreeNet
-------------
To use XTreeNet with MS-DOS Shell Task Swapper, select the
Prevent Program Switch option in the MS-DOS Shell Advanced
dialog box. For more information about specifying advanced
properties, see Chapter 8 of the Microsoft MS-DOS User's Guide
and Reference.


C:\DOS>
```

What happened? APPNOTES.TXT contains more information than can fit on your screen, so what doesn't fit scrolls off into computer heaven.

How can I keep it from scrolling off the screen so fast?

DOS allows you to tack on another command word to fix this problem. You must use the vertical bar followed by the word *MORE*. (The vertical bar is usually on the same key as the backslash, but you have to press Shift to get it.)

To see the whole file, one screen at a time, type this:

TYPE APPNOTES.TXT ¦MORE

The ¦MORE part of the command works just like the /P **switch** that you can use with DIR. It pauses the screen and displays the line -- More -- at the bottom (see fig. 11.2). Just press Enter or any other key to see the next screen.

Plain English, please!

In DOS lingo, a **switch** is simply some special information you give a command. Just as you'd ask a waiter for your filet mignon to be cooked "medium rare" or "well done," DOS commands sometimes need additional information, or switches, to do their job.

Fig. 11.2
Adding ¦MORE to the TYPE command makes DOS display a file one screen at a time.

```
APPNOTES.TXT

NOTES ON USING APPLICATIONS WITH MS-DOS VERSION 5.0
===================================================

This document provides important information not included in the
Microsoft MS-DOS User's Guide and Reference or in online Help.

Look through the following table of contents to determine
whether your application is included.

ATTENTION CODEVIEW AND INTEL ABOVEBOARD USERS
+++++++++++++++++++++++++++++++++++++++++++++++
Sections 1.1 and 1.4 contain critical information
about using Intel Aboveboard and CodeView with
MS-DOS 5.0.
+++++++++++++++++++++++++++++++++++++++++++++++

For information about installing MS-DOS 5.0 and using hardware
and networks with MS-DOS 5.0, see the README.TXT file.

The following topics are discussed in this file:
-- More --
```

I keep getting an error message, Bad command or file name**, and I know I'm typing the right letters!**

New DOS users often type the words exactly, but forget to put spaces between the command word (in this case, it's TYPE) and the name of the file that the command is supposed to affect. DOS needs that space between TYPE and APPNOTES.TXT so it can understand where the command ends and the file name begins. DOS knows how to TYPE, but it's a little weak on TYPEAPPNOTE.TXT.

Which files can I display with the TYPE command?

Text (TXT) files are readable to DOS because they don't contain special codes like boldface or italic. The APPNOTES.TXT file contains plain text, so it looks okay when you display it on the screen. Try looking at the file CHKDSK.EXE with the TYPE command and you see something that looks like super geek talk (see fig. 11.3). Because CHKDSK.EXE is a program file (the EXE stands for executable), it contains instructions only your computer can understand.

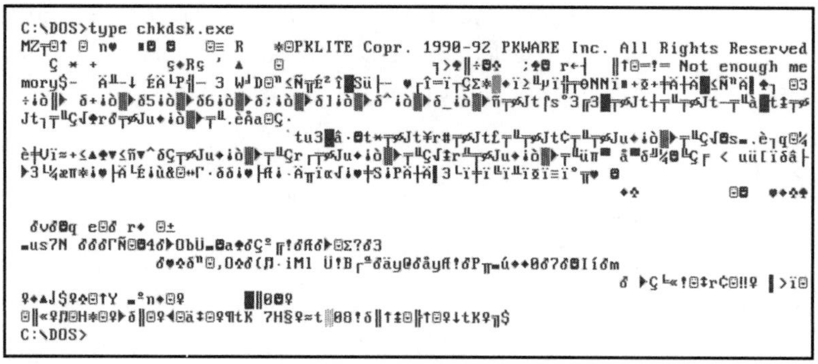

Fig. 11.3

Some files contain strange-looking information because they're not written for you to interpret.

When you tell DOS to TYPE a program file, imagine that you're commanding it to read the contents in English. It does its level best, but if the file wasn't in English in the first place, what you get is a mass of happy faces, beeps, and little accented letters. Don't be alarmed by all the beeps and funky characters—they're kind of annoying but they're not hurting anything.

All file names are not created equal

Sometimes, you can tell a lot about a file by its three-character **extension**. TXT files, for example, are probably text files that you can TYPE to the screen. DOC files may have come from a word processor.

Files that end in EXE or COM are always program files. That's a rule. They're not for looking at, they're for *loading* and *running*. Don't EVER save any of your data files using either of these extensions because DOS gets very confused.

Syntax and parameters—yes, you need to understand this stuff

You must type commands *exactly just so* in order for DOS to understand you. One slip and it's `Bad command or file name`. You're sure of entering things correctly when you use the proper **syntax**.

If you said "Apple please green the get," nobody would understand what you were talking about. That's because the English language has a set of rules (called **syntax**) that govern how you put sentences together to make sense. Now, you can probably figure out how this sentence should work ("Please get the green apple") because you understand the language and the syntax rules. Unfortunately, your computer doesn't. You have to follow the DOS syntax, or the computer won't understand what you want to do.

Each command has its own syntax and most of them follow a common pattern. (What's this? Something in DOS follows a pattern?) At the DOS prompt, you always type the command word first, followed by a space, and then type whatever else the command needs to finish the job. We call this "whatever else" a **parameter** (pronounced per-AM-uh-ter) for the command. So the whole command ends up looking like this:

command parameter

That's not so complicated, is it? You saw this command a few pages ago:

TYPE APPNOTES.TXT

It works because TYPE is a command that DOS knows, and APPNOTES.TXT is a file that it can find. You used APPNOTES.TXT as the parameter for the TYPE command—and you didn't even understand parameters then!

A parameter can be a file name, a directory or drive name, a path to one of those items, and so on. Whatever the command needs for DOS to carry it out. Don't worry; if DOS doesn't have enough information, DOS will tell you!

Copying a file is like digital cloning

One of the great things about disk-based information is that it's easy to copy. More to the point, you can make as many copies as you like. But why would you want to copy files?

- A copy of a file on a floppy is a more efficient way of sharing information with co-workers than it is to hand them a stack of papers and ask them to type it into their own computers.

- You should also make **backup copies** of all your important files, place them on floppy disks, and store them away from your PC. You never know when the digital demons will make off with your original data. (Just kidding. But stuff does get lost or destroyed sometimes, so it's good to have backups.)

To copy a file, you use the DOS COPY command. The COPY command needs two parameters: the first tells it what to copy and the second tells it where to put it. You type a space between the two parameters, so DOS can tell the what-to-copy part from the where-to-put-it part. Like this:

COPY *what where*

How to copy a file to another disk

To copy a file to another disk, first change to the directory that contains the file you want to copy. Then, type the command COPY followed by a space and the name of the file to be copied. Leave another space and then type the letter of the disk drive where the copy should appear followed by a colon (:). Remember to press Enter to send the command to DOS.

For example, to copy the file README.TXT from your DOS directory to a floppy disk, follow these steps:

1 Place an empty formatted floppy disk in drive A.

2 Type **C:** and press Enter. This command ensures that drive C is the current drive. If you KNOW that it is, you don't have to do it.

3 Type **CD \DOS** and press Enter. This opens the DOS directory if it wasn't already open.

4 Type **COPY README.TXT A:** and press Enter. (Leave a space after COPY and a space after TXT.) DOS copies the README.TXT file to the disk in drive A.

?Q&A ____

> **What does** `File not found` **mean?**
>
> This error message means exactly what it says: DOS can't find the file you named. Make sure you typed the file name correctly and that you have the correct directory open. If you can see the file name in the current directory, you can copy it. Just watch your spacing and your spelling.

Do I have to switch directories first?

Nope. If you know the location of a file you want to copy, you don't have to actually open its directory. Instead, you can just type the file's location as part of the COPY command. To copy NETWORKS.TXT from the DOS directory to drive A without opening the DOS directory, type this:

COPY C:\DOS\NETWORKS.TXT A:

Techno-geeks call this **specifying the path** to the file. I prefer to think of it as telling DOS the address where the file lives:

> "Go to drive C and then turn into the DOS directory. Once you're there, get NETWORKS.TXT and COPY it to drive A."

Notice that there are still only two spaces in this whole command. The **path** to the file is entered as one word because DOS considers it to be an integral part of the file name.

Or you can make a copy in another directory

If you just want to copy a file to a different directory on the same disk, just add the directory's name after the drive letter at the end of the command.

For example, to copy the README.TXT file to the WINWORD directory, type this:

COPY README.TXT C:\WINWORD

To copy the same file to the MYSTUFF directory (which is inside the WINWORD directory), you'd type this:

COPY README.TXT C:\WINWORD\MYSTUFF

If this seems complicated, imagine that DOS is a file clerk who moves files around at your beck and call. The trouble is that DOS is not intelligent enough to find the MYSTUFF directory by itself. You have to tell it to go to C: first, then open WINWORD, where MYSTUFF can be found.

 Q&A

> **What do I do when I see** `File cannot be copied onto itself?`
>
> This error message means that you're trying to copy a file into the same directory that the file resides in. Check your typing!

I don't want to type all that stuff

Do all these long path names have you lost? You can leave the destination path out of the command entirely if you change to the destination directory before you give the command. Suppose you want to copy the file LETTERS.DOC from a floppy in drive A to the DOCUMENTS directory in drive C.

Make C: the current drive, and then type **CD \DOCUMENTS** to change to that directory. Now type:

COPY A:LETTERS.DOC

That's it! Since you didn't type a destination, DOS just assumes you want to copy to the current directory and magically brings the file to where you are!

How to get rid of files you don't want anymore

The longer you live in a house, the more stuff you collect in the closets. Similarly, the more you use your computer, the more files you collect on your disks. As your hard drive fills up, you are often forced to do a little spring cleaning. Once a file has outlived its usefulness, you can delete it with the DEL command. For example, to delete the README.TXT file that was created in the previous section, type this:

DEL C:\WINWORD\NEWFILE.TXT

If you had already opened the WINWORD directory, you could just type this command:

DEL README.TXT

Remember that you don't need a path name when you're already in the right directory. The thing about the DEL command that scares people is that you never receive any feedback from DOS that the command worked. You are simply returned to the DOS prompt—no warnings or congratulatory messages of any kind.

?Q&A

Is a file really gone when I delete it?

Nope. It would take too long for DOS to actually remove the information from a file. The *next time* DOS wants space on the disk though, it will write over the information you "deleted." All DOS does when it deletes a file is destroy the first character of the file name and mark the file's disk space as "For Sale" to the next file created. This concept is the key to *undeleting* files in the next section.

!(Tip)

In case you run across the ERASE command someplace, it is identical to DEL— it does the same thing and uses the same syntax. It just takes longer to type!

Deleted the wrong file by accident? Undelete it!

Sooner or later, you're going to delete a file and then immediately wish you hadn't. At such times, it's good to know that DOS can probably bring the deleted file back for you by way of the UNDELETE command.

Suppose you just deleted a file called PROG.EXE from the C drive. You can bring it back by typing this command:

UNDELETE PROG.EXE

When you do, DOS will say that it found a file named "?ROG.EXE" and asks if the file it found is the one you want to undelete (see fig. 11.4). Press Y to answer yes, and DOS asks for the first letter of the file name. You can type any letter you want, actually, but it's obviously better to use the "P." Type the letter, and DOS tries to recover the file.

Fig. 11.4
The UNDELETE command can bring deleted files back from the great unknown.

```
UNDELETE - A delete protection facility
Copyright (C) 1987-1993 Central Point Software, Inc.
All rights reserved.

Directory: C:\
File Specifications: PROG.EXE

    Delete Sentry control file not found.

    Deletion-tracking file not found.

    MS-DOS directory contains    1 deleted files.
    Of those,    1 files may be recovered.

Using the MS-DOS directory method.

    ?ROG     EXE    29334  9-30-93  6:20a  ...A  Undelete (Y/N)?y
    Please type the first character for ?ROG    .EXE: p

File successfully undeleted.


C:\>
```

⊗<Caution>_| The UNDELETE command works reliably only if you use it immediately after deleting a file. The more you use your computer before trying to recover the file, the less likely UNDELETE will be successful. This is because other files may get saved over the data that was contained in the deleted file.

The UNDELETE command is included only with DOS versions 5.0 or later. If you have a DOS version older than 5.0, you should consider upgrading. Talk to your dealer if you're not sure how to upgrade.

You can change file names, if you like

Often, you'll want to change the name of a file. Maybe this week's sales are now last week's sales, or perhaps you simply don't like the name you originally gave to a file. The command REN is used to rename files in DOS. To use this command, just type REN followed by the file's current name and new name. For example, to change LETTER1.TXT to MYLETT.TXT, type this:

REN LETTER1.TXT MYLETT.TXT

This command has the same syntax as COPY but is very different in the way it works. With REN, you still have only one copy of the file when you're finished. COPY, as you know, can also change a file's name, but you wind up with two files—one with the old name and one with the new one.

As always, the usual rules about path names apply. If you're not in the directory with the file whose name you want to change, you have to either open that directory or type the complete path to the file:

REN C:\WINWORD\LETTERS\LETTER1.TXT MYLETT.TXT

If you use the full path to a file name as part of the REN command, don't bother typing it again as part of the new name—DOS doesn't need it because the file isn't moved anywhere by the command. If you do type it and make a mistake doing it, all you get is an error message.

What if DOS tells me Duplicate file name or file not found?

This means either that the file you want to rename doesn't exist or that there's already a file in the active directory that has the file name you want to use. In the first case, check your typing. In the second case, choose a new name.

When a file's in the wrong place, move it

Copying a file is like photocopying a letter. When you're done, you end up with the original plus a new copy. The COPY command is great for placing duplicates of files on another disk. When you want to just rearrange files to other directories on the same disk, MOVE is better. Your disk doesn't fill up with old forgotten copies of files because the originals are automatically deleted from their directories.

If you have DOS Version 6.0 or later, you can use the MOVE command. To move the file README.TXT from the DOS directory to your WINWORD directory, you'd type this:

MOVE C:\DOS\README.TXT C:\WINWORD

Notice that this command also resembles COPY, in that it has two parameters: a **source** and a **destination**.

I have DOS Version 5. How can I move a file?

If you have a version of DOS earlier than 6.0, you can still move a file, but you have to COPY it and then DEL the original:

COPY C:\DOS\README.TXT C:\WINWORD

DEL C:\DOS\README.TXT

What do I do when DOS asks about overwriting a file?

Sometimes, when copying or moving a file, you may see a message asking whether you want to overwrite an existing file. For example, when trying to copy CHKDSK.EXE, you might see this:

```
Overwrite C:\CHKDSK.EXE (Yes, No, All)?
```

This means there is already a file in the destination directory with that name. What do you want to do?

- Answer Y to have the new file replace the old one.

- Answer N to cancel the copy.

- Answer A when you're copying many files simultaneously and want to replace them all. You'll find out how to do that trick in a few minutes.

I can't find the file I want

Looking for a misplaced file can be like finding a needle in a haystack. Luckily, there's a trick you can use to make DOS find a file. Try typing this, but instead of typing *filename.ext*, type the name of the file you're looking for:

**CD **

DIR *filename.ext* **/S**

The **/S** makes DOS search all the directories and subdirectories on the drive.

Do I have to rename/copy/move/delete each file separately?

One daunting task that you will one day face is when you decide to copy an entire directory containing 50 or more files. Relax, you don't have to do it one file at a time. In fact, the command probably takes *less typing* than if you try to copy only one file…

How to use wild cards

DOS allows you to use something called a **wild card** (or **wild-card character**) that represents any file name. If you've ever played poker, you know that when you have a wild card in your hand, you're allowed to make that card equal to anything else in the deck. For example, if Jokers were wild and you held four aces and a Joker, you could say that you had five aces. (Bet BIG money on this one!) If you played like my friend Bill, you might say that you had four aces and a three or seven or Queen. (I love playing with Bill.)

The ? wild card matches one character at a time

DOS uses the question mark (?) as a wild card exactly like the preceding example. The ? can be used to replace *any one* character in a file name. Let's say I had nine files in my current directory and I had given them all names like LETTER1.DOC, LETTER2.DOC, LETTER3.DOC and so on, right up to LETTER9.DOC. I could copy all of them to a floppy disk in drive A: with the following command:

COPY LETTER?.DOC A:

The ? acts as a wild card that accepts any single character at that one position. The file names must still start with "LETTER" and end with "DOC." Since DOS takes any character at all where the ? appears, you might say it plays poker like Bill.

 **(Tip)**

> Since wild cards accept any character, just using one question mark in a command can conceivably affect 36 different files. (That's 26 letters and 10 numbers that could all appear in that one position.)
>
> You can avoid unpleasant surprises by using the DIR command with your wild card before you attempt a COPY or (heaven forbid) a DEL. The DIR will non-destructively *show* you the file names that match your wild card. Then, if you decide that these really are the files you want to erase, go ahead and type DEL followed by the same wild card.

You can use as many question marks in a file name as you desire. If you have report files with names like SALES93.REP, SALES84.REP, and SALES75.REP, you can include them all with SALES??.REP. This is fast and easy, but it only works if you have used some kind of obvious pattern when naming your files. A file named 95SALES.REP would not be included by your command.

The * wild card can match a bunch of characters

Once you find yourself straining to figure out a pattern in your file listings, it's time to learn about the super-duper all-inclusive wild card. The asterisk

(*) takes the place of any number of characters in a file name or its extension:

COPY *.REP A:

The file name *.REP refers to any file that has a REP extension and would automatically accept even a file like 95SALES.REP. If I wanted to copy every file in the directory, no matter what, I could use *.* as the file name. This means, "accept every file name and every extension."

Now try * and ? together

If you want to get really tricky, you can combine the different wild cards. For example, the file name SALES??.* means any file starting with SALES and two characters. The extension can be anything at all. Want to try one a little harder? The file name S*.??P would accept any file starting with S, as long as the last letter in the extension was a "P." Now you're really starting to understand computerese!

Copying, moving, and deleting by the handful

Suppose that you want to put backup copies of all your word processing documents onto a floppy disk. You might issue the following command:

COPY C:\WINWORD*.DOC A:

The wild card is simply plugged into the command where the file name would go. This one takes all files in the WINWORD directory that have the DOC extension and copies them to drive A.

You can move or delete files the same way:

MOVE C:\WINWORD*.DOC C:\LETTERS

DEL C:\WINWORD*.DOC

Never use *.* unless you're sure!

Beware the deadly *.* when you're deleting files! Because *.* refers to every single file in a directory, you can wipe out a huge amount of information with a single blow. DOS has one tell-tale message that appears on the screen when you're about to delete everything: "All files in directory will be deleted. Are you sure? (Y/N)" appears nowhere else. If you see this message at any time, stop and read the command you just typed. DOS has interpreted it as DEL *.*! Press Y if you are sure and N if you're not.

12

Doing Stuff with Disks (DOS)

Formatting a disk is like painting a parking lot. Until you draw those lines, nobody knows where to put their cars.

In this chapter:

- What do I do with this box of disks I just bought?

- Can I use a disk more than once?

- Rats! I didn't mean to format THAT disk!

- Backups? We don't need no stinking backups!

Now that you know how to move files from place to place, you're probably beginning to realize how handy those floppy disks are. You can use disks to store old files you need to keep but won't use very often. You can use them to keep an extra copy of files you use all the time (in case something happens to the original), or to move files from one computer to another.

In this chapter, you learn some of the basic DOS commands you use to work with floppy disks.

Teaching your disk how to drive

As you learned in Chapter 8, "Disks and Disk Drives," you usually can't use a new disk right out of the box—you have to **format** it first. Formatting a disk is a lot like painting the white lines for parking spaces in a parking lot. Until you get those spaces marked and numbered, nobody knows where to put their car. Likewise, until you format a floppy disk, DOS can't figure out where to store your files (or how to get them back).

⊗<Caution> Formatting a disk also wipes out any information that was on that disk before you started. (You can't paint the lines in a parking lot if the cars are still there!) This isn't a problem with new disks, but it can cause you a lot of heartache if you try it with just any old disk you find lying around. Always use the DIR command to see if the disk has anything important on it first (see Chapter 10 for more information about DIR).

❶(Tip)

Make sure that the disk you want to format matches the type of floppy disk drive you have and that the disk isn't write-protected. If you're not sure, go back to Chapter 8 and read about disk types and capacities.

Formatting a disk sounds like a highly technical task, but it's really very simple:

1 At a DOS prompt, type **FORMAT A:**. DOS asks you to insert a disk into your drive and press Enter. Do it. As DOS prepares the disk for use on your system, it displays messages showing its progress.

2 When DOS asks for a volume label, type any name you like, or just press Enter. DOS shows you some technical facts about your disk, including how much information it can hold.

3 When DOS asks whether you want to format another disk, press N on your keyboard. (Or press Y if you have another disk to format and start again at step 2.)

Figure 12.1 shows the entire formatting process as it rolls across your screen. When DOS is done formatting the disk, it's ready for you to use.

Fig. 12.1

DOS tells you everything you never wanted to know about your floppy disk.

```
C:\>format a:
Insert new diskette for drive A:
and press ENTER when ready...

Checking existing disk format.
Saving UNFORMAT information.
Verifying 1.44M
Format complete.

Volume label (11 characters, ENTER for none)?

    1,457,664 bytes total disk space
    1,457,664 bytes available on disk

        512 bytes in each allocation unit.
      2,847 allocation units available on disk.

Volume Serial Number is 1239-18CD

Format another (Y/N)?n


C:\>
```

What's a volume label?

When you format a disk, DOS asks if you want to give it a **volume label**. This is simply a name for the disk. A volume label is just like the sticky label you put on the outside of the disk. If the disk is already in the drive, though, it's pretty hard to see the sticker.

You can also use the volume label to help explain what's in your files. Squeezing a meaningful description into an eight-letter file name can be hard. For example, if DIR revealed files named JANUARY.95, FEBRUARY.95, and MARCH.95,

you still don't know what they *contain*. If the directory listing started with the message, Volume in Drive A: is BUDGETS, however, their contents would be more obvious.

What if you want to change or add a volume label to a disk without having to reformat it? Simple. Use the command, LABEL, followed by the letter of the drive your disk is in (for example, LABEL A:). DOS will ask you to type in the new volume label and you're done! You don't even have to pull off any sticky label gunk!

Q&A

> **What do I do when DOS tells me** `Invalid media` **when I try to format a disk?**
>
> `Invalid media or Track 0 bad - disk unusable`
>
> You probably have the wrong kind of disk in the drive. Specifically, you may have a high-density disk in a low-density drive. Check the disk's type, or try a different disk. See Chapter 8 for details.

Q&A

> **Why does DOS keep telling me,** `Existing format differs from that specified`**?**
>
> If you get this message when formatting, you probably have the wrong kind of disk in the drive. Remember that disks come in different density types or capacities. If your system has a high-density disk drive, DOS assumes you want to format a high-density disk. If you want to format a double-density disk instead, you must tell DOS to do it differently:
>
>   FORMAT A: /f:720
>
> /f:720 tells FORMAT that the disk should treated as a 720K, or double-density disk. Yeah, I know...you'd think the switch would be /s for "size," but /s is used for something else (to place system (boot) files on the formatted disk). Go figure.
>
> If you're using a 5 1/4-inch high-density drive and you want to format a double-density disk, you do the same thing, except the switch is /f:360 (for 360K, the capacity of that kind of disk).

Making an old disk like new

When you format a disk, two things happen. Any old data is erased and the magnetic "white lines" are repainted for the next set of files you plan to save there.

In the real world, parking lot attendants don't have to repaint the parking lot every night, they just have to sweep up the trash. If you want to wipe everything off a disk quickly, you can do a **quick format**, which only deletes the files without bothering to reformat.

By adding the /Q switch to the FORMAT command (*Q* stands for *Quick*), you tell DOS not to bother preparing the disk from scratch. Instead, DOS just erases all the data on the disk, leaving the disk blank. Just type

>**FORMAT A: /Q**

 Plain English, please!

What is a **bad sector**? A bad sector is a small portion of a disk that, for some reason, appears to be flawed and therefore unusable.

When FORMAT finishes, it displays a message about the amount of space on the disk. Sometimes this message includes a line such as x number bytes in Bad Sectors.

If you get a bad sector error, feel free to find another use for the disk. They make great coasters.

⊗<Caution> Never, *ever* use the FORMAT command with your hard disk unless you are preparing a new one. If you format your hard disk, you will wipe out all the data stored there, leaving you with a computer that can't even start up correctly.

①(Tip) Although a disk theoretically stays formatted forever, the little magnetic "parking lot" lines can fade away with time. It's a good idea to completely reformat an old floppy (without the /Q switch) from time to time so that DOS has a chance to discover any problems that may have cropped up.

Uh, oh. I think I just reformatted the wrong disk

Boy, are you in trouble! Well, maybe not. Any version of DOS 5 or higher includes a special command that can probably repair the damage. UNFORMAT can recover everything as long as you haven't placed any other files on the disk since the accidental format.

To resuscitate your files, type **UNFORMAT A:** (if A: was the disk you messed up) and read the dire warnings carefully. One or two key presses later, the lost data reappears. If you *don't* have UNFORMAT, swallow your pride and call your guru for help.

If all else fails, you can always revert to the backup copy of the floppy disk. You *did* make one, right? Well, if you don't have a backup copy, the next section shows you how to make one.

In case of fire, break glass and insert backup disk

Computing, like Mother Nature, can be an unpredictable thing. What if lightning strikes and your power goes out just as you finish writing that novel you've been working on for 10 years? What if your hard disk dies (it might)? What if your *floppy* disk dies (it might, too)? What if (eek!) your computer picks up a virus and it destroys all your data?

Sometimes we take the reliability of our computer equipment for granted. That's why it's important to get into the habit of backing up disks regularly. It's a simple process, it just takes some discipline.

⊛ *{Note}*___ | Actually, you should back up your entire system regularly, but that's a topic for a later chapter.

Making a backup disk is simply making an exact duplicate of the entire disk. You could copy the files one at a time, but that could take hours. Luckily, there's a more efficient way to copy an entire disk: the DISKCOPY command. It requires a disk containing the information to be copied and a disk containing, well, nothing. Just follow these steps:

1 At the DOS prompt, type **DISKCOPY A: A:** and press Enter. Yes, A: should be there twice—the first A: tells DOS where the source disk is, and the second A: tells it where the target is. They're almost always the same drive.

2 DOS asks you to insert the source disk (the one you want to make a copy of) into drive A: and press any key to continue. DOS starts reading the disk as soon as you press a key.

3 When DOS asks you to insert the target disk (the one you're copying to), do so and press any key. DOS starts writing the information to the new disk. (If the disk is not yet formatted, DOS will do that for you, too.)

4 With older versions of DOS, you may be asked to swap disks more than once. If DOS asks whether you want to write another duplicate of the disk, press N. (Unless you do, of course.)

5 When DOS asks whether you want to copy another disk, answer N.

Figure 12.2 shows an entire copying process as it appears on your screen.

Fig. 12.2
DISKCOPY makes it easy to copy a whole disk's worth of files at one time.

```
C:\>diskcopy a: a:
Insert SOURCE diskette in drive A:
Press any key to continue . . .
Copying 80 tracks, 18 sectors per track, 2 side(s)
Reading from source diskette . . .
Insert TARGET diskette in drive A:
Press any key to continue . . .
Writing to target diskette . . .
Do you wish to write another duplicate of this disk (Y/N)? n
Volume Serial Number is 18CE-2F85
Copy another diskette (Y/N)? n
C:\>
```

⊗<Caution> DISKCOPY works a little like FORMAT. It does not add to the existing files on the disk, it overwrites them. In addition, because the files are completely overwritten, you can't get them back with UNFORMAT.

In short, make sure your target disk doesn't contain any files you want to keep.

❓Q&A *What do I do when DOS tells me* SOURCE diskette bad?

When you try to copy a disk, you may see a message like this:

    SOURCE diskette bad or incompatible, copy process ended

This message means that the source disk is damaged, unreadable, or in a format that is incompatible with the drive that is trying to read it.

✳{Note} If your system doesn't have a fair amount of memory, it might have to copy the disk in chunks. The computer can only remember so much at one time, so it has to read a little, write a little, read a little, write a little. Just follow the instructions on the screen, don't mix the disks up, and you'll be fine. (It's still better than copying files one at a time!)

Doing Stuff with the System (DOS)

DOS is way too compli-cated—it uses more com-mands than a four-star general.

In this chapter:

- How can I get all that garbage off my screen?

- Can you at least give me a hint about how this command works?

- My friend's DOS prompt looks different than mine.

I f you've ever looked in your computer's manuals (and lived to tell about it), you know that DOS uses more commands than a four-star general. Most of DOS is way too complicated for mere mortals, but there are a few commands that are handy to know. That's what you'll learn in this chapter.

Wiping the slate clean

After only a few minutes of working in DOS, your screen gets cluttered with all sorts of garbage (see fig. 13.1). Although this junk might have been useful a few seconds ago, now it's just in the way. Fortunately, there's a very simple command that you can use to erase all that stuff from your screen: CLS (which stands for CLear Screen).

To clear your screen, just type **CLS** and press Enter (see fig. 13.2). That's it!

(Tip)

Don't worry about accidentally destroying data or anything like that when you use CLS. It only erases old screen messages. It has no effect on your disks or files.

Fig. 13.1

Your screen can get cluttered with a lot of useless text.

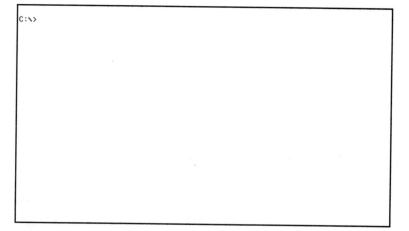

```
AUTOEXEC BAT          659 10-05-94    8:26p
WIN32APP    <DIR>         08-17-94    1:47p
PCMAGCD     <DIR>         10-03-94    5:05p
CORELDRW    <DIR>         08-31-94    1:22p
WING        <DIR>         09-26-94   11:46a
DPAINT      <DIR>         09-11-94    3:36p
MY_STUFF    <DIR>         09-20-94   11:26a
COMPLIB     <DIR>         10-03-94    5:07p
STU      BAT           18 04-21-94    3:40a
ST       BAT           46 10-04-94    2:01p
SNAP     EXE       42,421 06-08-91   10:34a
SAVE     EXE       27,061 06-08-91    9:52a
CONFIG   MY           305 06-03-94    2:22p
CASSLABL EXE        2,321 12-31-90    2:42a
CASSLABL ASM       29,513 12-31-90    2:41a
AUTOEXEC MY           795 06-03-94    2:21p
CSERVE      <DIR>         08-10-94    6:43a
MSVC        <DIR>         08-10-94    6:47a
MSWORKS     <DIR>         08-10-94    6:48a
PROWIN      <DIR>         08-10-94    6:50a
QUICKENW    <DIR>         08-10-94    6:52a
        46 file(s)        200,595 bytes
                      519,012,352 bytes free

C:\>
```

Fig. 13.2

To get rid of the mess, just type CLS and press Enter. Then, your screen gets a fresh, new face.

```
C:\>
```

Asking DOS for help

For some reason, computer manuals seem to be written for people who don't need them. The people who make DOS finally realized this, so starting with Version 5, they added the DOS Help system. And in Version 6, they made it even better! Now if you have a question about a DOS command, it's easy to find an answer fast.

Help! I don't remember what it's called!

To access the DOS 6 Help system, type **HELP** at the DOS prompt. You will see a screen like the one in figure 13.3, which shows MS-DOS Help's standard opening. As you can see, this screen lists all the DOS commands.

 **{Note}**

> The DOS 5 Help feature works a little differently than the DOS 6 Help system. We'll get to that in a minute.

Fig. 13.3
DOS can give you fast help whenever you need it.

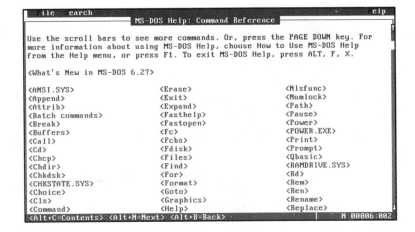

To get help on a specific command, arrow over to the command, then press Enter. Or, if you like, you can simply click on the command with your mouse.

 (Tip)

> If you don't see the command you want, press Page Up or Page Down to see more. There are so many commands, they don't all fit on the screen at once!

When you select the command, you see a screen like the one in figure 13.4, where DOS fully describes the selected command. Help displays all the information you'll probably need about each command, including a description, notes, and complete syntax. Additional information is available by selecting either the Notes or Examples button at the top of the screen. Use your Page Up and Page Down keys to see parts of the text that don't fit on the screen.

Fig. 13.4
DOS offers full
descriptions of all
of its commands.

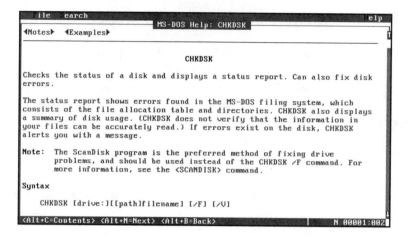

To exit the help system, you have to use the menu at the top of the screen. Use your mouse to click on the word Eile, then click on Exit. No mouse? No problem. Just press the Alt key, and press F for Eile and x for Exit. Now you're back at the prompt and ready to go.

I remember what it's called, but I forgot what it does

Okay, so you already know the name of the command you want. You just can't remember the other stuff you're supposed to type with it.

If so, you don't need to bother with Help's opening screen. Instead, jump right to the command by typing the command's name right after the HELP command. For example, to get help on the UNDELETE command, type this:

HELP UNDELETE

then press Enter. The Help system immediately displays the selected command's description (see fig. 13.5). This screen contains everything you'd ever want to know about the UNDELETE command. (And probably a lot you *didn't* want to know.)

 This is the *only* way to get help in DOS 5. You don't get to see a list of the commands.

Fig. 13.5
The help screen for the UNDELETE command.

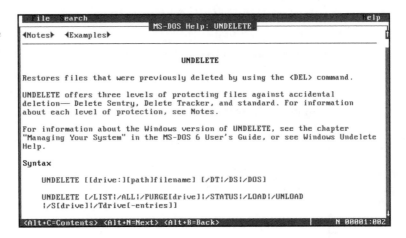

```
 ile   earch                                              elp
                        MS-DOS Help: UNDELETE
◄Notes►   ◄Examples►

                              UNDELETE

Restores files that were previously deleted by using the <DEL> command.

UNDELETE offers three levels of protecting files against accidental
deletion— Delete Sentry, Delete Tracker, and standard. For information
about each level of protection, see Notes.

For information about the Windows version of UNDELETE, see the chapter
"Managing Your System" in the MS-DOS 6 User's Guide, or see Windows Undelete
Help.

Syntax

    UNDELETE [[drive:][path]filename] [/DT!/DS!/DOS]

    UNDELETE [/LIST!/ALL!/PURGE[drive]!/STATUS!/LOAD!/UNLOAD
    !/S[drive]!/Tdrive[-entries]]

<Alt+C=Contents> <Alt+N=Next> <Alt+B=Back>              N 00001:002
```

> For even quicker help, try the FASTHELP command. It just gives you a quick reminder of how to use the command you need without all the technical mumbo-jumbo. For example, typing FASTHELP FORMAT brings up a short description of the FORMAT command.
>
> Typing the command FASTHELP by itself brings up a complete list of all DOS commands with a brief one-line description.

Creating your own DOS prompt

When you're working in DOS, that old C:\> prompt comes across as pretty boring and unfriendly. You don't have to put up with that! You can change your prompt to reflect your mood, give a friendly greeting, or simply tell the exact time. The trick is to use DOS's PROMPT command.

Changing your prompt for now

Suppose that, for now, you want your DOS prompt to show the current path name followed by the message "Please type your command, darling." Just type this command and press Enter:

PROMPT $p Please type your command, darling

In this command, the word PROMPT tells DOS that you want to change the way the prompt looks. The $p in the command is a special code that tells DOS that you want to see the *path* in the prompt. The "Please type your command, darling" part is text that appears literally in the DOS prompt. As you can see in figure 13.6, changing the DOS prompt enables you to give your computer a little more personality.

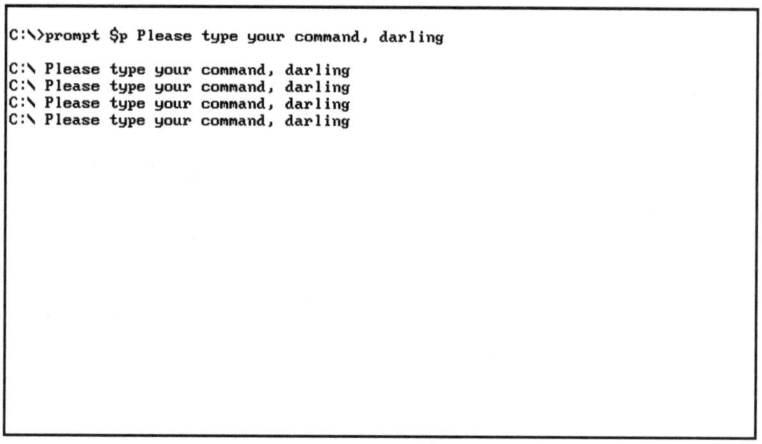

Fig. 13.6

A customized DOS prompt can make you feel more at home with your computer.

```
C:\>prompt $p Please type your command, darling

C:\ Please type your command, darling
C:\ Please type your command, darling
C:\ Please type your command, darling
C:\ Please type your command, darling
```

(Tip)

Being able to see what drive and directory you're in is pretty useful. No matter what else you want your prompt to say, its always best to include the $p somewhere in there.

There are many other special codes besides $p that you can add to your prompt command. You can have your prompt show the time ($t), the date ($d), your DOS version ($v), and more. You can get that little ">" character at the end of the regular prompt with $g. You can use more than one code together, as in tdvg. To see all the things you can add to your prompt, type HELP PROMPT.

Although your DOS prompt looks very different now, it is still the same old DOS prompt. You still type your commands at the flashing cursor, just as you did before.

If you decide that your prompt isn't as nice as you expected, you can always go back to the original by typing:

PROMPT pg

Or, of course, you can try again with something different. Change it every day if you like, or whenever the mood strikes you.

Remember, this change is only temporary. The next time you turn on your computer, it goes back to the way it always was before. This may be a good thing, because you can always restart your computer if you get confused. If you come up with a really good one, though, you might want to make the change permanent.

Changing your prompt and making it stick

When you get up in the morning, there's a whole list of things you have to do to get out the door and on your way. Your computer's the same way. It has to go through a **startup routine** each time it's turned on.

Part of this routine is reading a special command file on your hard disk called AUTOEXEC.BAT. As DOS finds this file, it performs all the commands it contains before it turns control over to you. This is the perfect place to change your DOS prompt. Just follow the steps below:

Plain English, please!

What's an **AUTOEXEC.BAT** file? Any file that ends in BAT is called a **batch file**. Batch files contain bunches of DOS commands that are executed in a particular order.

AUTOEXEC.BAT is simply a batch file with a special name—DOS knows to look for this file on the hard disk every time the computer is turned on.

Unlike other program files (like those that end in COM or EXE), a batch file is a kind of program that can be written and edited by any user. When the same series of DOS commands is entered often enough, it becomes worthwhile to put those commands in a batch file.

1 Switch to the C drive (by typing **C:**), then make sure you're at the C:\> prompt. (Type **CD ** and then press Enter if you're not.)

2 Type **COPY AUTOEXEC.BAT AUTOEXEC.OLD** and press Enter. DOS makes a copy of your AUTOEXEC.BAT file for safe keeping. If something goes wrong, you can use this backup copy to change things back the way they were.

3 Type **EDIT AUTOEXEC.BAT** and press Enter. DOS runs its special Editor program and loads the AUTOEXEC.BAT file into it (see fig. 13.7).

Fig. 13.7

Although yours will look different, here are the first several lines of my AUTOEXEC.BAT file.

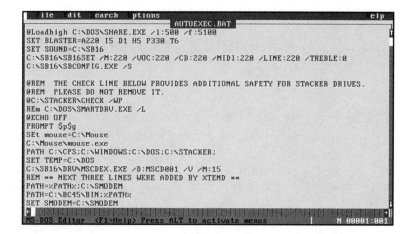

4 Use the down arrow key to get all the way to the end of the file (see fig. 13.8). If there's already a line somewhere in this file that says PROMPT, you can ignore it for now.

Fig. 13.8

Use the down arrow key to reach the last line of AUTOEXEC.BAT.

5 On the last line of the file, type the command **PROMPT $p What Next?** and press Enter (see fig. 13.9).

Fig. 13.9

Place the custom prompt command at the end of your AUTOEXEC.BAT file.

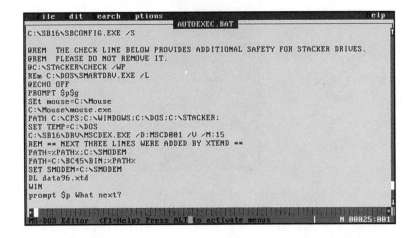

6 Save your changes by selecting the File menu's Save command (see fig. 13.10). (Use your mouse, or press Alt-F and then S.) DOS saves the new AUTOEXEC.BAT file.

Fig. 13.10

Save the file after you add the prompt command.

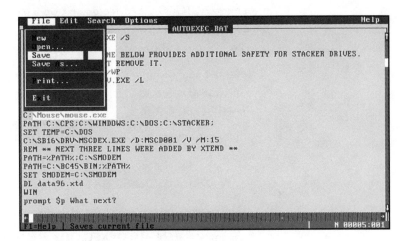

7 Quit the editor by selecting the File menu's Exit command (see fig. 13.11). You are transported back to DOS.

Fig. 13.11

Use the editor's Exit command to return to DOS.

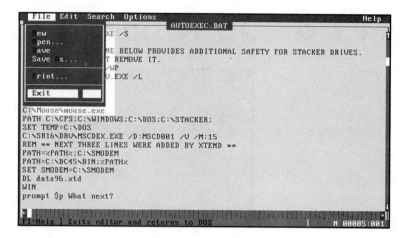

To get your new prompt installed, just reboot your computer (by holding down Ctrl+Alt and pressing Del) so that DOS reads through its new wake-up file. Now you can truly amaze your friends with your DOS trickery!

My new AUTOEXEC.BAT file doesn't work! What now?

If your new AUTOEXEC.BAT file doesn't work right, you may have mistyped something or accidentally changed another line as well. As long as you remembered to do step 1 above, you can fix things easily. Here's what to do:

1 Restart your computer, and when the words Starting MS-DOS... appear, press your keyboard's F5 key. This stops DOS from reading your AUTOEXEC.BAT file.

2 When the DOS prompt appears (it may look a little strange, like C>), type this

DEL AUTOEXEC.BAT

This deletes the file you changed. It doesn't work anyway, right?

3 Then, type **REN AUTOEXEC.OLD AUTOEXEC.BAT**. This renames the old file so that DOS can find it the next time it "wakes up."

4 Now restart your computer to put everything back the way it was before you tried to change it.

How Do I Do Windows?

Baffled and bored by that big, black DOS screen? Windows was designed for people who would rather move pictures around than memorize a bunch of cryptic commands.

You've probably already noticed that DOS is a little finicky when it comes to interpreting what you type. Well, Windows was developed as a response to users everywhere crying out for something easier to use. It is a **graphical user interface** (or **GUI**—sounds like "gooey") that sits on top of DOS and lets you accomplish the same things as in DOS by manipulating little pictures and objects on the screen with your mouse.

I got Windows with my computer. What good is it?

Think of Windows as a collection of dashboard controls for your computer. All dashboards have a speedometer, a way to turn on the lights, a fuel gauge, etc. All Windows programs have the same basic things: a way to open a file, save a file, get help, etc. The programs all look a little different, but you can figure out how to work the basics in a few seconds.

The major advantage of using Windows is that all the programs you use work pretty much the same. Therefore, each new program you buy is progressively easier to learn. By the time you hit your third Windows program, things start looking real familiar.

How to make Windows start automatically in your system

In Chapter 13, we told you how to make your personal DOS prompt a permanent part of your computer. You had to modify the last line of your system's AUTOEXEC.BAT file. Windows is loaded exactly the same way, except the last line of the file must be the WIN command.

If you want Windows to load automatically every time the system is turned on, follow the numbered steps in the *Prompt* section of Chapter 13 (especially the part about making a backup copy of the file first). Simply substitute the WIN command (or *x:\directory*\WIN, where *x:\directory* is the drive and directory where

Windows is installed on your system, if the Windows directory is not in your PATH statement in AUTOEXEC.BAT) where we tell you to type in your new prompt.

If your computer has a menu (e.g., "Press 1 to start WordPerfect, Press 2 to start Lotus 1-2-3," etc.) that appears each time you reboot, you'll probably need to modify the menu program rather than your AUTOEXEC.BAT file. If you didn't create this handy menu system, go find the person who did and have them show you how to make the necessary changes.

How to get Windows up and running

Probably the only similarity between DOS and Windows is that they both need to be started somehow. DOS loads automatically when your computer is turned on, but there are several ways to get Windows started. If you bought your system with Windows installed, Windows may start automatically when you turn on your system. If so, you're all set.

If you find yourself staring at the DOS prompt after turning on your system, take a deep breath and count to five. Then, try starting Windows by typing WIN and pressing Enter. If this doesn't work, try changing to the Windows directory (use the command CD \WINDOWS). Then type WIN again.

 Q&A

What do I do if I still can't get Windows started?

If you've tried to start Windows and none of the methods work, you either don't have Windows installed on your system, it's been installed incorrectly, or some other problem has occurred. If you have the original diskettes and you know how, reinstall Windows from scratch. If you need help, contact the store where you bought your computer.

The Program Manager does just that: It manages your programs

When Windows starts, you see a big box, or *window*, on the screen (see fig. 14.1).

66 *Plain English, please!*

What's a **window**? A window is just a rectangular area of the screen with something in it. Later you'll see how to open several windows with a different program in each one. The Program Manager window contains group windows and can contain program windows, etc. 99

Fig. 14.1
A Windows session almost always starts off with Program Manager, which is the usual way to, well, manage your programs.

Menu bar

Desktop

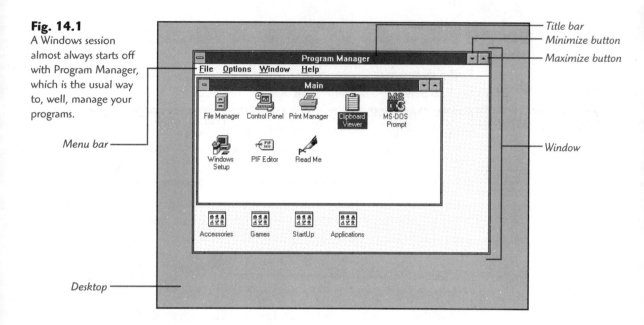

Title bar
Minimize button
Maximize button

Window

Program Manager is a typical window. It's rectangular and has a lot of icons and menus and things. To use all these window features, you should have a mouse. You *could* use your keyboard, but it's just not quite as fast as the mouse.

What are all these little pictures?

Program Manager is the main access point for all the programs you use in Windows. The square pictures at the bottom of the screen are special **icons** that represent **program groups**.

A program group is nothing more than a way of organizing your programs into categories that make them easy to find. Windows automatically gives you programs divided up into the following groups: Main, Accessories, Games, Startup, and Applications. (If you're hooked up to a network, you will also have a program group called Network.)

How do you use the mouse with Windows?

Windows really is at its best when you command it with a mouse. Using one isn't as complicated as brain surgery, but it does take some practice. So, before you go any further, look at table 14.1, which shows the things you should learn to do with your mouse.

Table 14.1   Mouse Actions

Action	How to do it
Point	Place the mouse pointer over an item (such as an icon or a menu) on the screen.
Click	Press and release the left mouse button.
Double-click	Click twice quickly.
Drag	Place the mouse pointer over an item, press and hold down the left mouse button, and move the mouse. The object you're pointing to gets dragged across the screen. Release the mouse button to drop the object.

You may have seen this table before. It's in Chapter 9. But it's important enough that we're repeating it here.

A fun way to practice using your mouse is to play a few games of Windows Solitaire, a program you learn to start later in this chapter.

The mouse works best if you relax

For most new users, even holding a mouse doesn't come naturally. Put your right hand on your mouse and look at yourself. Is your elbow way up in the air with only the tips of your fingers touching the little rodent? Then you're doing it wrong and your arm will fall right off from fatigue after a few minutes.

Think of the mouse as a convenient place to rest your whole hand. Drape it across the mouse with your first two fingers placed lightly over the buttons. The mouse should touch your entire palm. Let your wrist and your whole forearm touch the table top. Now relax those tight muscles and just "droop." If it's not comfortable, you're not relaxing enough. Droop some more.

When you're ready to click a button, the way your hand drapes over the mouse should keep it from jumping around when you press with your index finger. Don't stab with your finger—just press down lightly.

It takes a bit of practice to make the mouse move where you want it. Ever notice how Queen Elizabeth waves? Her wrist just kind of pivots to the crowd. Move your mouse the way the Queen waves. Just a little wrist action is all you need to scoot the pointer across the screen.

I don't have a mouse to control my pointer. I have something else.

If it's a ball in a hole, which looks like the top of a roll-on deodorant, it's a **trackball**. Trackballs are usually found on portable ("laptop") computers. You might also have something that looks like a mini-joystick with a couple of buttons. These other devices can be mastered as easily as the mouse—you just have to spend a little time getting that hand-eye coordination together.

This mouse has a mind of its own!

Having a few mouse orientation problems? That's OK. It doesn't come naturally to anybody, but then again, neither does a pencil. Unlike the pencil, which you had to adapt to, you can use Windows to make the mouse adapt to you! Later in this chapter, you will see how you can change the way the mouse works.

How to use a Windows menu

Along the top of the Program Manager window are the words File, Options, Window, and Help. Place *the tip* of your mouse pointer over the word Window and press and release your left mouse button one time (a mouse action called **clicking**). A menu drops down from the word, showing you all the choices available (see fig. 14.2). The words on the drop-down menu are commands that you can give to Program Manager. Just click with your mouse on the command you want. The menu disappears and Windows does what you asked it to do. Sure beats typing backslashes!

Fig. 14.2
The menu bar contains drop-down menus that contain the program's commands.

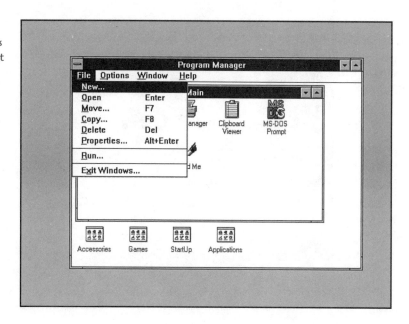

(Tip)

If you open a menu by accident and decide that you don't want to do any of the options displayed there, you can close it again by clicking once more on the same command that opened it. Click once on Window and the menu appears. Click again on Window and it goes away. Or you can press the Esc key on your keyboard, which is the way to get out of just about anything in Windows.

There's a special menu tucked away in the window's Control-menu box, too. To see this menu, click once on the Control-menu box at the top left of Program Manager's window (see fig. 14.3). See the Close command? This command is used to leave Windows and return to DOS. You can also select the Close command by pressing Alt+F4 on your keyboard.

<Caution>

Never close down Windows by turning off your computer. When you exit Windows and return to DOS, Windows checks to make sure that all your programs are properly closed and that all your open documents are properly saved. If you just turn off the power, Windows never gets a chance to check this stuff and you might lose some valuable work.

Fig. 14.3
The Close command
exits Windows and
returns you to DOS.

Control–menu box

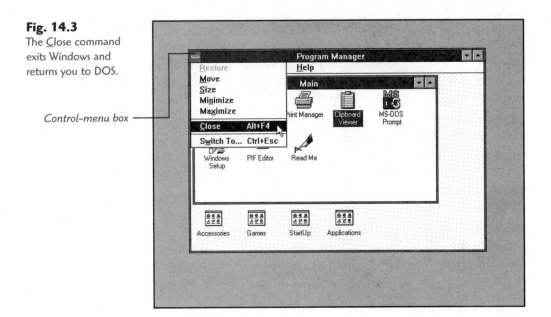

Windows that stretch, shrink, and scroll

As you get more familiar with Windows, you'll find that screen space is a
precious commodity. Just like papers that sit on top of each other on a
cluttered desk, each open window tends to cover up at least a portion of
some icon or window on the screen. For this reason, it's important to understand how to adjust the size and placement of a window.

This window is too small. How can I change it?

Want the biggest window possible? Use the *Maximize button* (that's the "up-
pointing" triangle in the top right corner of the screen), which enlarges a
window to take over the entire screen. To use the button, just click it once
with your mouse. Once a window is maximized, you don't need that button
anymore, so the Maximize button changes into the Restore button (the
double-headed arrow shown in fig. 14.4), which returns the window to its
original size when you click it. You maximize a window when you want to
see all of a program clearly and you don't mind it covering up any other open
windows or icons.

Fig. 14.4

A maximized window has a Restore button, which returns the window to its original size when you click it.

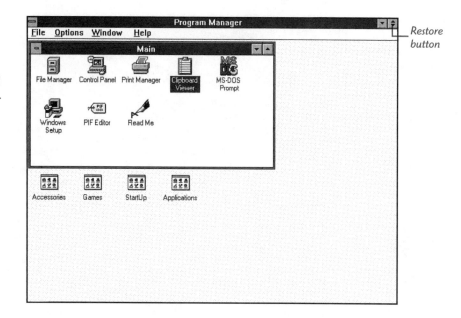

Restore button

Okay, now I want this window out of my way

The Minimize button is a way of shrinking a window down so small that it changes into a tiny picture, or **icon**, at the bottom of the screen. You do this if you just want to set a program aside for a minute to do something else. Minimizing a window is like pushing your phone off into a corner of your desk until you need to make a call: It clears more desktop space for you to work.

If you click the Program Manager's Minimize button (the down-pointing triangle), you see a screen like figure 14.5. Program Manager is still there, but it's off in a corner. To restore the window to its original size, double-click the icon—or click once to display the icon's menu, from which you select the Restore command.

> **What happens to all the things in a window when I resize it?**
>
> Don't worry about losing the contents of a window because you minimized it or covered it up with something else. Just because you can't see something doesn't mean it's gone for good! When you resize a window, you're just changing the appearance of it—you're not deleting things from your computer.

Fig. 14.5
A minimized window becomes an icon that sits at the bottom of the screen, ready to be called back with a click of the mouse.

You can make the window almost any size with the mouse

See the thick border around the Main window? If you put your mouse pointer right over this border, the pointer changes to a double-headed arrow. You can do this over any of the four sides or any of the four corners of a window. Try this and see that the arrow is sometimes straight up and down, sometimes sideways, and sometimes at an angle.

This double-arrow shape means that you can now drag the window's border to a new size. To do this, press and hold down the left mouse button while moving the mouse in one of the directions the arrow was pointing. When you do, the window's outline sticks to the mouse pointer and goes wherever it goes. When you release the mouse button, the border gets unstuck, and the window shrinks or grows to fit the new outline.

 (Tip)

The different parts of a window's border enable you to change the window in different ways. When you drag the left or right window border, you change the width of the window. When you drag the top or bottom window border, you change the height of the window. Finally, if you drag a border corner, you change the window's width and height simultaneously. Try it!

Scrolling through the world of Windows

If you drag a window's border so that it is smaller than the stuff it contains, scroll bars appear at the side or bottom of the window (see fig. 14.6). Scroll bars let you to see information that doesn't fit in a window.

Windows and multitasking

One buzzword you hear a lot lately is **multitasking**, which just means running more than one program at a time. (*True* multitasking is a little more complicated. But this is what most people mean when they use this word.)

How does this work? Let's say you've got your Windows word processor going. Now, you'd like to use your spreadsheet program at the same time. No problem. Just start up the spreadsheet program, too.

When you run a Windows program, it appears in its own window. Because these program windows can overlap each other, there's room for any number of them on the screen. This means that you can start as many programs as your computer's memory allows.

How does Windows know which program you're using at the moment? Easy. Although you can have many programs going simultaneously, only one can be active. The active program is the one that's ready to accept your commands and is always the program on top of all the others.

The band across the top of the window (called the **title bar**) is usually a different color in the active program than it is in the programs you're not actually using. This helps YOU remember which window is currently active.

Here's a little trick you can show your friends: Use the Alt+Tab key combination to switch from one window to another. To do this, hold the Alt key down while pressing and releasing the Tab key. What happens? Each time you press the Tab key, you'll see an information box for each of the windows you currently have open. It's almost like a Windows Lazy Susan! Make sure you keep that Alt key pressed the whole time, though—as soon as you let go of Alt, Windows switches to the program whose icon was displayed the last time you pressed Tab.

Fig. 14.6

Some windows have scroll bars, which enable you to see information that doesn't fit in the window.

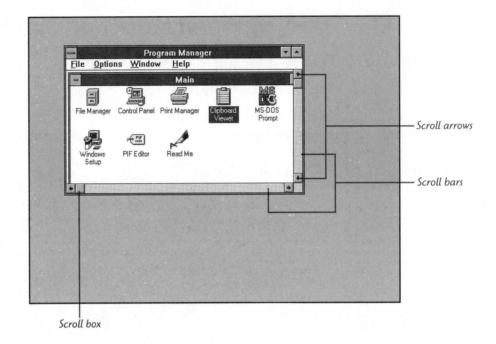

Scroll arrows

Scroll bars

Scroll box

Figure 14.6 shows the scroll bars and their parts: scroll arrows at each end, a scroll box (the square block in the middle), and the scroll bar itself. These parts work together to let you see information in the window.

Click on a scroll arrow to move the window slightly in the direction the arrow points. To move a screenful at a time, click in the gray area on either side of the scroll box. To quickly move anywhere in the window, drag the scroll box to a new position.

(Tip)

Although you can use a window's scroll bars to see more information, it's more convenient to maximize a window in order to see as much as possible at once. It's a lot easier to edit a letter when you can see four paragraphs at a time than it is when you can see only a few lines. Tiny windows are really only used when you have more than one window open at a time.

Now that you understand icons and mice, here's how to DO something in Windows

Windows is a lot more than just a playground for your mouse. To really start using Windows, you need to load a program or two. The first step to running a program is opening one of the program groups at the bottom of the screen.

Finding your programs

Program Manager is a lot like a library that has separate rooms for various categories of books. To read a book in a library, you go to the right room, find the book, and then open it. Similarly, Program Manager is a library of Windows programs. Think of the different groups as different rooms where the programs are stored. To use a program, you open its group, find the right icon, and then double-click the icon to start the program.

In figure 14.7, you see that Program Manager shows a window named Main, as well as several icons named Accessories, Games, StartUp, and Applications. Having the Main window open is like being in the main room of the library. Where are the other rooms? That's what the icons represent. Just double-click an icon to open it up like Main.

Fig. 14.7

The Program Manager window organizes your programs into groups.

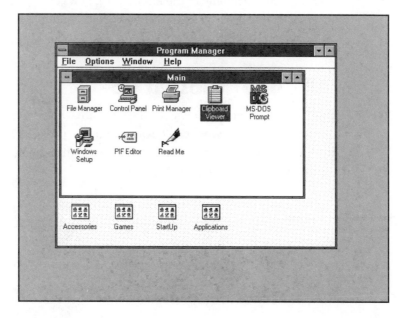

When you're ready to leave the room and close the group, just click the Minimize button with your mouse. The group window will return to its original icon size.

Sometimes, program-group icons get hidden under other open program groups. To get at these icons, you can minimize any windows that are in the way. Another way to get at hidden program-group icons is to choose them from the Program Manager's <u>W</u>indow menu. All the groups are listed there. Clicking on any of the names will automatically open that group and bring it to the top of the pile.

I want to try one of these programs. How do I start?

Ready to start using Windows programs? How about something easy and safe for your first project? For example, to start the famous Solitaire for Windows game, double-click the Games icon to open the Games program group (see fig. 14.8). Then, double-click the Solitaire icon. Although it's only a game, Solitaire for Windows is an excellent training ground for practicing your mouse techniques (or at least that's what I tell my boss when she catches me playing it in the middle of the afternoon!). You get to point, click, double-click, and drag cards all over the green, felt tabletop. Use the menu to redeal or change the rules!

All done? Close it up

Just like when you put away the deck of cards when you're done playing the card version of Solitaire, you'll want to put the program away (called **closing** the program). To do this, double-click the Control-menu box in the window's upper left corner (see fig. 14.9).

Fig. 14.8
The Games program
group contains the
famous Solitaire and
Minesweeper Windows
games.

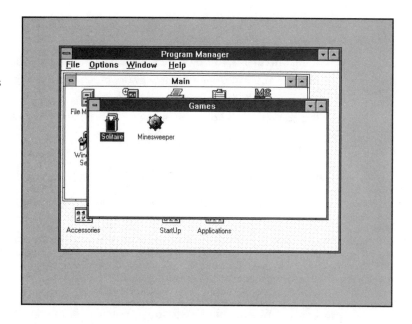

Fig. 14.9
Double-click a
window's Control-
menu box to close
the program.

Control-menu box

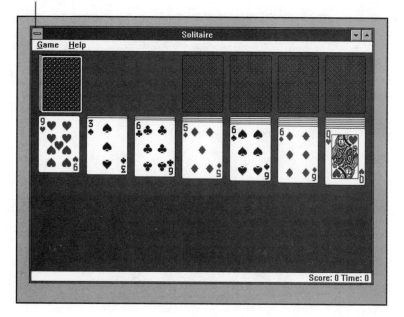

Plain English, please!

The **Control-menu box** is the little square in the upper left corner of every window. You can close a window by double-clicking the Control-menu box. Or, you can display the control menu by clicking the Control-menu box once. The control menu holds commands for moving and closing the window. **99**

Hopping from group to group

When you close the Solitaire program, you'll see the Games group that's still open. If you want to switch back to the Main program group and use something in there, simply click once inside any part of the Main window that you can see on the screen. When you do, the Main program group jumps on top of the Games program group (like in fig. 14.10). If you want to close a program group completely, click on its Minimize button or double-click its Control-menu box. When you close a program group, it goes back to being an icon at the bottom of the Program Manager window.

Fig. 14.10

In this illustration, Main is the active window. It is on top of all other windows and its title bar is darkened.

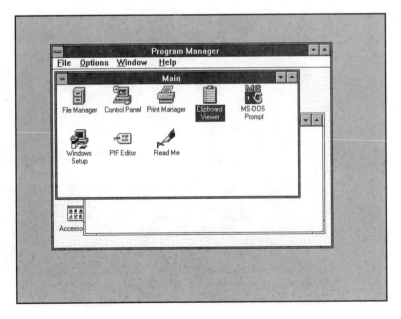

Dialog boxes let you tell Windows *exactly* what you want

Maybe this sounds a little nuts, but sometimes you have to talk to Windows. Of course, Windows doesn't actually speak. Instead, it pops up a special kind of window called a **dialog box**. Dialog boxes may have important messages in them, or empty spaces for you to type in extra info that Windows needs to complete a command successfully.

To see an example, choose the E̱xit Windows command from Program Manager's F̱ile menu. (Click on F̱ile, then E̱xit Windows.) A dialog box called *Exit Windows* pops up on the screen (see fig. 14.11).

Fig. 14.11
The Exit Windows dialog box asks you *if* you're sure you want to leave Windows.

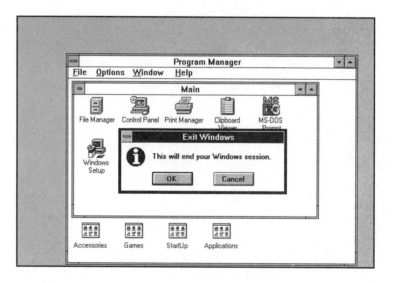

Think of the dialog box as a way to enter parameters for a command, just as DOS needs parameters for its commands. If you just tell DOS to "COPY" without adding any file names after it, you get an error message. If you just tell Windows to "RUN," it's polite enough to ask where and how far. If a dialog box asks you a question, answer it. If you wish you'd never brought the subject up in the first place, select the Cancel button. The Cancel button is almost always a safe way to change your mind about a command. The OK button allows you to quit Windows and return to the DOS prompt.

When you browse through any menu in any Windows program, you notice that some of the commands are followed by an ellipsis (that's three dots to you and me). The ellipsis means that lurking back there is...a dialog box.

You can adjust Windows, just like your TV

You can adjust some Windows settings with a program called **Control Panel**. Using Control Panel is like fiddling with the knobs on your color TV. You can change the color, set the time and date, adjust the sound and, yes, even tinker with your mouse.

The Windows Control Panel may be a little too much like a color TV's controls. If you fiddle with things you don't know anything about, you may have to call in a 14-year-old to fix it. Feel free to browse around and look inside icons, but be very careful about changing unfamiliar settings.

To use Control Panel, first double-click the Main program group to open it. Then double-click Control Panel's icon. Control Panel pops up, as you see in figure 14.12. The contents of your Control Panel window may differ from the items shown in figure 14.12, depending on whether your system has a sound card, is hooked up to a network, etc.

In Control Panel's window are icons that work like those TV knobs we talked about. The icons represent the things about Windows that you can change. Let's stick to the mouse settings, which are pretty safe. To customize your mouse, double-click the Mouse icon. When you do, the Mouse dialog box appears (look at fig. 14.13). (If you're on a network, you're probably using a different version of Windows, and your Mouse dialog box will look somewhat different from the one shown in fig. 14.13.)

Fig. 14.12
Control Panel lets you customize your Windows system.

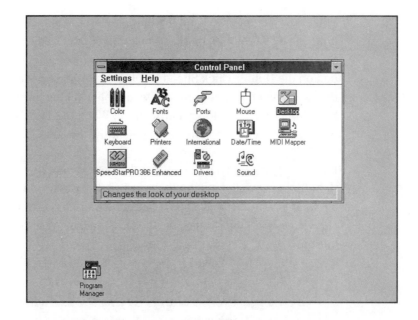

Fig. 14.13
The Mouse dialog box enables you to change how your mouse acts.

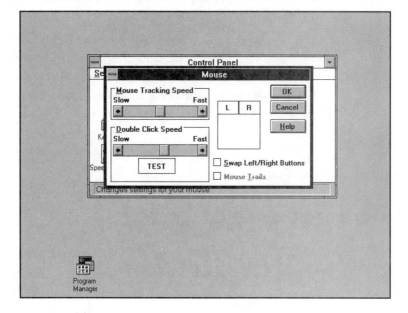

What now? If you have trouble pointing with the mouse, slow it down by dragging the scroll box on the Mouse Tracking Speed scroll bar to the left. On the other hand, if you can't seem to double-click fast enough, drag the scroll box on the Double Click Speed scroll bar a little to the left. After you make this adjustment, test your mouse by double-clicking the TEST box. If you still have trouble, slow it down a little more. When the TEST box changes color every time you try a double click, you know the settings are right for you.

Finally, if you happen to be left-handed, you can swap your mouse's left and right buttons by clicking in the Swap Left/Right Buttons box. When you do, an X appears in the box. Then, your mouse's right button will act like the left and vice versa. When you're finished customizing your mouse, click the OK button.

I've changed some things in the Mouse dialog box, and now I can't get my mouse button to work at all! What'd I do?

You have no idea how many people get messed up by putting an X in the Swap Left/Right Buttons box. Once they do it, they can't fix it because they don't know that they have swapped the functions of the left and right mouse buttons. Just use the right mouse button to get back to the Mouse dialog box, and uncheck the Swap Left/Right Buttons box.

How do I get out of here?

When you're finished with Windows and you want to return to DOS, just double-click the Control-menu box in the Program Manager window's upper left corner. As you saw earlier, Windows then asks you if you really want to quit. Click the OK button and the DOS prompt appears.

15

Let File Manager Do the Dirty Work

In this chapter:

- What do those little yellow folders mean?

- How do I see the files and directories on a disk?

- How do I create and remove directories?

- How do I look at another drive?

- I want to see two drives at once.

Windows' File Manager is the PC equivalent of your own personal file clerk, administrative assistant, and full-time maintenance crew, all rolled into one!

The File Manager in Windows is a handy program that does file and disk management tricks, but without those impossibly cryptic DOS commands. BUT you still need to know some basic DOS *concepts*. That is, you still need to know what a directory is and why DOS restricts you to funny, truncated file names, like WIN.INI, WINWORD.EXE, and LETTER1.DOT. If you're not too clear on these concepts, look at Part III of this book.

A quick tour of File Manager

File Manager is a program that comes free with Windows. Because it is considered to be fairly important, it's located in the Main group and sports a rather appropriate icon: a filing cabinet. Open the Main group with a double-click of your mouse and then give the File Manager icon a double-click, too (see fig. 15.1).

Fig. 15.1

Where is File Manager? Right in Program Manager's Main program group. Just look for the picture of the tiny file cabinet.

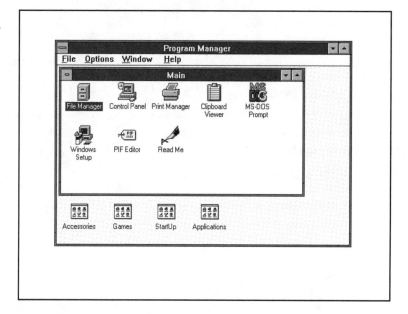

File Manager, shown in figure 15.2, shares many features with other windows you should be familiar with by now. The top right corner has two buttons for minimizing or maximizing the window. The top left corner has the Control-menu box. (That's where the Close command is when you want to exit File Manager.) You'll find pull-down menus across the top and scroll bars along the bottom.

The row of disk-drive icons near the top of the File Manager's window is your connection to all the disk drives on your system, including CD-ROM drives and network drives if you happen to be connected to a network. Click on these icons to switch from one drive to another. It's almost like flipping a page in a book. The drive window changes to show the files and directories on the disk.

You know which drive is **active** (the C: drive in most cases) because its icon will be surrounded by a rectangle. In figure 15.2, File Manager displays the files and directories in drive C:, the active drive.

Fig. 15.2

File Manager starts off appearing to be even more complex than DOS, but soon you begin to understand how it displays a drive for you to see. Here you see the files and directories on C:.

Control-menu box · Minimize button · Maximize button · Main pull-down menu · Disk drives · Active drive · Scroll bars

{Note} — Depending on your equipment setup and your versions of Windows and DOS, your File Manager screen may look or operate slightly different than shown in this chapter.

Finding files and searching directories

This book's chapters on DOS explain the concepts of directories and files. Although File Manager lets you communicate with DOS through icons instead of commands, you still must deal with directories and files.

But Windows has a much more visually interesting way of showing you the structure of your hard disk and identifying the things that are on it. On the left side of the drive window, you see a column of little yellow file folder icons with names next to them. Each file folder represents a directory on your disk. Each folder contains the files within that particular directory.

- To open a file folder and look inside, just double-click its icon. The little yellow file folder actually opens up.

- When a file folder is opened, the files and directories inside the file folder appear as names and icons in the right side of the window. For a full explanation of what the icons mean, turn to the section "How to peek into a file" in Chapter 16.

- You can double-click up and down the column of folders and quickly see all the files inside any one of them. The DOS DIR command was never like this!

- If there are other file folders (directories) inside the selected one, they are shown on the right side of the window along with the files. If you want to see them as part of the **tree structure** on the left, double-click the directory that they are stored in. The hidden branch of sub-directories will be displayed (see fig. 15.3) and you can click on those subdirectories now to see what they contain.

Fig. 15.3

File Manager shows directories on the left and their contents on the right. What could be easier?

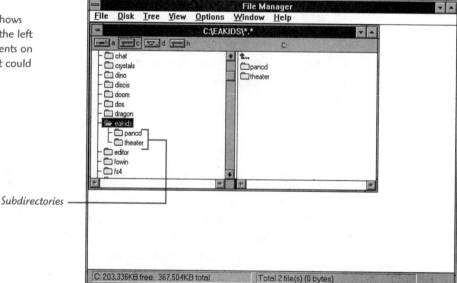

Subdirectories —

①(Tip)_____ If you want to see all the subdirectories on a disk quickly, just select <u>T</u>ree from the menu. Then select Expand <u>A</u>ll, and the complete directory tree will unfold magically before your eyes.

①(Tip)_____ If you like, you can change the size of each **pane** in the drive window. To do this, place your mouse pointer over the narrow vertical bar just to the right of the scroll bar for the left window pane. When the mouse pointer changes to a double-headed arrow, press and hold the left mouse button, and drag the bar a little to the left or right.

Making new directories and dumping old ones—in a flash!

Of course, you can use File Manager to make your own directories or to get rid of directories you no longer want. To make a new directory, follow these steps:

1 Click the file folder that will hold the new directory. If you want a directory to be located directly off the root, click on the top folder icon that has the backslash (for example, C:\).

Fig. 15.4
Select the file folder that will hold the new directory.

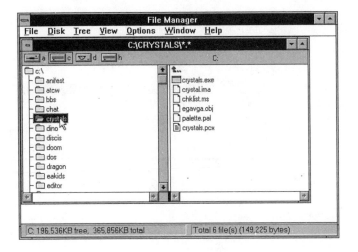

2 Select File, Create Directory. The Create Directory dialog box appears.

Fig. 15.5

You use this dialog box to create a new directory. Simple as pie.

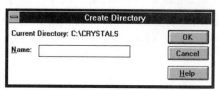

3 Type the name of the new directory, then press Enter or click the dialog box's OK button.

Fig. 15.6

Presto! The new directory appears in the File Manager's drive window.

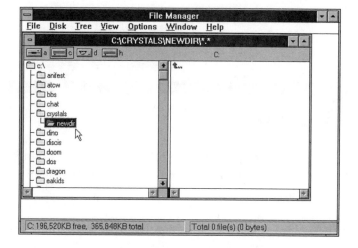

Getting rid of a directory is almost as easy. Here's how:

1 Select the directory you want to delete, and then press your keyboard's Delete key (or select the File menu's Delete command). The Delete dialog box appears.

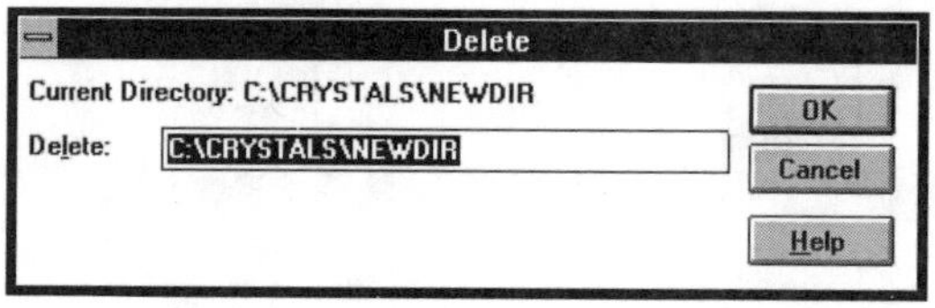

Fig. 15.7

Cleanup time. You use this dialog box to zap any directories you no longer need.

2 Click the OK button. The Confirm Directory Delete dialog box appears.

Fig. 15.8
Just making sure that
you want to send this
directory into oblivion.

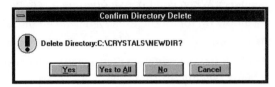

3 Click the Yes button.

4 If there are any files in the directory, the Confirm File Delete dialog box appears. Click the Yes button to delete the file. If you know that there is more than one file in the directory, click the Yes to All button.

Fig. 15.9
Click Yes if you really
want to deep-six a file.

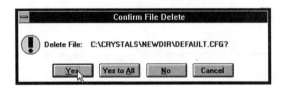

If you had your cursor on the root directory of drive C: and pressed the Delete key on the keyboard, you could wipe out an entire hard disk in one fell swoop. Did you notice the Yes to All button in the Confirm *Directory* Delete dialog box? Clicking Yes to All is like saying, "Stop asking me on each one. I know what's there and I don't want any of it." The Confirm *File* Delete dialog box works the same way.

 Be very careful about selecting the Yes to All button. Be *absolutely* sure that's what you want to do. When in doubt, click the Cancel button and first examine the files you're trying to delete.

You can even see more than one drive at a time

Like a savvy administrative assistant, File Manager knows how to do *lots* of things. Not only does it show you the whole drive at one time, it can also show you more than one drive at one time. Eat your heart out, DOS!

Just double-click the icon of the new drive you want to see (not a single, a double-click). When you do, like opening a second book, you get another drive window on top of the first. Can't see all of both windows? Use the Window menu's Tile command to position the windows one above the other or side by side (depending on your version of Windows), so you can see them both clearly (see fig. 15.10).

Fig. 15.10

Two drives for the price of one! File Manager shows you more than one drive at a time for your viewing pleasure.

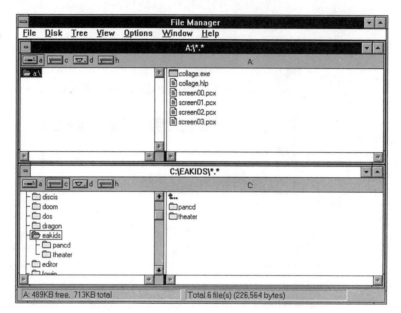

(!) *(Tip)*

In some versions of Windows, when File Manager tiles two windows, it places them one above the other. This is a little dumb because the directory tree listings in each drive run vertically and you never get to see much of the drive without scrolling.

When you select Window, Tile, hold down the Shift key on your keyboard. The windows will appear side-by-side instead. Dazzle your office mates with this neat trick!

16
Doing Stuff with Files (Windows)

Now that you know how to work File Manager, you can start doing useful stuff. But first you need a little more File Manager basic training. (Sorry!)

In this chapter:

- How can I see what's in a file?

- I want to make an extra copy of a file

- This file won't go away!

- Uh oh, I think I lost a file

- How can I work with groups of files instead of just one at a time?

The average Windows user would rather walk across hot coals than type in a lot of confusing and long-winded DOS commands. Luckily, Windows users can get File Manager to handle most of the drudgery.

⊛ {Note} File Manager varies slightly from version to version, depending on your setup. Your version may not look or act exactly like that shown in this chapter.

How to see more information

When you type the DIR command under DOS, you get more than a list of file names. The list includes "no-charge" extras such as the size of the file and when it was created. Many people really like this information and are disappointed when it doesn't show up in File Manager. Well, it's not really missing. You can see the full file info anytime you want to, or you can slice and dice the file info to suit your needs.

To see all file information, click on the View menu when you're in File Manager, then select All File Details. After that, the file window looks something like figure 16.1, with the files arranged in a single column. Each row in the window shows all the information for a file. When a file list is quite long, it will never fit in the one little window. Simply click the scroll bar at the right side of the window to see the rest of the file names.

Fig. 16.1
File Manager can still show you all the file details if you change the View options.

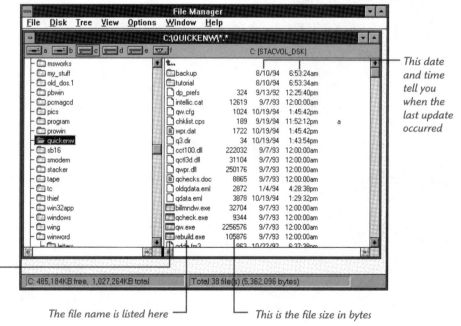

This date and time tell you when the last update occurred

The icon in this column indicates what type of item it is

The file name is listed here

This is the file size in bytes

If you select the View menu's Partial Details option, the Partial Details dialog box appears (see fig. 16.2). Here, you select which file info you want to see. Deselect File Attributes if you like. Or go all the way and deselect Last Modification Time as well; then you'll see only the date and size of each file.

Fig. 16.2

Customize how File Manager displays your files, by choosing to see as much or as little information as you like.

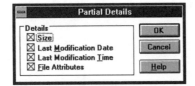

You can sort the list a different way, too

File Manager lets you list your files in a number of different orders. In most cases, you'll probably want to arrange files alphabetically so you can quickly find them by name. On other occasions, however, you may want to see which files were modified most recently. Or, maybe you want to see which files are hogging up the most disk space. Because you have different needs at different times, File Manager lets you decide how to view your files: by name, by type, by size, or by date. Just pull down the View menu and choose one of the Sort options.

It says my file has a rash?

The All File Details option shows you a little more than you bargained for. There's a *new* column of info at the right-hand side that's filled with very strange letters. You might see r, a, s, or h in this column; they can even be combined together into ra or sh or who knows what. You're allowed to ignore them, but if you must find out, here's what they mean.

The letters are called **file attributes** and are like a secret code that tells DOS how to handle that file. The letter r means that the file is **read-only** and shouldn't be deleted (must be important, huh?). An s is noteworthy too because this is a **system file** that makes the computer work! The little a next to most of your files means that the file has not been backed up since its last modification. (You might want to read Chapter 34 soon.) If there are any files with an h, count yourself lucky. You're looking at a **hidden** file that's normally invisible to DOS users. Isn't Windows cool?

How to peek into a file

In the last chapter, you were introduced to the drive and directory icons, respectively. If you look closely at File Manager's file window, you'll see several other icons. These represent individual files, as explained in the following table.

A Quick Table of File Manager's Icons

Icon	What this icon means
	These icons are files that Windows recognizes as programs. They all have the extension COM, EXE, or BAT. You can double-click these icons here to run the program.
	These files are associated with a certain Windows application (Excel, WordPerfect, Paintbrush, and so on). Windows knows which program saved this file on the disk. You can look at one of these files by simply double-clicking the file name. Windows gets the program, then the file, and loads them both into memory, giving you access to all the features of that file and that application.
	The files with the blank-page icon aren't currently associated with any Windows application, which means you can't view them by double-clicking. (Try it. You get an error message, but it doesn't hurt anything.)

How file associations work

When you answer the phone at your house, you typically find out two things right away: who's calling and who they want to talk to. Then you call the appropriate person to the phone, clamp your hand over the mouthpiece and whisper "It's the plumber" or something appropriate. This is pretty much how file association works. A double-click on a file name is like the phone ringing, indicating that a file needs attention. File Manager answers the call, determining from the file extension which program the file wants to "speak with."

 Just as your 10-year-old probably wouldn't want to field the call from the plumber, a graphics program like Paintbrush doesn't want to be asked to handle a word processing document or a spreadsheet. Associating a file extension with the wrong program can result in a total communication gap whenever you double-click files with that extension.

After File Manager calls the appropriate program, it whispers "It's FISCYEAR.XLS" or "It's FLOWCHRT.DGM" or whatever the name of the file is, so that the program knows exactly which file needs to be opened.

Copying and moving files

File Manager lets you use your mouse to perform copies and moves. You simply drag the file name from one place in a window to another. Before you can start copying and moving files with File Manager, though, you need to know some of the assumptions it makes about your actions:

- If you drag a file from one place to another on the *same* disk, File Manager assumes you want to *move* that file rather than *copy* it.

- If you drag a file from one disk to another, File Manager assumes that you want to *copy* the file to the new location and keep the original wherever it was.

Copying a file

Because of the assumptions File Manager makes, there are two ways to copy a file using your mouse. To copy a file from one disk to another, first open a window for both disk drives (refer to Chapter 15) by double-clicking the drive letter icon. Tile the windows if necessary. Then click on the name of the file you want to copy. Hold down the mouse button and drag the file name from one window to the other (see fig. 16.3) and let go when you get there to drop the file. File Manager copies the file to the new location.

This operation is much easier if you have File Manager show both drive windows simultaneously by selecting the <u>T</u>ile command from the <u>W</u>indow menu.

Fig. 16.3

With File Manager, you can copy files by dragging them with your mouse.

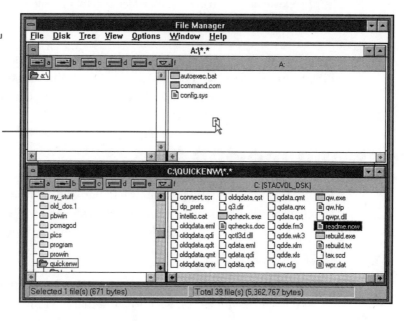

When dragging a file, this mouse pointer shows that the file is being copied

File Manager copies the file to the directory where your mouse is pointing when you drop the file. For example, if you have the mouse pointer over a directory called MYSTUFF when you drop the file, the file gets copied into the MYSTUFF directory. If you don't want the file in any directory, drag it to the root directory at the top of the directory tree.

To copy a file from one place to another on the same disk, hold down the Ctrl key and then drag the file with the mouse. The Ctrl key tells File Manager to copy the file rather than move it.

Moving a file

Moving files in File Manager is as easy as copying, especially if you're moving from directory to directory on the same disk. To do this, just drag the file and drop it on the directory icon where you want it to go (see fig. 16.4).

Fig. 16.4
You can also move files
by dragging.

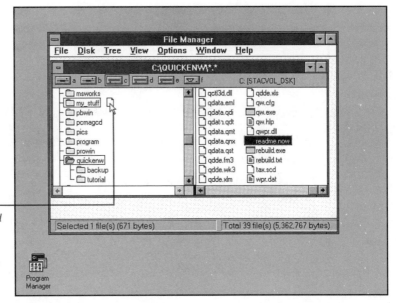

*Notice that the
document icon attached
to the mouse pointer
doesn't contain a plus
sign; therefore, the
document is being
moved and not copied*

To move a file to another disk, open a window for both disks so you can see
what you're doing. Hold down the Shift key, and then drag the file from one
disk window to the other. The Shift key tells File Manager to move the file
rather than copy it.

Q&A

*I thought I copied something but instead moved it. How
can I prevent this?*

Choose Options, Confirmation and make sure that the Mouse Action option
is selected. That way, you'll always get a pop-up dialog box requesting confirmation when you drag a file.

Deleting a file

Erasing files with File Manager is pretty easy, too. Just click on the file to
select it and then press the Del key (or choose File, Delete). When the Delete
dialog box appears (see fig. 16.5), click the OK button to do it, or click the
Cancel button if you change your mind.

Fig. 16.5
The Delete dialog box gives you a chance to change your mind about deleting a file.

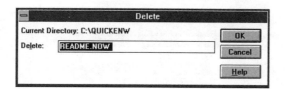

Delete

Current Directory: C:\QUICKENW

Delete: README.NOW

OK   Cancel   Help

?Q&A

What does `This is a system, hidden, or read-only file` ***mean?***

If you try to delete a file that has a system, hidden, or read-only attribute, Windows warns you first. These files are usually pretty important, so it's unusual to wipe them out. Windows will let you delete them if you're sure you want to.

Renaming a file

Sometimes, file names wear out their usefulness, and you need a fresh name to reflect what the file has evolved into. You can use File Manager to change a file name.

To rename a file, first select it. Then choose File, Rename (see fig. 16.6). Type the file's new name, and press Enter. Choose Cancel if you change your mind and want to keep the old file name.

Fig. 16.6
The Rename dialog box is File Manager's way to let you change a file name.

Rename

Current Directory: C:\QUICKENW

From: README.NOW

To:

OK   Cancel   Help

Q&A ⎤ ***Why is Windows showing me the Error Renaming File dialog box? Help!***

Every file in a specific directory must have a unique name. You're probably trying to use a name that has already been assigned to another file. (Or you might have tried to use a character that's illegal as part of the file name.)

Finding a lost file

When you get a lot of files and directories on a disk, it's easy to forget that special place where you put a file so it wouldn't get lost (ha!). Luckily, File Manager has a handy command for finding those files that have wandered off.

To locate a specific file with File Manager, choose File, Search. You'll get the Search dialog box (see fig. 16.7) where you can type the name of the lost file and indicate which directory File Manager should look in first. (To search your entire hard disk, make sure this says C:\, and select the option Search All Subdirectories.)

Fig. 16.7
When you select the Search All Subdirectories check box, File Manager searches not only the directory you typed in the Start From box, but also every subdirectory inside that directory. If you deselect this check box, File Manager searches only in the named directory, ignoring all subdirectories.

Search
Search For: ***.NOW**
Start From: C:\QUICKENW
☒ Search All Subdirectories

OK Cancel Help

After you type the file name and starting directory, click OK, and File Manager scans your disk for files that match the file name you requested. When it's done, File Manager displays the search results in a new window. The list in this window shows every occurrence of the requested file (there may be several with the same name in various directories). Look over the list for the location of the exact one you want.

?Q&A

> **I don't remember the exact spelling of the file name I need to find.**
>
> No problem—you can use DOS wildcards (see Chapter 11 for a refresher). For example, you can tell File Manager to search for the file *.EXE, in which case it would find every file with an EXE extension. Never use *.* as a search criterion, because File Manager will simply list every file on the disk, which doesn't help too much.

Dealing with groups of files

It's possible, right in the file window, to select any group of files and then perform an action on that group. Let's see how it's done.

Selecting files that are in sequence

To select a group of files that are listed all together in a window, click on the first file to highlight it. Then press and hold the Shift key, then click the last file in the group. When you do, all the files between the two clicked files become highlighted (see fig. 16.8). Since all these files are now ready for some kind of action, this isn't a good time to press the Del key. (Or maybe it is, if you want them all gone!)

Fig. 16.8

Selecting groups of files with File Manager is as easy as a couple of clicks.

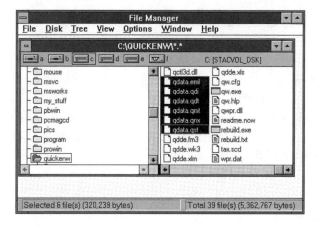

Selecting files that are out of sequence

What if the files that make up your desired group are not listed together in the window? No problem. Click the first file name, and then add any number of files to the group, one by one (see fig. 16.9) by holding down the Ctrl key and clicking each additional file name.

Fig. 16.9

You can even select a bunch of files that are not grouped together in the file window.

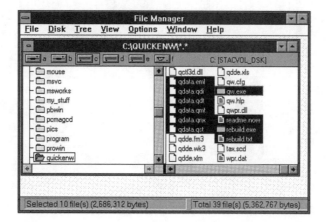

Copying, moving, and deleting groups of files

Once all the files are selected, you can drag the entire group to copy or move them as desired. For example, you can drag the group to a new directory on the same disk (see fig. 16.10) and the entire group of files will be moved. As you might expect, you can drag the group to another drive, and the entire group will be copied—very handy when you want a backup copy of important files!

 Q&A

> **I decided I don't want to do anything with this group of files. What should I do?**
>
> Click on any file name without holding down Shift or Ctrl, and your group is no longer selected.

Fig. 16.10
You can copy or move an entire group of files simply by selecting the group, and then dragging to another icon or window in File Manager.

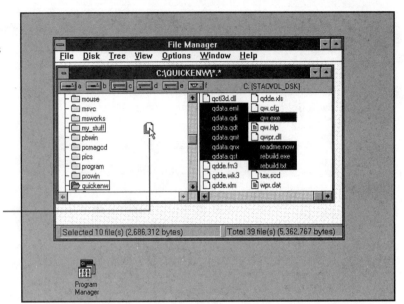

This mouse pointer indicates that multiple files are being moved

17

Doing Stuff with Disks (Windows)

In this chapter:

- How do I format new disks?

- Can I format used disks to erase them? How?

- Do I really care about write-protection?

- How do I copy disks in Windows?

If you're in Windows, formatted floppies are just a click (or two) away!

You've already seen that Windows makes file management a snap. Your mouse enables you to copy and move files much more quickly than you can in DOS. And Windows' File Manager is no slouch when it comes to working with your disk drives, either.

Formatting disks in Windows: It's so easy!

Despite all the visual differences between Windows and DOS, one thing never changes. If that floppy disk has never been formatted, it's of no use to anybody. Yes, Windows can do that for you—formatted floppies are just a click (or two) away.

*{Note}* You never know when you're going to need a formatted disk in a hurry, so most people format all their floppies as soon as they open the box. These far-sighted and industrious people (who floss twice a day and have their oil changed regularly) have a big supply of formatted disks available, which helps them avoid the horrors of accidentally formatting a disk that already has some valuable information on it.

How do I format a new disk?

File Manager is your one-stop program for dealing with files and disks. To format a disk, load File Manager and then slip the floppy disk into the drive. It's a good idea to double-check the contents of the disk, so always click on the *drive* icon at the top of the window, just to see if there's anything on the disk you should know about. If an Error Selecting Drive dialog box pops up (see fig. 17.1), saying the disk is unformatted, then *great!* Just select the *Yes* button with the mouse and continue.

Fig. 17.1
File Manager detects an unformatted disk and asks if you want it formatted now.

*<Caution>* If you click the drive icon and no error message appears, then the disk in the drive is already formatted and may even contain something you want to keep. Look closely at the file window to see what's there.

OK, now that you really do know that your disk needs formatting, I won't put you off any longer. Open the Disk menu, then click Format Disk. When you do, you see the Format Disk dialog box (just like the one in fig. 17.2).

Fig. 17.2
No commands to type!
The Format Disk dialog
box makes formatting
disks a walk in the
park.

Now, just follow these steps:

1 In the <u>D</u>isk In list box, select the drive that holds the disk you want to format.

2 In the <u>C</u>apacity list box, select the type of disk to format. (If you're not too sure about disk capacities, take a look at Chapter 8; the section titled "How much can they hold?" covers the subject nicely.)

②Q&A ⎡ ### So how do I use these list boxes?

Windows goes out of its way to help you make decisions. One way it does this is by letting you choose things from lists. In Windows, lists are represented by list boxes—small boxes with an arrow button at one end. You click the arrow to see the list of available options, then click an item to choose it from the list. Your choice appears in the box, and you get to enjoy this really great feeling of control.

3 When you're done selecting drives and disk types, click the OK button. Windows then asks whether you're sure you want to format the disk.

4 If losing all the data on the disk doesn't give you a cold sweat, go ahead and click the <u>Y</u>es button. Windows gets to work and formats the disk.

5 After Windows is done, it brings up the Format Complete dialog box (see fig. 17.3). This box not only tells you how much stuff you can store on the new disk, but also gives you a chance to format another disk in case you're doing a whole box of them (see our previous note about industrious, far-sighted people). Click the <u>Y</u>es button to keep formatting, or click <u>N</u>o to stop.

Fig. 17.3
Want to format more disks? Just click the Yes button and keep going.

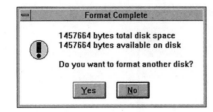

Q&A

Windows is telling me that it Cannot format disk, *so what do I do?*

First, make sure you have a disk in the drive that's been selected in the list box. Also, make sure that the disk is the type you selected in the Format Disk dialog box. (Trying to format a 720K, low-density disk as a 1.44M, high-density disk is sure to make File Manager whine.) Finally, make sure that the disk isn't write-protected.

So what is write-protection?

Write-protection means the disk drive isn't allowed to change the contents of the disk in any way. This feature is very handy for guarding that information you never, ever want to copy over or otherwise lose from the disk. Chapter 8 discusses write-protection in more detail and even shows you what the write-protection devices look like on disks.

(Tip)

If you find yourself trying to format a disk that's been write-protected, maybe you should check to see *why* someone write-protected it. You know, if the road's closed, there may be a reason!

What can the FORMAT command do for my used disks?

In Chapter 12, you saw that DOS can perform a **quick format** that erases a floppy disk without actually rewriting the little magnetic lines that define where the files are stored. This operation cuts the formatting process in half, which makes it much faster, and generally pleases everyone.

So, guess what? File Manager can perform exactly the same quick-format function, and you don't even have to type any of those DOS commands with slashes. Just put the disk into your drive and select the Format command from File Manager's Disk menu. When the Format Disk dialog box appears, select the drive as you normally would, but then click on the Quick Format option (see fig. 17.4). Click the OK button and you're off to the races. Talk about a fast format!

Fig. 17.4

Save time when formatting previously used diskettes. Use the Quick Format option and have at it!

 **{Note}**

If a disk has been around for a while, you may want to skip the Quick Format and do a full format instead. This gives Windows a chance to refresh the disk by redrawing the "white lines around the parking spaces." At the same time, it finds any problems with the disk before you find them the hard way.

Copying disks: It doesn't have to hurt!

Nothing protects your data better than keeping back-up copies on another disk. The bottom line: keep a duplicate of every file that's important to you. If you can't afford to lose it, copy it!

The problem with copying files is that moving them around one by one can take a lot of your valuable time. Luckily, you can copy whole diskettes quickly with File Manager, so you won't have any excuse for putting your backup off till tomorrow. It doesn't even matter how many files are on the disk. Since the entire disk is copied anyway, one file or one hundred files takes the same amount of time.

To make a backup copy of a disk, all you need is the **source** disk (the one you want to copy) and a **destination** disk (to hold the copy). Before you begin the copy process, make sure the destination disk holds absolutely nothing you want to keep. The Copy Disk process will whack out anything currently on the destination disk and replace it with an exact copy of the information on the source disk. You will swap the source and destination disks as the copy process continues.

To achieve the blissful state of disk-backup security, follow these painless steps:

1 Select <u>D</u>isk, then <u>C</u>opy Disk from File Manager's menu bar. The Copy Disk dialog box appears (see fig. 17.5).

Fig. 17.5

The Copy Disk operation is as simple as it looks.

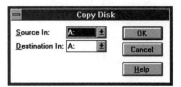

2 Click the dialog box's OK button. The Confirm Copy Disk dialog box appears, warning you that all data on the destination disk (the one you're copying to) will be erased (see fig. 17.6).

Fig. 17.6

Did you check that destination disk to make sure it's OK to erase anything lurking there?

3 Click <u>Y</u>es. The Copy Disk dialog box appears, asking you to put the source disk into the drive (see fig. 17.7).

Fig. 17.7

The source disk goes in first.

4 Put the source disk into drive A, and click the OK button. Windows copies the data from the disk into the computer's memory. A status report line appears in the box, telling you what percent of the process is completed.

5 When a different Copy Disk dialog box appears, you're halfway through! Insert the destination disk into drive A, and click the OK button. Windows copies the data from your computer's memory to the destination disk.

⊗<Caution>

Remember, File Manager makes a perfect copy of the original disk and erases anything that had been on the *destination* disk. (You don't run into this when you're doing only a file copy, so it's easy to get confused.) So be sure that you're not mistakenly copying the blank destination disk to the source disk that *was* full of files, or your day is going to be really messed up. To prevent this sort of mishap, write-protect the source disk.

⊘Q&A

What do I do when Windows tells me Unable to copy disk**?**

Here are a few things to check: Did you remember to put a disk in the drive? If so, either the source disk or the destination disk may be defective. (Let's hope it's not the source disk.) Try popping the disk in and out of the drive to make sure it's seated properly. Better check that both disks are the same density rating, as well. Finally, make sure the destination disk isn't write-protected.

18

Doing Stuff with the System (Windows)

In this chapter:

- These screen colors are boring. Can I change them?
- Dress up Windows with wallpaper, screen savers, and patterns
- Want to start Windows programs automatically? Here's how

Want to add colorful pictures or custom colors to your screen? You can change your screen so it looks the way you want it to!

The options in customizing DOS are limited to changing your prompt and a few other goodies, as you discovered in Chapter 13, "Doing Stuff with the System (DOS)." Windows, on the other hand, lets you change a wide variety of settings to make your work area more comfortable and friendly.

The stuff in this chapter is just for fun. Nothing here will hurt your Windows setup—although it might hurt your eyes if you choose hot pink, chartreuse, and mauve as your screen colors!

Making Windows look the way you want

 Most of the options that let you add bells and whistles to your Windows setup are found in **Control Panel**. Look in the Main program group for the Control Panel icon and double-click it to open the Control Panel window (see fig. 18.1).

_____ Your version of Control Panel won't look exactly like this figure. You'll probably have fewer icons, more icons, or just different icons. It all depends on what kind of software you have!

Fig. 18.1
Control Panel lets you adjust colors, fonts, mouse sensitivity, and even change the language of your keyboard!

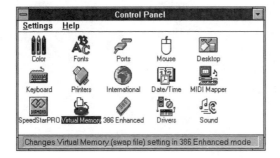

Changing the screen colors

You may find that the Windows default colors are kind of bland. Want to add some zip? Double-clicking the Color icon is like a trip to a psychedelic paint store (see fig. 18.2). Click on the arrow next to the Color Schemes list box, and you can see all the ready-to-go color schemes. Just click a color scheme to make it active. You even get a little preview showing how the scheme will affect all the elements of the Windows system. When you click the dialog box's OK button, your Windows colors change to the color scheme you chose.

_____ Is the color scheme you selected a little too flashy? Change it again! Double-click the Color icon in Control Panel, and choose another scheme. Conservative? You can restore the original colors by choosing Windows Default as the color scheme.

Fig. 18.2

Windows comes with a lot of color schemes that you can use instantly. For a glow-in-the-dark version, try Hotdog Stand or Plasma Power Saver. If you're into warm and relaxed, maybe Ocean or The Blues will be your favorite.

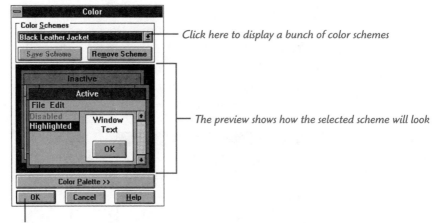

Click here to display a bunch of color schemes

The preview shows how the selected scheme will look

Click here when you have something you like

Want to have some fun? Click the Color Palette button. A new section of the dialog box opens and lets you change individual colors for parts of the Windows screen. In the preview box, click the part of the screen you'd like to change. Then click the color you want from the Basic Colors set. (If you feel REALLY adventurous, click the button that says Define Custom Colors and fool around with your own little paint palette!)

When you're done, click Save Scheme and assign a name to your custom color set. Then choose OK. You can change the individual colors again any time you want.

Wallpapering the desktop

Wallpaper is an image or design that appears behind Program Manager. You don't see it unless Program Manager is minimized or sized to be smaller than full-screen. (See Chapter 14 for details on resizing windows.)

Wallpaper takes a lot of memory to display. If you turn on wallpaper and then your computer seems to slow down, turn the wallpaper off. It's only for fun, anyway.

Windows comes with a wide selection of wallpaper designs—from tasteful and neat to busy and ostentatious. Double-click the Desktop icon in Control Panel to see the available choices (see fig. 18.3). In the Wallpaper section of this dialog box, click on the arrow to display the list of available wallpaper files. Just choose a name that sounds good, and click the dialog box's OK button. *Presto!* A surprisingly snazzy desktop appears (see fig. 18.4).

Fig. 18.3
The Desktop dialog box lets you change several features about your Windows desktop. Wallpapering is only one of the choices.

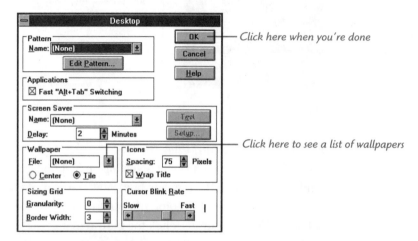

Click here when you're done

Click here to see a list of wallpapers

Fig. 18.4
This figure shows the EGYPT.BMP wallpaper in use. Other neat designs include redbrick, argyle, and zigzag.

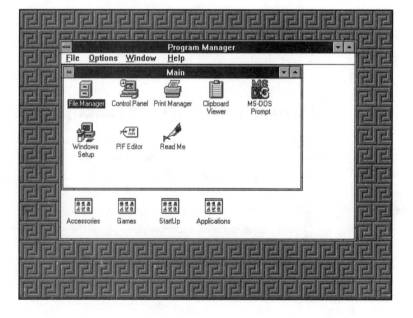

Q&A

> **My wallpaper just appears in the middle of the screen. Why doesn't it cover the screen?**
>
> If the wallpaper you choose is fairly large (for example, if you make your own design with Paintbrush as explained in the sidebar at the bottom of this page), you should click the button marked Center in the Wallpaper section of the Desktop dialog box. This gives one large, centered image on your screen. Most of the wallpapers that come with Windows require that the setting be changed to Tile. This fills the screen with multiple copies of an image that has been saved at a small size.

Adding a screen saver

Screen savers are special programs that automatically take over the display when a computer is idle for a certain amount of time (see the monitors stuff in Chapter 7 for an explanation of how this works). Although Windows doesn't come with screen savers as fancy as those you can buy at the store, it does give you a few neat choices.

To set up a Windows screen saver, go back to the Desktop dialog box. In the Screen Saver section, click the arrow to display a list of screen savers currently on your system (see fig. 18.5). Click one to install it. (Later, if you want to remove it, choose None from the list.) Want to see how the screen saver will look? Click the Test button for a preview.

Make your own wallpaper

Wallpaper is created from a special kind of picture file called a **bitmap** (that's why the file name has a BMP extension). You can make your own BMP files with Paintbrush, the drawing program that comes with Windows. Draw the design you want in Paintbrush. Save it to disk as a BMP file in your Windows directory. Then it will appear in the list when you go back to the Desktop dialog box, so you can choose it from the list.

Fig. 18.5
Screen savers fill the
screen with moving
images when the
system has been idle
for a specific period
of time.

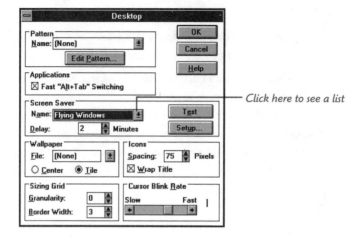

— *Click here to see a list*

To set the amount of time the computer must be idle before the screen saver
appears, click on the arrows next to the Delay box. Some screen savers have
settings you can change, like personalized messages or colors. You get to
these options by clicking the Setup button.

②Q&A _____ ┌── **OK, the screen saver is running. How do I turn it off?**

To get back to work, move the mouse or press a key. The safest key to press is
the Ctrl Key.

Other stuff you can play with in Control Panel

In addition to using a wallpaper, you can add a pattern to the Windows
desktop behind Program Manager. In the Desktop dialog box (as usual), click
the arrow in the Pattern section and choose a pattern. Scottie, Waffle, and
Weave are all pretty interesting. You can even doctor the pattern by choosing
one and then clicking the Edit Pattern button.

{Note}

The pattern you choose is used as a background for the little boxes around minimized program icons. Don't follow this? Don't worry—just remember that if you can't read the icons, the pattern is probably at fault.

A pattern WITH a wallpaper isn't really a good combination. Try it and see what kind of weird visual things you can create—but don't expect to be able to work well this way.

The Sound settings are really fun, but you can't use sound without a sound card or a special file called a **speaker driver**. (These two speaker drivers— SPEAK.EXE and SPEAKER.DRV—are generally available from Microsoft, various bulletin boards, and so on.) If your system has a sound card, or you got a speaker driver from somewhere, you can control what noises or tunes you hear when Windows starts, shuts down, encounters an error, and so on. The system uses WAV (pronounced "wave") files. Lots of people have WAV files available—bits of movie dialog, funny sounds like "uh oh," etc. Check with your computer dealer if you want more details on using sound.

Control Panel lets you play around with a lot of other settings, too. Unfortunately, some of these controls can disable or screw up parts of your system. Check for instructions in your Windows documentation or the Windows Help system. In general, don't try the following things without knowing what you're doing:

- **International** adjusts Windows for use with languages other than English. This icon can give you an Icelandic keyboard if you're not careful.

- **Fonts** adds or deletes various type styles for your printer. You can't add any if you don't buy them, and then they come with instructions. If you just experiment, you might end up deleting the ones you already have.

- **Ports** is for advanced brain surgeons only. Changing stuff in here can make your modem or your mouse play dead.

- **Printers** adds a new printer if you buy one or kills an existing one if you don't. Don't fool around with this one without help.

- **386 Enhanced** deals with settings for the CPU and memory. Don't play with this stuff unless you're willing to pay for a fix-it guy afterward.

- **Drivers** helps you install extra hardware for your computer. The manufacturer should tell you exactly what to do.

If you're always in a hurry, open your programs automatically

Do you get up in the morning to a fresh pot of coffee, brewed automatically by your coffee maker? Convenient, isn't it? Well, Windows offers some simple preprogramming of its own. How would you like to start Windows and find your favorite programs open and waiting?

If you use the Calendar or Schedule program, it could be open, displaying your appointments for the day. Maybe you use a spreadsheet or word processing program and want to get started immediately. No problem!

How to set them up...

Look around in Program Manager for a program group named StartUp. If you don't have a StartUp group, choose File, New, Program Group, and click OK. Type **StartUp** and click OK. When you open the StartUp group, it's probably empty (see fig. 18.6). Any programs you add to it will be started automatically when you start Windows.

Fig. 18.6
Whether you create the StartUp group or it already exists, it's probably empty.

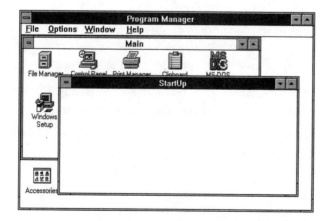

Use the following steps to place your favorite program(s) in the StartUp group:

1 Open the StartUp program group.

2 Now open the program group that has the first program you want. For example, if you want to start Notepad automatically when you start Windows, open the Accessories group. (That's where Notepad is.)

(Tip)_____ | Resize the windows so you can see both groups easily.

3 Press and hold down the Ctrl key. Click the icon you want and drag the icon to the StartUp group (see fig. 18.7). When you're there, let go of the mouse button and then the Ctrl key. Windows copies the icon into the StartUp group.

4 Keep adding icons as you like. But see the next section if you don't have lots of memory.

Fig. 18.7
If you forget to press Ctrl, Windows moves the icon instead of copying it. Just drag it back where it belongs and start over.

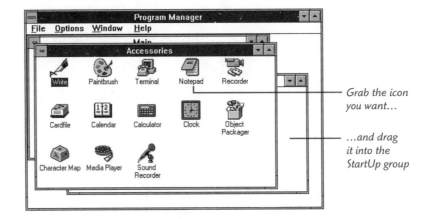

Grab the icon you want...

...and drag it into the StartUp group

...or take some out

Every time you add an application to the StartUp group, it takes Windows a little longer to get started. This is because Windows not only has to load itself, but also all those extra programs. As the electronic memory of the PC gets filled with these programs, you may notice the overall speed of the computer decreasing as well. For this reason, you may want to reduce the number of programs in the StartUp group.

You may have already figured out that deleting the icon from the StartUp group is all it takes. Before you do this, make sure that the icon still exists in another program group. You will probably want to be able to use that program in the future!

When you're ready to dump something from the StartUp group, click the icon and then press Del. Windows displays the Delete dialog box. Click the Yes button to delete the icon, or click No if you change your mind.

(!) (Tip)

If you delete an icon from Program Manager, you don't delete the program itself from the disk. You just remove an easy way to get it started. (Not unlike throwing away your car keys, actually.) You can restore the icon, and it's pretty much like finding your car keys. See your Windows documentation or the Help system for details.

19

My Written Work Has to Look Good—Tell Me about Word Processors

A word processor's job is to make your writing efforts look good, whether this means a grant proposal, a term paper, or the most stunning grocery list you've ever seen.

In this chapter:

- Other than letters and memos, what can I produce with a word processor?

- How is word processing different from typing on a typewriter?

- Hot new features of today's word processors

- Take a look at some of the best word processors

It's safe to assume that 99.9 percent of all home computers have a word processor of some kind installed on them. In fact, it's very likely that your operating system has a built-in word processor with limited capabilities, but to get all the features you want in a word processor, you might feel the need to also buy a commercial one.

✱{Note} ⎸ A **word processing program** is generally just called a **word processor** in the computer industry (and in this chapter). The term **word processor** also applies to a piece of hardware much like an electronic typewriter, but that equipment isn't discussed in this book.

What can I do with a word processor?

Basically, you can use a word processor to do anything you used to do with a typewriter. Because word processors are flexible and smart, the things you can do with your documents are practically limitless. You can move things around, fix problems, and change the whole shape of a document with remarkable ease.

You'll find that many of the limitations on what you can produce will come from your printer rather than your word processor. With the right paper or forms, here's a partial list of things you could make with your word processor:

- File folder labels
- Disk labels
- Business cards
- Greeting cards and invitations
- Menus

- Letterhead
- Newsletters
- Brochures and fliers
- Banners
- Bumper stickers

Most programs throw in extras, too

Remember when power steering, power brakes, and an automatic transmission were options on most cars? Well, these days, all of those are standard features on nearly every car. The new generation of options includes things like sunroofs, anti-lock brakes, and separate temperature control for each seat. Word processors have likewise evolved—some features that once made a splash on the PC software scene for being brand-new and different are taken for granted now because almost every word processor on the market includes them. Among these well-established features are

- Adding headers and footers
- Inserting footnotes
- Using different character fonts in a variety of sizes

- Changing text to **bold**, *italic*, <u>underlined</u>, <u>double underlined</u>, ~~strikethrough~~, and more

- Checking for spelling errors (in some programs, checking for grammatical errors, also)

Word processor features that remind me of car airbags (that is, many modern word processors have them, but some don't, even though they ought to) include the following:

- Adding lines or boxes in a variety of widths and styles

- Inserting digitized photos and artwork

- Making charts and tables with newly entered data or by linking to data that already exists in a database

- Drag-and-drop editing (you really gotta have a mouse for this sleight-of-hand stuff!)

- Creating a table of contents or index automatically

- Executing complex macros

Plain English, please!

A **macro** is just a bunch of commands that do a specific job, which you save as a unit. Macros are handy for automating repetitive tasks. You might, for example, create a macro that swaps transposed letters in a word. 🙷

Do I have to spend a fortune to get a decent word processor?

Many new PCs come with a variety of software packages, including a word processor. If yours didn't, however, you'll probably be interested in knowing how much a good word processor will cost.

Word processors can be expensive, with street prices of $300 or more. However, there are ways to avoid spending such big bucks. One way is to purchase a **competitive upgrade** package. You can only do this, however, if you already own another word processor and are "trading up" to the new one. Another way is to purchase **software suites**. See Chapter 24 for details.

How to jazz up those boring documents

*This newsletter page uses a **three-column layout**. Note the **vertical and horizontal lines** that are used to separate the columns and other elements on the page.*

*You can add a variety of **graphics** to most word processing documents. This scanned photograph straddles two columns and adds visual interest and balance to the page.*

THE LAKES

Contained within the National Park are three very famous, and pulchritudinous, lakes. The first you come to by jaunting car is the Lower Lake, also called Lough Leane. The second, or Middle Lake, is also called Muckross Lake. The third is simply known as the Upper Lake. In addition, don't miss Torc Mountain and its stupendous waterfall. Water from the Devil's Punch Bowl rushes over Torc's 60' waterfall, gushing and glorious, it is a sight you will not want to miss.

THE PEOPLE

Of course, as we have said before, the people of Ireland are its main tourist attraction. Their warm, friendly smiles await your visit. Their music greets you; their song welcomes you. Men resting along the side of the road from working in the peat bogs. Their worn, shiny suits a symbol of days gone by. The women, with their rosy red cheeks, shopping for fresh bread and potatoes; chatting with their

beauty and solitude of the landscape, and the love of life from the people. It is a memory to cherish your whole life through.

MUCKROSS ESTATE

Also located near Killarney, County Kerry, is a tremendous National Park called Muckross Estate. Over 10,000 acres of mountains, lakes, and green, green flora preserved by the Republic for your enjoyment. Cars are not allowed on the estate; there are, however, alternatives. You may rent or bring your own bicycle. Or take a jaunting car. Jaunting cars line the entrance to the park (as well as line the streets of Killarney), ready to transport you to this scene of serenity and beauty. The horse-drawn carriages are driven by gents who spin tales and weave stories of old Ireland, Killarney, Muckross, and the fairies.

Your first stop on the Estate is Muckross Abbey. A Franciscan Abbey built in the 15th century,

it is one of the best kept and restored abbeys in all of Kerry. Your next stop is Muckross House. A monumental 19th century home donated, along with the land, to the people of Ireland by its former owners. The house is filled with intricately hand-carved furniture, home-made crafts, tapestries, and original art works. The basement contains a stable, and fully stocked print shop, pub, blacksmith shop, kitchen, and weavers shop; all have presenters working as you tour, answering any and all questions.

*A variety of **fonts** and **font sizes** creates different types of emphasis in certain parts of the page.*

TRAVEL AIRLINES

presenting our
Spring Specials

Round Trip to Shannon	$695
Round Trip to Dublin	$795

Restrictions and limits apply
Call for information and prices

CALL TOLL FREE
1-800-009-9900

*Centered text provides emphasis and enhances readability. Note the use of **white space** to make information easy to read.*

Graphics lines such as this create a page border and add visual interest.

Clip art can add drama or even humor to your documents. With most word processors, you can move clip art or inserted pictures, and the program adjusts the text to flow around the new location.

Building a masterpiece

You'll probably end up using your word processor to type everything—not just documents that need to look great (like quarterly reports and monthly newsletters) but rough transcripts of phone conversations or even notes to your significant other.

The first thing you do with a word processor is create a new document, which you'll eventually save in a file on disk. This task is a lot like sticking a new piece of paper in a typewriter. Some word processors have a new document ready to go as soon as you start them. Others make you choose a command (such as New on the File menu) before they'll give you a clean window in which to type your document.

Just start typing

Once you have a new document started, type everything you want on the page, just as you would with a typewriter. The big difference is that mistakes you make with your word processor aren't permanent—you just press the Backspace key to get rid of the troublesome characters and then retype the word.

Fig. 19.1

All word processors have a command for starting a new document, that leads to a blank page like this.

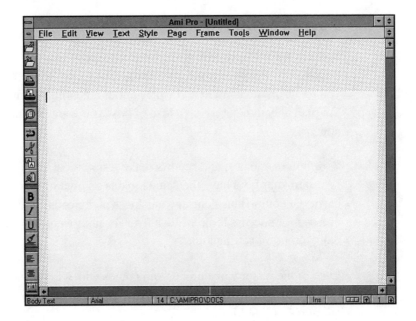

Another difference is that you don't press the Enter key at the end of each sentence like you use the carriage return with a typewriter. Today's word processors all perform **word wrap**, so you only press Enter when you've finished a paragraph.

 Plain English, please!

Word wrap means that your cursor (often called the **insertion point**) goes down to the left edge of the following line when the word you're typing won't fit in the margin.

Edit the heck out of it

In the old typewriter days, producing a second draft of a document was as much physical labor as it was mental; you had to retype the whole thing.

A word processor makes editing a document as easy as rearranging magnets on a refrigerator. Decide which parts of the document need to be lifted, moved, or added. The rest of your writing stays put on the screen as you use commands—like Copy, Cut, Paste, and Replace—to move the parts around, so you never have to retype anything that was done properly the first time.

Fancy it up

You can spruce up as you write, or add the pretty stuff when you're done typing—fancy borders, different fonts, tables, etc. The latter approach lets you focus on the content and worry about adjusting the presentation later, but plan ahead to get a rough idea of how you want the final document to appear.

Your letters, memos, and reports make a statement about you. Should a memo to your boss have the same look as an invitation to a surprise birthday party? Of course not. Your new business plan needs a nice, conservative, dressed-for-success look, while a flyer for next week's big sale demands a bold, attention-getting look.

Each of the major word processors comes with a huge wardrobe of accessories to help you dress your documents appropriately—for success, or to get attention, or just for fun.

Get it out on paper

When you have a dazzling document, you're ready to print. Printing a document is probably the most complicated task you'll have to do with a word processor (outside of figuring out when to use "who" and "whom"). This is because you have to make sure that the printer and word processor can work together.

If you use a Windows-based word processor, Windows handles most of the printing details for you, making sure that what comes out on the page looks the same as what's on the screen. If you're using a DOS-based word processor, though, you may need to refer to your word processor's manual to be sure that you have both the word processor and the printer set up correctly.

Save it for posterity

Another great thing about word processors is that once you create a document, you can save it onto a hard disk or floppy disk. Then, anytime you like, you can open the document (that is, display it on the screen) and print a few extra copies, or do additional editing.

The latest and greatest word processors

Each word processor has its own strengths and weaknesses. It's crucial that you decide which tasks matter most to you and choose a word processor that excels at those tasks.

Windows comes with its own word processor, Write (it's in the Accessories group). Before you spend a lot of money on a word processor, try Write to see whether it'll do enough things to satisfy all your word processing needs. Write isn't as powerful as the major word processors, but it's good enough for most home computer users.

Microsoft Word for Windows

The Windows version of Microsoft Word (called Word for Windows or just WinWord for short) has long been a consumer favorite (see fig. 19.2). This is thanks to its ease of use, its full supply of state-of-the-art word processing features, and its extra goodies.

Fig. 19.2

Microsoft Word for Windows is one of the leading word processors because of its solid selection of standard features and healthy dose of extras.

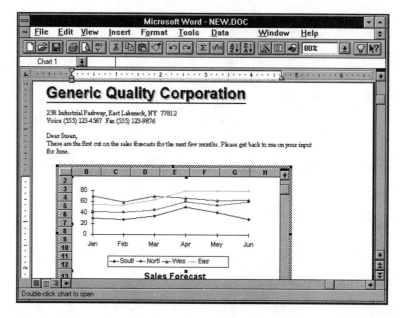

Word, like all major word processors, features a spelling checker and grammar checker, along with customizable toolbars and menus. Word has automated many activities, including checking spelling (it can catch errors as you type) and adding numbers to numbered lists (it can pop up each subsequent number for you). Word also handles special chores like adding borders, graphics, and tables to a document.

 Plain English, please!

A **toolbar** is a row of on-screen buttons, with each button representing a command that you can give to the program. To issue the command, you just click the button with your mouse. **99**

Word includes a graph maker, an equation editor, numerous **Wizards**, and WordArt (see the sections below for explanations of the last two). In addition, Word ships with many templates for getting documents started quickly, as well as with prewritten business letters.

 ### Plain English, please!

A **template** is a document that has been created and laid out for you. To use a template, all you do is open it with your word processor and fill in the blanks with your own text. Think of templates as electronic versions of those preprinted forms you can buy at a stationery store. Figure 19.3 shows an invoice template.

Fig. 19.3
This invoice template is one of a dozen templates that Word provides to help you create business documents quickly.

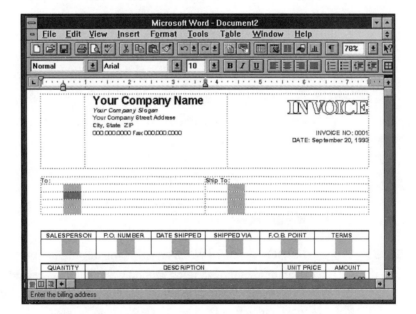

Wizards

To make creating documents easier, Word includes Wizards, which are automated helpers that lead you, step by step, through the creation of a certain type of document. Working with a document type you've never dealt with before is as easy as following on-screen instructions. Word includes Wizards for fax cover sheets, letters, memos, résumés, etc.

WordArt

WordArt is a mini-program or **applet** included with Word that helps you turn plain text into fancy artwork. You can do zany stuff with WordArt, such as twisting words and phrases into unusual shapes, for use as logos and letter-head, for example. WordArt lets you stretch, bend, distort, and colorize letters and words. It's a snap to use. And once you create something in WordArt, you can resize, move, or copy it into another document using the Windows Clipboard.

WordPerfect for Windows

The Windows version of Novell's WordPerfect (see fig. 19.4) includes toolbars, templates, spelling checker, drawing, charting, and more. With the latest version (6.1) of WordPerfect for Windows you can:

- Assemble a variety of charts (for example, pie, bar)

- Fax documents from within WordPerfect for Windows

- Copy formats from one section of text to another

- Create mini-spreadsheets

- Assign special effects (color, shapes, shadowing) to text

- Create and edit graphic images with WP Draw, a scaled-down version of WordPerfect Presentations

The DOS version of WordPerfect is probably the most popular word processor of all time. Although it lost ground when Windows exploded in popularity, the DOS version of WordPerfect 6.0 is still a very impressive program. In fact, it looks and acts deceptively like a Windows program.

Fig. 19.4
WordPerfect for Windows is the newest version of the world's most popular word processor.

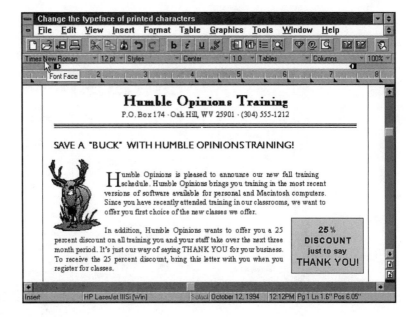

Ami Pro

Although Lotus Development Corporation's Ami Pro (see fig. 19.5) is not as popular as Word for Windows or WordPerfect for Windows, it's the easiest to use of the major Windows word processors—especially when it comes to complex things like page layout. With Ami Pro, for example, it's especially easy to create newsletters and documentation, thanks to its graphics capabilities and its ready-to-use templates.

 Plain English, please!

Page layout is the process of determining how a page will look. This process includes setting margins, positioning headlines, creating headers and footers, and choosing styles for paragraphs.

Fig. 19.5

With its superior graphics handling and outstanding templates, Ami Pro deserves to play in the majors.

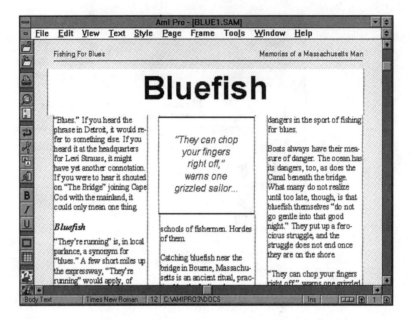

In addition, Ami Pro's superior graphics-handling ability helps set it apart from its competitors, as does its lightning speed during operations such as printing. Like most modern word processors, Ami Pro's screen includes a toolbar at the top and a status line at the bottom, from which you can quickly select character types and styles.

In addition to the usual spelling and grammar checker, Ami Pro sports handy tools for making the program work the way you want it to. For example, you can create a new icon, place it on the toolbar, and assign a macro to the icon. Presto! You've got your own custom command button.

20

I Crunch Numbers—Tell Me about Spreadsheets

In this chapter:

- What's a spreadsheet, and why do I need one?

- Parts of a spreadsheet

- Text, numbers, and formulas

- The "Big Three" Windows spreadsheets

- Spreadsheets that work with DOS

You've seen a sort of spreadsheet if you've ever seen a baseball scoreboard.

A spreadsheet is pretty much like a scoreboard, with rows and columns. But you don't need a scorekeeper; you can change and update information instantly, correct mistakes without erasing, and even whip up a chart or graph showing statistics at a moment's notice. You can use a spreadsheet program for all kinds of instant calculations, such as finding the amount of interest you'll pay on a loan.

What's a spreadsheet program good for?

Numbers, of course, are the heart of the spreadsheet. Very few people use a spreadsheet program to write letters or memos, although you can do that with recent versions. Most of the time, you use a spreadsheet program to handle anything where you want columns and rows of numbers, you need financial calculations, or you want to show statistics in a graph or chart:

- How much money did your business make last year?

- What was the average grade earned by your students on the last test?

- Which meetings are being held in which ballrooms or suites, and at what time?

- How much did your advertising expenditures increase over the last five fiscal years?

Figure 20.1 shows a typical spreadsheet. In this example, the owner of a very small restaurant calculates costs and profits. Notice the bar graph that shows at-a-glance which product line is most profitable.

Fig. 20.1

A typical spreadsheet program, with rows and columns.

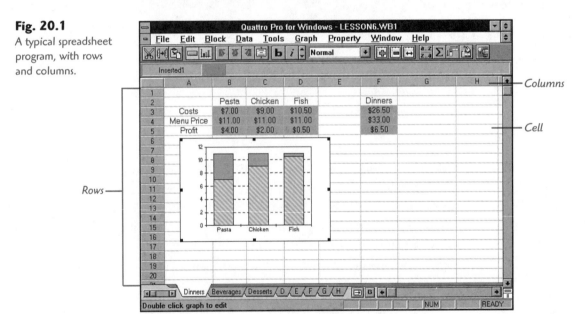

A very important spreadsheet feature is the ability to recalculate constantly. As you insert new information, the spreadsheet can recalculate totals instantly, so your information is always up-to-date.

Another very useful part of current spreadsheet programs is the ability to do "what-if" thinking. This lets you try to come up with the "best plan" in the easiest manner. Suppose you increased your production output for the second half of the year. What kind of profit could you expect to make? Would it offset the additional production costs, such as overtime?

How is a spreadsheet different from an accounting package?

A spreadsheet isn't a substitute for a business accounting software program. Rather, a spreadsheet typically handles the big picture, such as total sales for a month. An accounting software program records the details that make up those sales.

Parts of a typical spreadsheet

The intersection of a column and row is called a **cell**. Spreadsheets have millions of cells. You simply scroll the screen horizontally or vertically to view the ones outside the current view.

Just like houses on a street, the cells are given unique addresses. Most spreadsheets use letters to name the columns of cells. Numbers are used to name each row. The upper-left cell in a spreadsheet is A1. The cell below that is A2. The cell one place to the right of A1 is B1, etc. A rectangular bunch of cells—either a single column or row or multiple columns or rows—are called a **range** or a **block**, depending on the program you use (see fig. 20.2).

Fig. 20.2
Each spreadsheet cell
has a unique address.

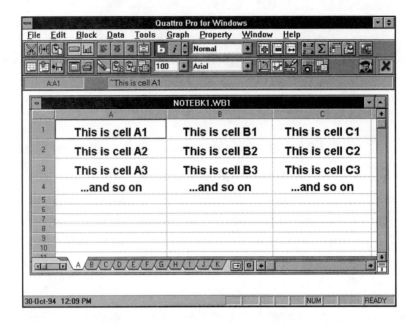

Spreadsheet cells can be filled with numbers, text, or formulas.

Basic spreadsheets just have numbers and text in cells

Text in a spreadsheet is often used to describe a row or column, such as GROSS SALES, JANUARY, PROFIT, etc. You can also write paragraphs that explain the information in the spreadsheet, annotate graphs, and so on.

Recent spreadsheet programs allow extensive formatting of numbers and text. In many cases, the programs include special features that automatically format the spreadsheet. You can choose from quite a variety of formats that include shadow boxes, drop shadows, color bars, various type sizes and typefaces, and so on.

Formulas

The true power of the spreadsheet is the formula. Formulas command the spreadsheet to do a calculation. A spreadsheet may have formulas that tally the interest on an outstanding loan or simply total a range of values.

For example, you could add up 12 monthly sales numbers, one for each month of the year, which appear in column A. The formula might look like this:

```
A1+A2+A3+A4+A5+A6+A7+A8+A9+A10+A11+A12
```

If you change any of the numbers being added, the total changes automatically. For example, if you have a revised sales figure for June (in cell A6), just pop that new number in the cell. As fast as you can press Enter, your spreadsheet changes the total at the bottom of the column.

 (Tip)

> These days, you don't even have to type most of a formula. Modern spreadsheet programs let you click the cells you want to add, subtract, or whatever. You can even drag the mouse over a bunch of cells at a time to select a column, a row, and so on.

Formulas also let you multiply, divide, and subtract, as well as perform other math operations.

Functions are even more powerful than formulas

If you don't want to keep typing the addresses of individual cells to make a formula, or even clicking the ones you want ("A1 *plus* A2 *plus* A3…") gets pretty boring), try a **function**. Functions are just built-in formulas. The manufacturers of spreadsheet programs pretty much know the kinds of things you need to do, and have already thought up formulas for most situations.

For example, virtually all spreadsheet programs have a function that adds a column or row of numbers, because everybody who uses a spreadsheet needs this formula at some point. Remember the example from a few paragraphs ago?

This formula says that you want to add the contents of cell A1, A2, A3, and so on through cell A12. Here's how the equivalent function might look, depending on what spreadsheet product you use:

@SUM(A1..A12)

=SUM(A1:A12)

These two formulas say exactly the same thing as the earlier formula: You want to add up all the numbers in cells A1 through A12. And the result will be identical, too.

The @SUM in the first example is pronounced "at sum."

Keep in mind that the program doesn't care which way you do it, but the function saves on typing for you. Some spreadsheets even have buttons on a toolbar that you can click to enter the function you want—talk about convenience!

What-if calculations

Remember, cells with formulas recalculate results if you change any of the numbers used for the formula. This automatic "ripple effect" allows you to create financial plans, plugging in different assumptions. The automatic recalculation then immediately shows you the impact of the new numbers.

Spreadsheets are even smarter than you think!

One of the coolest features in a spreadsheet (and very labor-saving!) is the ability to copy your formulas from one cell to another. This doesn't sound like any big deal, because you can copy and paste in almost any program.

The big difference in a spreadsheet program is that when you copy a formula, the program is smart enough to guess what you're trying to do, and help you fix the formula so it works somewhere else!

For example, look at figure 20.3. Notice the amount `84,708.96` in cell C12? You can't see it in this picture, which shows the results rather than the formula, but that's a calculation for the amounts in the cells above—all in column C. If you copy that formula and paste it into cell B12, though, the program assumes that you want to calculate with the amounts in column B, not column C, and fixes all the addresses in the formula. You don't have to do a thing!

Fig. 20.3

This may become your favorite part of using a spreadsheet. If you have lots of columns or rows to calculate, let the program figure out what you need.

You can copy this formula...

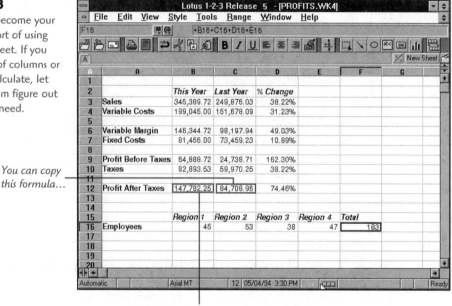

...to here, and the program adjusts the addresses automatically

Color and pictures, too!

Spreadsheets are well-known for their ability to turn a slew of numbers into an insightful (and even pretty) pie chart or bar chart. There are also 3D charts, line charts, histogram charts, and many, many more kinds! These charts often can be displayed in the corner of the spreadsheet, and the size of bars or pie slices automatically changes as you change your numbers (see fig. 20.4).

Fig. 20.4

A typical bar chart—
one of several chart
types available in
spreadsheets.

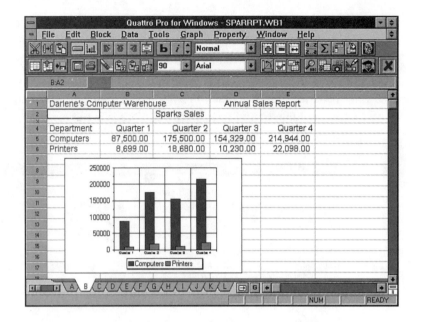

To improve reading, you can color your worksheet. You can paint an entire worksheet, color specific ranges, add tinted drop shadows and cell borders, or set off a chart by adding special shading.

The "Big Three" Windows spreadsheets

Like car manufacturers, spreadsheet software has evolved into the Big Three: Lotus 1-2-3, Excel, and Quattro Pro. All share many common features, while each has specific strengths. For example, all use the tabbed-notebook approach to three-dimensional spreadsheets.

Another novelty being adopted is the editing of cell contents in the cell. You used to edit the cell contents in a narrow box at the top of the screen. Now, your eyes no longer have to bounce between the cell and the box. Both Lotus 1-2-3 for Windows and Excel offer this **in-cell editing**.

Lotus 1-2-3 for Windows

Think of Lotus and most people think of the world's number-one spreadsheet program, 1-2-3 (see fig. 20.5).

Fig. 20.5

Lotus 1-2-3 is available in DOS and Windows versions. Here's Release 5 for Windows.

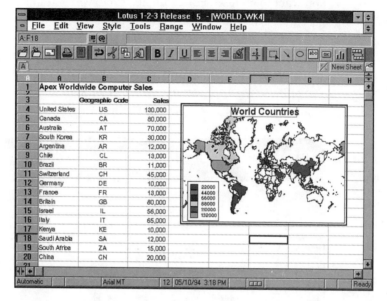

One of the best parts of Release 5 is a nifty mapping feature. You can view your data geographically—by state, region, or country, for example. You'll find maps of the United States, Canada, Mexico, Japan, and Europe, as well as 1,500 cities worldwide. You even can map your data by ZIP code.

Another cool feature is SmartMasters, a collection of 11 ready-made **templates** for common spreadsheet tasks. A template is the framework for a particular task (such as an income statement, personal budget, etc.)—it contains all the formulas for the task so that all you have to do is insert your specific numbers. For example, with a few clicks of your mouse, you can create budgeting, expense tracking, direct mail spreadsheets, and more.

Microsoft Excel

Microsoft Corp.'s Excel is full of significant features, such as true 3D worksheets, and "IntelliSense," the ability of the spreadsheet to sense what you want to do next. For example, Excel will automatically enter a closing parenthesis to your formula so you don't have to.

Excel works very well with other Microsoft programs, such as Word for Windows. Excel 5.0 also provides useful what-if capabilities and includes Visual Basic for Applications, which is a programming language you can use to automate tasks and even build your own programs.

Fig. 20.6

Excel offers more keyboard and mouse shortcuts than you could ever master.

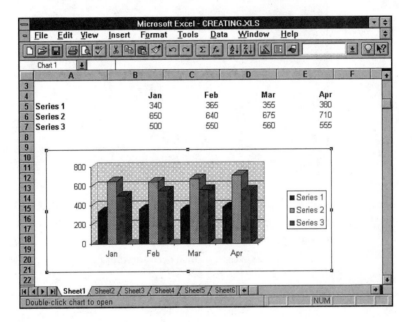

Quattro Pro for Windows

Quattro Pro 6.0 (a program that is now owned by networking giant Novell through its WordPerfect Corp. subsidiary) offers a little something for everyone, from the beginner to the power user. Toolbars make a wide variety of commands available with the click of a mouse.

Like 1-2-3's templates, Quattro Pro has Experts that automate creating budgets, what-if analyses, and bullet charts. The Formula Composer shows complex spreadsheet macros as a tree structure. With this feature, you can easily handle the most difficult spreadsheet macros (see fig. 20.7).

Fig. 20.7

Quattro Pro is one of the easiest spreadsheets to use.

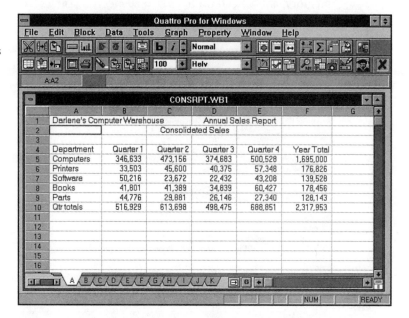

Spreadsheets that work with DOS

Using a DOS spreadsheet could be like going down a dead-end street. As the world further embraces Microsoft Windows, there is likely to be little improvement to existing DOS products. Still, a DOS spreadsheet program can operate on older, slower computers in the office.

Lotus 1-2-3 for DOS

Lotus 1-2-3 Release 4.0 for DOS (see fig. 20.8) adds a souped-up interface and a spelling checker, and lets you assign names to ranges of cells. A status bar at the bottom of the screen shows at a glance the current cell's number format, named style, and font. You then can change those settings with a few clicks of the mouse.

A handy note feature lets you add Post-It-style notes to any cell. The note can be displayed full size, shrunk to a tiny yellow triangle, or hidden.

Release 4.0 for DOS is best for people who have a fast computer, 1.5M of memory, and a need for a 3D spreadsheet. If you lack any of these, you may be wise to stay with the older version of 1-2-3.

Fig. 20.8

Lotus 1–2–3 for DOS has undergone its last face–lift.

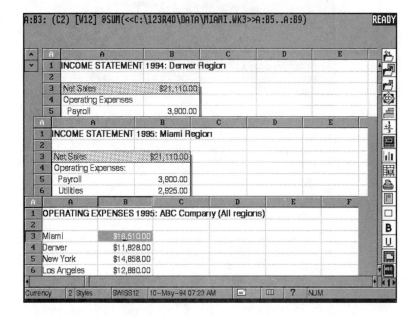

Quattro Pro for DOS

Quattro Pro for DOS 5.0 is an excellent value for a DOS spreadsheet. It includes a "slide-show" facility for showing charts one after another. It also can directly use database files from Paradox 4.0. Figure 20.9 shows Quattro Pro 5 for DOS.

Fig. 20.9

Quattro Pro offers multiple-window capability, even in the DOS version.

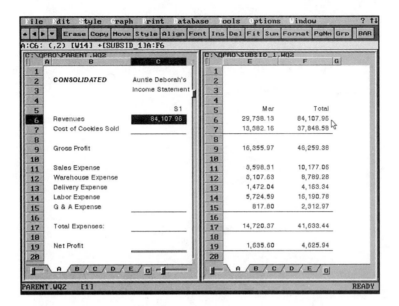

While Lotus 1-2-3 for DOS uses extended memory to handle large worksheets, Quattro Pro for DOS uses your hard disk for extra memory. As a result, the program runs okay with as little as 512K of memory and on the oldest PCs. However, the drawback for this backward compatibility is that calculations may take longer. Also, the size of your spreadsheets is limited. (However, most spreadsheets aren't very large, anyway.)

21

I Manage Lists—Tell Me about Databases

If you've ever used an address book, you're already an expert at using databases.

In this chapter:

- A database is like an index card file
- What can I use a database for?
- Some of the more popular programs

Ask any computer guru what a database is, and you may hear that a database is "a collection of data structured and organized in a disciplined fashion so that quick access is possible to the information of most interest at the present time." Your response, of course, is "Could you translate that to English, please?" For the simplified version, read on!

You already know what a database is

You might not realize it, but you've no doubt used a database before. Very simply put, a database is a collection of information. For example, an address book is a database. Think of a database like this:

- You collect similar types of information from different sources (your friends' addresses and phone numbers)

- You store them all in one place (in an address book)

- You can look up a single **record** ("What's Uncle Bob's address in North Carolina?")

- You can **query** to find out various things that are similar about each record ("How many of my relatives live in North Carolina?")

- You can perform **calculations** on the data ("If I added together all my friends' ages, what would the total be?")

- You can prepare **reports** based on the data or calculations ("Print address labels for all my friends who have birthdays this month.")

What's so great about a computerized database?

There are several fantastic elements involved with computerized databases:

- **Maintenance.** Like life itself, a database is always changing. Just look at the scribbles in your own address book. If you keep your database on a computer, updating—or **maintenance**—is a snap!

- **Space.** A computerized database stores a lot of information in a small amount of space. You would need hundreds of address books to store the amount of information you can store in just one computer database. Also, the database doesn't take up any extra room on your desk.

- **Speed.** Think about how long it takes to flip pages and find an address. A computer database can find your addresses in a mere fraction of the time.

- **Efficiency.** If you have all your addresses stored in a database, you can print them on envelopes or mailing labels. You no longer have to type or hand-write each address on each envelope.

What kinds of things can I store in a database?

Just about anything! You might keep financial data in a database and make decisions about how to manage and invest your money based on that data. Catalog all your favorite recipes, your baseball cards, or your CDs, tapes, and videos.

A business can keep virtually all the information it needs in a database. This information may include data about its customers, employees, salaries, and its product line.

Anatomy of a database

To make the database's job easier, it stores information in groups known as **records**. A single record might be all the information you have about your friend Jim: his wife's name, their anniversary, the names and birthdays of all their kids, where he works, and so on.

One record usually contains several types of information. Thus, records are divided into separate **fields**. Here are some typical field types:

- **Character fields** are typically used for names, addresses, and other alphabetic information.

- **Date fields** store information such as a birthday, anniversary, or purchase date.

- **Time fields**, such as 12:01 p.m., can be used to show exact times, such as what time a customer's order was delivered.

- **Logical fields** are for yes or no answers, such as "Anniversary card sent?" or "Shipped?".

- **Number fields** track numbers and money. For example, how many children each person in your address book has, or the total amount due on a customer's order.

- **Memo fields** might hold instructions on how to get to a friend's house, special shipping instructions, or other extraneous information.

By breaking down all this information, the database can work more efficiently and answer your questions a lot faster. If you want to find the names of all your friends in California, the database only needs to search character fields that you have probably labeled "State." It doesn't have to read every single field in every single record to find the answers.

Relational versus flat–file

An address book is a good example of a **flat-file database**. All the information about a particular subject is stored in a single place.

A more sophisticated type of database is a **relational database**, which enables you to store related information in several places and link the information together. Why do this? Because relational databases eliminate redundant information.

Imagine you have a database of a doctor's patients. This database may have fields for their names, addresses, and so on. You also must track each patient's visit. In a flat-file database, you would have to add several fields for each doctor visit—Visit 1, Visit 2, Visit 3, etc. As the years go on, adding these new fields for subsequent visits would make the database ugly and unwieldy. Some patients would have only a few Visit fields, but the hypochondriacs would have scores of them.

In a relational database, you create the following databases that contain only a few fields:

- Database 1 contains all the patients' names, addresses, and insurance information.

- Database 2 contains information about each office visit, such as the patient's name, the date, and the fee.

- Database 3 contains information about the doctor's diagnoses, such as the patient's name, symptoms, and the prescription written.

If you link the patient database (Database 1) to the visit database (Database 2) through a common thread called a **key field** (in this case, the patient's name), you create an efficient relational database.

Once linked, all the related information is retrieved quickly and without much effort from you. For example, to see all the visits for a particular patient, you call up the patient's record in Database 1 by entering the name (the key field). The rest of the information (in Databases 2 and 3) would be readily available by pressing a few keys.

✳ {Note} ───── A relational database is very powerful, but it can be a lot harder for beginners to create.

Okay, I know what I want. Now what's available?

A variety of database programs are available. The following list provides some features to look for:

- The **search** feature helps you find the information you want without having to know fancy programming code. The best search is called **query-by-form.** This means you just enter in the field what you are looking for. For example, if you wanted to search for your friends and relatives who live in New York, you enter "NY" in the State field.

- **Sorting** organizes information in the order you want. You should be able to sort in either **ascending order** (1 to 10, A to Z) or **descending order** (10 to 1, Z to A). Sorting by last name, state, birthday, etc. should be simple.

- **Data entry validation** and **default values** ensure that the data entered is correct. If your database knows what city is assigned to every ZIP code, you might have your database look at the ZIP code to make sure the city and state were typed correctly.

- **Importing data** and **exporting data** should be a snap. Lotus Approach, for example, can use files that are in Paradox, dBASE, or FoxPro format. If the information is easily exported, you can use it in other programs. For example, you could export an address to your word processor to use in a letter.

- **Programming features** are found in some high-end, complicated databases. Others include **macro** capabilities that record your keystrokes for later playback to perform certain tasks. For example, if you routinely sort and print your address list by birthday, you can record the process once and then assign it to a particular keystroke to use in the future.

- Designing **forms** and **reports** should be easy. Most databases support various report formats

{Note}

The following sections describe some popular Windows-based and DOS-based databases so you can see some of the features of these packages. But many other databases are available. In addition to Access, for example, Microsoft offers FoxPro, a higher-end database for those with programming experience. Be sure to consult with your software dealer for details before choosing a database package.

If you use Windows...

Windows databases offer the best balance between ease of use and power. Windows-based databases provide a friendlier face to your data entry. Instead of typing "Yes" or "No" in a field, you can click a button. For multiple-choice fields, you can just click a choice from the list.

Approach

Approach for Windows (see fig. 21.1) was one of the first easy-to-learn and easy-to-use relational database products available for Windows. Approach is perfect for business persons, consultants, and even developers who don't want to be pulling their hair out over a complicated programming language.

Fig. 21.1
Lotus Approach is one
of the newer data-
bases, but it has grown
up fast!

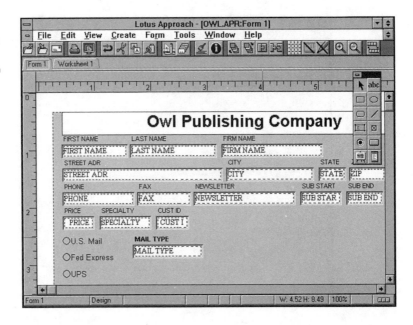

The icing on the cake is the addition of special reports for analyzing your
data in a different light and a charting feature for viewing colorful graphs
of your data. Even a spell checker is included.

Access

Microsoft Access (see fig. 21.2) has burst onto the database scene within the
last couple of years as a middle-of-the-road package. Although it's somewhat
easy to use, Access is still aimed at the database developer. In fact, Access
includes a programming language.

Access 2 includes plenty of features that make it easy to use, such as Wizards, cue cards, and other learning aids. By using **Wizards**, you can automate
many database tasks. For example, if you also have Word for Windows 6, the
Report Wizard can run a mail-merge to generate instant form letters.

Fig. 21.2

Access is Microsoft's database software.

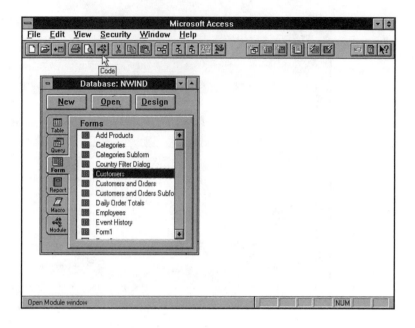

Paradox for Windows

Paradox for Windows from Borland International has always been a bruiser of a database. In the hands of an experienced developer, the program really packs a wallop. With Version 5, Paradox for Windows is an all-around better product: more compact, more powerful, and easier to use.

Fig. 21.3

Paradox for Windows from Borland International. Although it resembles Microsoft Access, Paradox offers somewhat different features.

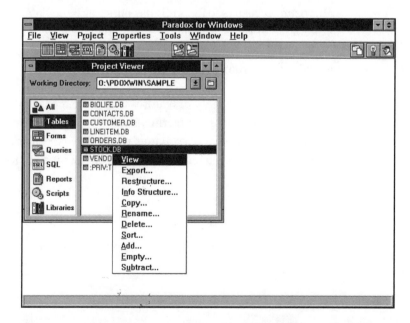

Like Access and Approach, Paradox includes interactive on-line helpers (Borland calls them **Experts**). Experts contain more forms and reports than Wizards, and they show you a preview of sample output so you'll have less backpedaling to do if you choose the wrong layout.

dBASE for Windows

dBASE for Windows—also from Borland International (see fig. 21.4)—is intended for use by hard-core dBASE programmers. The program enables developers of dBASE for DOS programming to easily move to the Windows version.

Fig. 21.4

Keep in mind that dBASE for Windows is intended for people who know some programming.

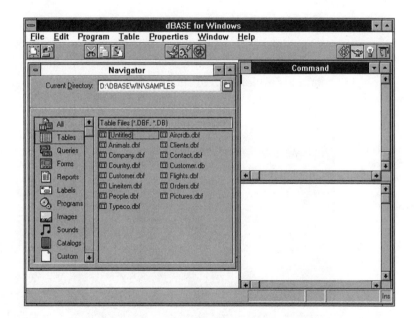

The prompt (a single dot) found in the DOS version is replaced in dBASE for Windows with the **Command Window**, allowing commands to be executed on-the-fly. Although dBASE for Windows provides a complete set of tools for creating forms, queries, and menus, you also can work visually or directly with code.

If you don't do Windows...

Generally, DOS database programs aren't nearly as friendly or easy as Windows to figure out on your own, but if you don't use Windows, you don't have much choice, huh? On the other hand, DOS-based programs have a tendency to run faster, so your database work could speed up with one of these programs.

⊛ {Note} _____ | dBASE III and dBASE IV were so popular that their file format (.DBF) *is still used for sharing data between programs. If you keep your own database but send it out to a service that does your mass mailings for you, they'll probably want your files sent to them in DBF format—regardless of what program you use.*

dBASE for DOS

Borland International really breathed new life into dBASE when it released dBASE 5 for DOS. It's a welcome upgrade for professionals who expect to continue developing and supporting DOS-based dBASE programs. The latest and greatest dBASE is shown in figure 21.5.

Fig. 21.5
DOS programs seem to be learning tricks from their Windows brothers—like how to be more friendly.

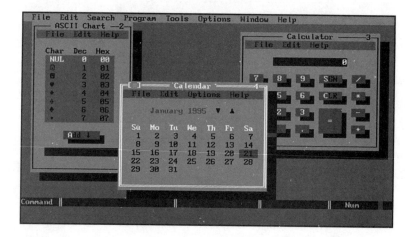

Thanks to new technology, the new dBASE provides improvements in performance:

- The compiler, which lets any dBASE database run as a stand-alone program, now is built-in. (It was sold separately before.)

- dBASE 5 for DOS provides a graphical view of your data that relies heavily on using a mouse.

Q&A for DOS

Want a friendly DOS word processor and simple database rolled into one? Consider Q&A for DOS from Symantec. Check out figure 21.6.

Fig. 21.6
Nice and easy *is* Q&A's big selling point.

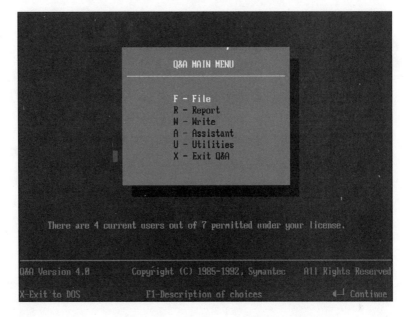

Q&A's word processor is simple, even for the occasional user. It has an excellent spell checker and thesaurus. Q&A also provides the **Intelligent Assistant**, which enables you to type your requests in simple English. For example, enter "Find all my clients in New York City" and the program turns those words into a search.

Developing a database also is a snap. You simply type the fields you want and then select what type of field each is. For example, typing in Firstname, Lastname, Address, City, State, and Zip and selecting them all to be character fields is enough to build a simple address list. The built-in word processor makes it a breeze to do mail-merges and form letters.

For groups of users, Q&A includes multiple levels of password security and it can be run on a network by several people at the same time.

22

I Do Slide Shows—Tell Me about Presentation Graphics Programs

The computer has re-placed the camera and the graphic artist for creating slides and overheads—especially for business presentations.

Originally, "slide" shows were literally that—photographs were developed in a slide format, and flipped through one by one on a big screen. An alternative method was an overhead projector with images hand-drawn or transferred onto transparent film.

Now presentation graphics programs, which you can buy for $500 or less, enable you to use a *computer* to create **slides** (sometimes called **pages**) with text, graphs, or clip art images such as a company logo.

Using the computer to create presentation materials has two major advantages:

- It automates creating text and charting data, so that anyone can build attractive slides quickly and easily. Figure 22.1 shows an example of one presentation program, PowerPoint 4.0.

- It lets you view the slides in a variety of formats—printed out, on-screen, and more—so that you can use the slides for a variety of business purposes.

Fig. 22.1
Presentation graphics programs like PowerPoint 4.0 for Windows (shown here) let you create slides with text, charts, and graphics.

You can even add graphics to make your slide show more interesting.

The software did most of the work involved in charting this data.

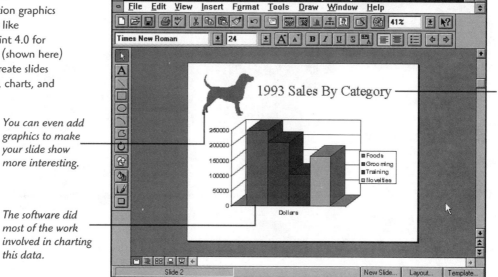

This slide has a large heading to explain what it's about.

What can I do with a presentation graphics program?

Of course, you can create a traditional business presentation—a series of slides that you display to an audience with a slide projector—explaining the data on each slide as you go along. Fortunately, you're not limited to just that traditional format. Here are more ideas:

- Create printed reports, handouts, or notes to use while you're speaking.

- Traveling with a laptop computer? Use the laptop to display your sales presentation. In charge of employee training? Create an informative slide show that new employees can view on-screen.

- Create self-running slide shows that can play on any computer—regardless of whether the presentation graphics program is installed on that computer.

- Explore multimedia by adding sound to a slide show.

⊛ {Note}_____

> Multimedia presentations generally require that your computer have a sound card, CD-ROM drive, and speakers.

- Use a highlighter feature to circle and underline key data while you're presenting your slide show on-screen. John Madden would love this!

- Send your slide show to a company specializing in presentation graphics program output, and get 35mm slides or color transparencies made.

How to start your own slide show

When you start a slide show file, you pick a "look" for all the slides by choosing a **master** (or **template**) for the slide show. The master sets the default colors, margins, etc. for all the slides you create. This saves you from having to set the colors and other settings each time you create a slide. It's like an artist who always starts with a blue canvas because she always paints seascapes. Most presentation programs come with at least a dozen different masters (see fig. 22.2).

❶ (Tip)_____

> The only limit on the number of slide shows you can create is the physical limit of storage space on your hard drive.

Fig. 22.2
Most presentation graphics programs offer a dozen or more looks you can choose for your slide show. Here, PowerPoint lets you preview a template in a similar way before picking it.

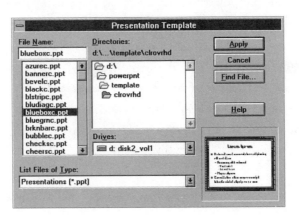

The master controls the color of the slide backgrounds and any background graphics that appear. It also determines what fonts and colors are used for slide text. Lastly, it controls the appearance of graphs, including such things as how graph parts are labeled. The master ensures that no matter what you're showing on the various slides in your show, all the slides look consistent. You look like a pro without even trying.

What if I pick a master and decide later that I don't like it, or it doesn't print out the way I want it to? Do I have to redo the entire slide show?

No way! You can change the master at any time. When you choose a new master, your presentation program automatically applies the new look to each and every slide.

Once you get to be a real pro with your presentation graphics program, you can create and save your own custom masters.

I'm not an artist; how do I design a slide?

Each slide contains a **chart**. Charts hold text, data, and graphics in different combinations. Each combination of elements is called a **slide layout** (sometimes called a **chart type**). Along with slide show masters, each presentation graphics program comes with several preformatted slide layouts. You simply choose the one you want, and the program displays a slide with placeholder areas that you fill in with your data (see fig. 22.3).

What if I want to do something totally unique? Am I stuck with one of the prefab layouts?

Preformatted slides are only there to serve as shortcuts when you're doing routine stuff. You can create a slide from scratch by making areas for text, graphs, and clip art wherever you want them.

Fig. 22.3
The New Slide dialog box in PowerPoint lets you choose what combination of elements will appear on a slide.

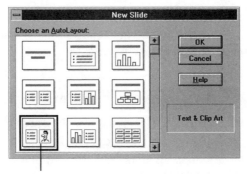

Thumbnails show different slide layouts. Click the one you want, then click OK.

After you select a layout for your slide, the program takes you to its main screen, where your brand-spanking-new slide is displayed. The slide will have **placeholders** for various elements, as you can see in figure 22.4.

Fig. 22.4
Presentation graphics programs give you placeholders on a slide so you can add your text and data easily. In this case, the slide has predefined areas for a title, bullet list, and clip art.

Now add the text

When you activate the text placeholder, a blinking cursor appears. Just start typing, pressing Enter whenever you want to start a new line or create a new bullet item. If you make a mistake, just use Backspace or any other technique you'd use in a word processing program to correct the mistake.

In most programs, you can use the Windows Clipboard to copy and move text within and between placeholder areas.

When you're finished filling in a text placeholder, simply click outside the placeholder to deactivate it. If you need to change the text later, click or double-click the text again to reactivate it for editing.

I really can't draw graphs by hand (ugh)

Certain math and science classes (you know the ones) required you to spend hours drawing little charts and geometric shapes on graph paper just to prove you could connect the dots. With presentation graphics programs, you don't have to do anything by hand. Creating a graph (even an organization chart) takes about three steps in most programs:

1 Activate the placeholder for your graph.

2 Fill in the data you want, including any necessary labels at the tops of columns or left side of rows, and then return to the slide (see fig. 22.5).

Fig. 22.5

Click a cell (the box where a row and column intersect), type the value, and press Enter or click to move to another cell.

3 Choose the type of graph you want (see fig. 22.6).

Fig. 22.6

You can choose a new look for your chart at any time—while you're creating it, or anytime later.

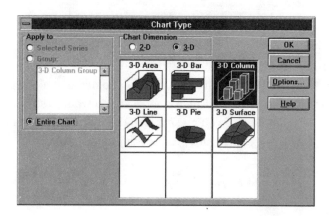

I need some clip art

You can increase the entertainment value of your slide shows by using **clip art** that comes with your presentation graphics program to accent your slides. In general, you click an icon or choose a command, choose the illustration to add, and finally drag on a slide to define the area where the art will be inserted. If you've scanned in your company logo or have created a drawing in another graphics application, you can place that on your slide, too.

Adding more slides

 After you finish creating a slide, you'll usually need to add others to the slide show. Adding a slide is generally a matter of clicking an icon, like the one next to this paragraph (from PowerPoint). Alternatively, you usually can select a command to insert the new slide.

Okay, now I want to see the whole slide show

Most presentation graphics programs let you choose from several different working views:

- Slide-by-slide—usually called something like the **slide editor view**, lets you see one full slide at a time. The figures earlier in this chapter illustrate this view. Not only can you add text and other elements in this view, but it's also the best view for formatting the slides.

- **Outliner view** lets you view your slide show as an outline of the slide text. Use this view to arrange the order of the information in your slide show (see fig. 22.7).

Fig. 22.7
Outlining a slide show
is just like working in
outline view for a word
processor. This is
PowerPoint's outliner.

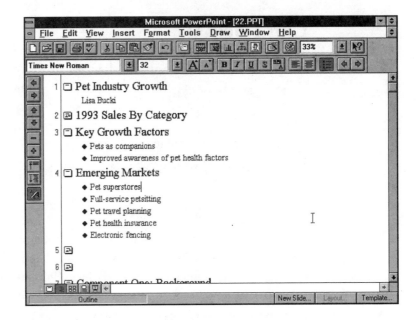

- Most presentation programs offer a view of the slide show with a
  thumbnail picture of each slide (see fig. 22.8). This view lets you
  reorder slides (often just by dragging one to a new location) based
  on the information they contain and their appearance.

Fig. 22.8
Use this view to drag
slides to a new position
in the slide show.

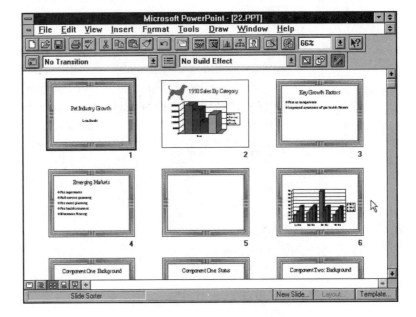

Can I print?

Of course! Most programs let you print the show slide-by-slide with each slide at full-page size. In addition, you can print each slide with a list of speaker notes or print reduced-size slides for use as audience handouts. Some programs even let you print the slide show outline.

How do I have real slides made?

Special service bureaus will take the slide show you created and make 35mm slides of it. To make this work, you usually have to install a special file that comes with your presentation graphics program. Then, you create an output file and send it to the service. Each program comes with instructions for working with service bureaus.

What about on-screen slide shows?

Most presentation graphics programs give you two ways to view your show on-screen. You can start the program and use a command to put away the program's window and show the slides at full-screen size. Or, if you want to show your slide show on a computer that doesn't have the graphics program installed, you create a **runtime version** of the slide show. You can copy this runtime version to any computer, and, even if that computer doesn't have the presentation graphics software, it will run your slide show.

Getting graphic with Windows

In general, if you're using a suite of Windows programs like Microsoft Office, Lotus SmartSuite, or Novell PerfectOffice, you should stick with the presentation graphics program that's part of that suite. This lends a lot of convenience to creating slide shows and reports, because the suite programs are geared to work together smoothly.

However, if you're not working with a suite of programs, the choice is up to you. The following is a look at each of the most popular presentation graphics programs and what they can offer you.

PowerPoint

The latest version of PowerPoint for Windows, Version 4.0, is part of the best-selling Office suite of applications from Microsoft, but you can also buy it separately. Most of the screen pictures earlier in this chapter show PowerPoint. PowerPoint offers all the features described earlier in this chapter, and more. One of its real strengths is built-in Wizards.

66 *Plain English, please!*

Wizards are little programs that make it easier for you to create a slide show. 99

Freelance Graphics

Freelance Graphics for Windows, from Lotus Development Corp., is part of the SmartSuite group of products. It's easy to use and offers predesigned SmartMaster templates to make it easy for anyone to develop attractive slides. To get started with Freelance, you can use its QuickStart tutorial, which walks you through several key features of the program (see fig. 22.9).

Fig. 22.9
Freelance Graphics for Windows offers quite a bit of help to get you started with the program.

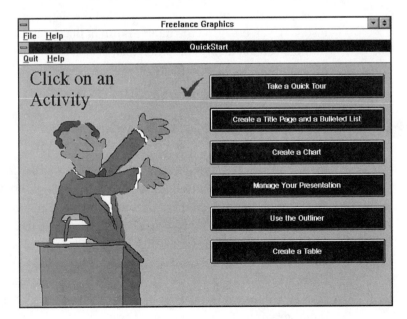

CorelDRAW!

Corel Systems in Canada has long been a leader in the graphics field. Their CorelDRAW! program has evolved from being the leading drawing program for Windows users to being a collection of tools geared to make your PC a fully-featured graphics studio. One of the tools that comes with CorelDRAW! is CorelSHOW, a separate program for creating slide shows (see fig. 22.10).

Fig. 22.10
CorelSHOW allows you to easily create presentations with the option of using CorelDRAW! 5.0's powerful capabilities.

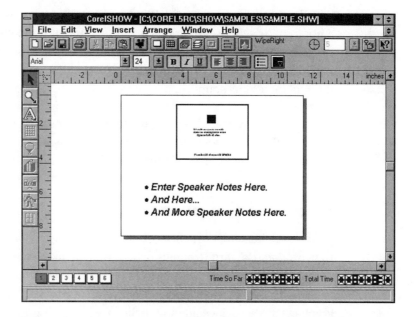

What version of CorelDRAW! should I buy?

If you don't need any of Corel's other graphics features and just want a low-cost solution for making quick-and-dirty, very simple slide shows, Version 3.0 will work for you. If you are looking to expand your graphics capabilities and want to take advantage of other CorelDRAW! features, consider Version 4.0 or 5.0, particularly the CD-ROM version if you have a CD-ROM drive. Both come with extra fonts and clip art that in themselves could be worth the extra cost. If you are still unsure what version you need, you may want to start with 3.0 and purchase an upgrade if you find you need more capabilities. (You might even save some money buying and upgrading 3.0; check out the prices before you buy.)

Where Corel excels is in the clip art arena. More clip art comes with CorelDRAW! than with most other presentation graphics programs, and CorelDRAW! gives you the capability to edit that clip art, which you may not be able to do in other presentation graphics programs.

WordPerfect Presentations

WordPerfect Presentations for Windows is part of the new PerfectOffice Suite from Novell. Presentations is full-featured; it provides several views for creating slide shows; excellent galleries of slide show masters, QuickArt clip art, and graph designs; and capabilities for making your slide show interactive and for adding sound.

To help you work with the program, Presentations offers **coaches**, which walk you through any procedure. The **Show Expert** (similar to a PowerPoint Wizard) gives you suggestions for content as you're building a slide show.

Harvard Graphics

Software Publishing Corp. now offers a Windows version of its smash hit DOS product Harvard Graphics, which was the market leader for many years (when DOS was king). This program matches other Windows offerings feature-for-feature, enabling you to develop numerous kinds of charts and graphs. It also provides point-and-click tools, so it's easy to work with.

(Tip)

Recently, Software Publishing Corp. introduced Harvard Spotlight for Windows, a $129 program that lets you preview and rehearse slide shows from PowerPoint, Freelance, or Harvard Graphics.

Getting graphic with DOS

DOS presentation graphics programs are somewhat limited in what they offer, particularly in the quality of on-screen graphics. They also don't have the point-and-click capability that makes Windows presentation graphics programs easy to use. Here's what's available:

- **Harvard Graphics**—Version 2.3 of this program was the market leader until it was eclipsed by Windows graphics programs. Version 3.0 of Harvard Graphics for DOS added improved features, including Windows-like menus and enhanced drawing tools.

- **WordPerfect Presentations** has been popular among users of the WordPerfect word processing program. If you're a loyal user of WordPerfect for DOS, this presentation graphics program may appeal to you.

23

Help Me Get Organized!

Better organizing and prioritizing of your work improve your personal productivity and let you get more done in less time.

In this chapter:

- What is an information manager?
- Can I track all my contacts and to-do lists?
- How can software help me stay organized?
- Can anything help organize my whole company?
- What are they going to organize next?

Information managers are programs that act much like your very own personal assistant. These programs come in two basic types: programs designed for individuals and programs designed to organize groups of people or entire companies. Both types of information managers are intended to prevent you from overlooking important tasks, meetings, commitments, and golf outings.

Using an information manager can help organize much more than just tasks and meetings. Information managers can do the following:

- List all the phone calls you need to complete today.

- Enable networked information managers to check co-workers' schedules for conflicts and automatically set up meetings that everyone can attend.

- Remind you to get a gift for a friend's birthday.

- Prioritize your daily tasks so that the important work gets done first.

- Track completed work, so you can tell someone exactly when you finished a certain report.

- Let you check your workload for the day, week, or month at a glance.

- Provide a central location for ideas and project information that helps keep everyone informed of the latest developments.

Getting yourself organized

Being organized can't guarantee you a promotion, but getting your act together certainly can't hurt you in your climb toward the big bucks. Better organizing and prioritizing of your work improve your personal productivity and let you get more done in less time. What a concept—more work in less time. If your organizational skills and memory could use a boost, you can benefit from using a **Personal Information Manager**, or **PIM**.

 Plain English, please!

The word "personal" in Personal Information Manager indicates that the software is designed to work with an individual's information, and isn't designed to track the schedules and events for large groups.

Information managers that do track information for groups are called **groupware**. I happen to think that the acronym **GRIM** (GRoup Information Manager) would have worked, but no one in the industry bothered to ask me.

Which PIM should I use?

Choosing which PIM to use depends on what type of assistance you need the most. You'll want to look at several different PIMs before making a final decision. If possible, talk to someone (preferably someone who seems organized) who uses the PIM you are considering and see if this person likes the way it works.

If you have tons of external contacts, work in telemarketing or outbound sales, or need a sort of all-in-one tool, then Symantec's ACT! program is a great choice.

If most of your work is done within your company, and you need to track projects, show up for meetings, and maintain useful to-do lists, then a product like Lotus Organizer fits the bill.

Each of these products is discussed later in this chapter. Remember that no matter which PIM you choose, the only way to make it work for you is to use it consistently.

A PIM for keeping in touch: ACT!

ACT! is a great PIM for people who need to keep in touch with a large number of people. ACT!'s many features make it especially useful for people in sales, public relations, or market research. ACT! has many built-in features, such as the following:

- ACT! can store an unlimited number of contacts (there is a practical limit, however, because your computer doesn't have endless resources) and lets you track up to 70 different items per person or company. Figure 23.1 shows a typical contact record.

- ACT! can schedule and prioritize as many calls, to-do items, and meetings as you care to enter. As an added bonus, it will bug you until you complete each call and to-do, and attend each meeting—at least until you tell it to leave you alone! The software also prints out reports that show you exactly what you need to do for the day, week, or month (see fig. 23.2).

Fig. 23.1
The database lets you keep track of everything you need to know about each contact.

Which company does she work for?

What was her secretary's name?

What do I need to say when I call?

How did she find out about us?

What should I call her?

When should I call her?

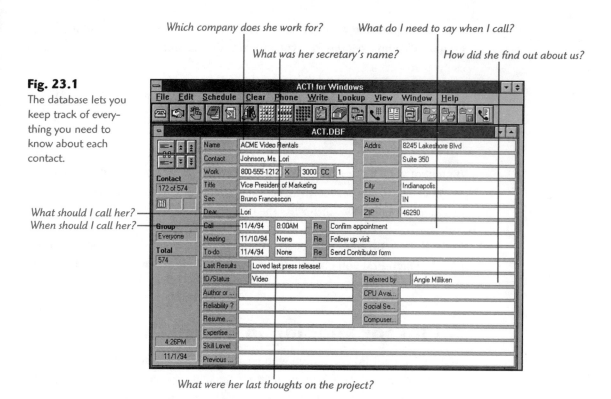

What were her last thoughts on the project?

Remember that thing with Karen…

Fig. 23.2
ACT! shows you what you need to do for the week.

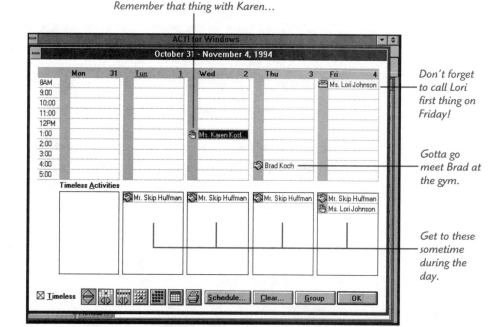

Don't forget to call Lori first thing on Friday!

Gotta go meet Brad at the gym.

Get to these sometime during the day.

- ACT! has a built-in word processor that is perfect for short business letters. The word processor works with the database, so mass mailings are a breeze.

- A report generator lets you create any kind of report you like—from a "what I did this week" report for your boss, to a "whose birthdays are coming up this month" for yourself!

PIMs for internal organization: Organizer

Maybe you're already a supreme schmoozer and can remember your customer's names, what time is best to call them, and so on, but your weakness lies in a total lack of organization. Perhaps there are a million meetings a month at your company, and you're expected to be at most of them. Or there are 60 projects underway at once, and you're involved in four dozen of those. You've tried to get the most out of your day planner, but can only fit so much on each page, and it's common for people to call you from the conference room to tell you that a meeting you were supposed to attend has started without you. It's time to consider a PIM such as Lotus Organizer.

Suppose you have a meeting with your boss every Thursday at 10 a.m. You're such a busy and dedicated worker (naturally) that you occasionally forget the time and arrive at your boss's office late—or worse, not at all. If these meetings were entered in Lotus Organizer, your computer would beep and flash a message on your screen telling you when it's time to leave for one (see fig. 23.3). A PIM such as Organizer helps to prevent CLMs (career-limiting maneuvers) like skipping meetings.

Fig. 23.3

Now you'll never be late, as long as you're close to your computer.

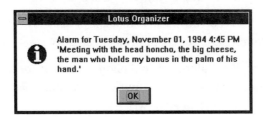

Organizer is great for scheduling meetings (you can schedule a recurring meeting once and Organizer takes care of filling in all the future dates!), maintaining to-do lists, and keeping a name and address list. By far, Organizer's greatest strength is that it's easy to understand and use. It looks and acts just like organizer notebooks you're used to seeing (see fig. 23.4).

Fig. 23.4

Organizer looks just like a normal organizer notebook—and you'll never forget your pen.

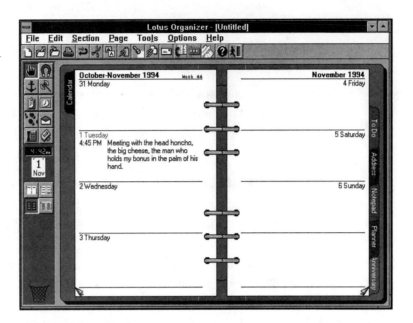

{Note}

Each PIM has its own personality and quirks. Because you have to work closely with your PIM, make sure you find one you really like. One of my favorite moments in Organizer is when I drag a meeting or to-do task and drop it in the trash can. Poof! The meeting or task burns up in the can!

Even though Organizer is easy to use, it still has plenty of power. Here are some of the jobs Organizer does well:

- Views your schedule by the day, week, or 30-day calendar.

- Schedules recurring tasks and displays tasks by priority, targeted completion date, status, or project category.

- Keeps track of addresses and phone numbers for everyone you know (and then some—go ahead, put your congressman in there; you never know when you'll need to write!).

- Schedules future phone calls and lets you view upcoming calls by name, date, company, category, or status.

- Tracks all your great ideas on Organizer's handy Notepad feature.

- Here's a lifesaver: You can enter anniversary dates and display them by year, month, category, or zodiac sign (geez!). Organizer reminds you to send a card, buy flowers, or check the phase of the moon.

Organizer also has features that are designed for a group scheduling environment. When used on a network with Lotus Notes, Organizer adds to its great PIM capabilities and becomes part of a very powerful groupware information manager. You can also use Organizer to tap into cc:Mail, another Lotus program that lets you send messages to other people on your network. See Chapter 30 for more about e-mail programs.

Getting everyone organized

The benefits of increasing productivity (and thus profits) through better organization are no secret to business. The same features that make PIMs useful to individuals are extremely useful to businesses.

How do you get everyone organized at once? You link a bunch of PIMs together and come up with something called **groupware**. Groupware programs allow you to schedule everyone's time and to-do lists, keep everyone updated on projects, and have a central location for employees to test ideas.

A PIM for the whole company!

So, how do you turn a bunch of independent PIMs into a program that can manage the resources of dozens, maybe even hundreds, of people and projects? The first step is to get everybody connected somehow. That requires the business to install a network and get everyone hooked up to that network.

 Plain English, please!

A network is a bunch of individual computers that are connected so that they can share each other's information. Different types of networks are discussed in Chapter 29, "Networks: Getting Connected."

Once everyone is connected via a network, the next step is to choose a groupware product. There are several groupware products available. Some, like Windows for Workgroups, are good for scheduling and minimal project management, but not much else. Other groupware products, like Lotus Notes, are incredibly powerful, flexible programs that can change entirely the way a company works. The type of program you should use depends on your needs and on how much you're willing to spend to maintain the system.

Scheduling's a snap!

Scheduling capability is one reason that groupware is growing in popularity. Whether it's meetings or project deadlines that litter your calendar, chances are you can benefit from groupware.

Let's all meet somewhere

Suppose you want to schedule a meeting with 20 co-workers. Normally, you'd pick up the phone and start calling everyone, trying to find a mutually agreeable time to meet (unless you're the boss, in which case "they'll meet when and where I tell 'em, and they'll like it!"). In many cases, you spend more time setting up a meeting like this with multiple participants than you spend at the meeting itself.

With a groupware product like Windows for Workgroups or Lotus Organizer (recall that Organizer, while simple to use, has a lot of hidden groupware power), everyone's schedules are available for the computer to check. Instead of calling everyone, you tell the software the names of the 20 people with whom you want to meet, and it tells you the earliest available time when everyone is free to attend. If that time is okay with you, the program automatically puts your meeting on everyone else's schedule. If that time is bad for you, the software finds another time when everyone's available.

It's due how soon?

The scheduling functions of groupware are great at keeping small projects on track. If you place a project's milestone goals on everyone's schedules simultaneously, it's less likely that tasks or to-dos will be forgotten.

Automated scheduling, as useful as it can be, is only the tip of the iceberg of groupware benefits. The real power of groupware comes in harnessing the imagination and idea power of a company's most valuable asset—its employees—as explained in the following section.

Organizing company resources

Simple groupware programs are good at keeping track of meetings, people, and commitments. But what if you want to organize the development of a complex new product, or develop better ways for employees to contribute ideas that help the company? This is where a program like Lotus Notes can be a tremendous benefit.

Powerful groupware products like Notes handle scheduling and small project-management tasks with ease, but Notes really shines in a large company with hundreds (or thousands) of people and dozens of projects.

Making big companies nimble

Notes is helpful because it lets a large business quickly deliver, receive, organize, and act on information from many sources. A good way to picture Notes groupware is as a huge corporate bulletin board that every company employee can see from his or her desk. Now, make this bulletin board extremely well-organized so that all the notes on the board aren't overwhelming. Next, link the notes on the bulletin board to all of the company's resources—accounting, sales, manufacturing, production, marketing, and so on. Finally, link the notes together so that everyone gets accurate, up-to-the-minute information whenever they need it.

With a system like this in place, large businesses can act as quickly as small businesses and actually benefit from their size and numerous internal resources.

Sharing big ideas

Notes also makes it easier to share ideas. You've heard of simple ideas that have saved companies tons of money. Without Notes, a great idea might have to cross many desks, sneak past several bureaucrats, and dance around company politics before it gets evaluated. Now, employees can put ideas on the bulletin board for the whole company to see. The good ones can be implemented immediately, and the bad ones make everyone laugh!

What are they going to organize next?

It's time for a look ahead at some pending developments in information management. Both in and out of the workplace, your life is sure to become more automated (which hopefully means less complicated).

The future of organization software

The next step in groupware will allow people in different geographic locations to work together as if they were sitting at the same table.

State-of-the-art groupware products allow multiple people to work on the same document at the same time, and to see what each other is doing to the document. These products integrate live video and sound, so that when you are at your desk working on a document with someone in another state, you can see a face and hear a voice via your computer. These products are in development and demonstration stages now, but with technology's rapid pace, they'll probably be an integral part of business life before long.

Organizing your life after work

The next steps in information management may help organize your personal life. New on-line systems should make it possible for you to schedule routine tasks from a computer at your home. How about ordering your car's license plates from a home PC instead of standing in line at the license bureau? Or scheduling your vacation—including all airfare, accommodations, dinner reservations, and golf outings—from a home PC? What about ordering ice cream across the Internet (see Chapter 33 for the full scoop on the Internet). Sound wacky? You can already order pizza electronically (in California, of course), and airline and hotel reservations already are on-line. If you can imagine a way to computerize some aspect of your life, somebody's probably already working on it.

Integrated Packages and Suites

It started as a marketing gimmick. Microsoft put several programs into a single box, labeled it Microsoft Office, and sold it cheap.

In this chapter:

- What's a software suite?
- How is a suite different from an integrated package?
- Which is better for me?
- Meet the top-selling software suites

Imagine you're writing your quarterly budget report with your favorite word processor and need some figures from a spreadsheet file. No problem. You just click on the special toolbar, jump over to the spreadsheet, grab the figures, and pop them into the word processor. Even better, you bring the numbers in as a linked table. That way, not only does the table look great, but when you update the numbers in the spreadsheet next week, your report will be updated automatically.

This typical scenario embodies the heart and soul of software suites, the bundles of vendors' top word processing, spreadsheet, and database programs sold for one rock-bottom price.

How "suite" it is

What's in a typical suite? A **software suite** will often include at least these programs:

- word processing
- database
- spreadsheet
- presentation graphics

Fig. 24.1

Suites usually include a special toolbar (look near the upper right corner of the window) that lets you jump back and forth between the various programs.

SmartCenter toolbar

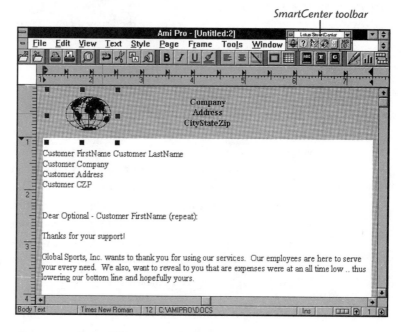

Microsoft's popular Microsoft Office suite includes:

- Word for Windows (word processor)
- Excel (spreadsheet)
- PowerPoint (presentation graphics)
- Access (database)
- A client license for Mail. (If you don't have Microsoft Mail on your network, you might as well throw away the Mail part.)

Fig. 24.2
The Microsoft Office
application menus and
toolbars are consistent
among the different
programs.

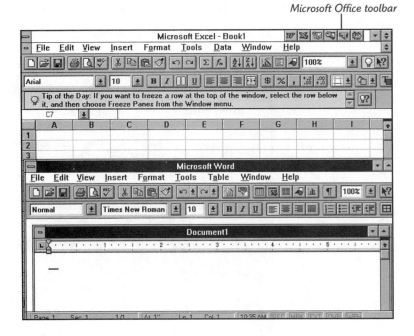

Microsoft Office toolbar

Lotus SmartSuite includes the following programs:

- Ami Pro (word processor)
- Freelance (presentation graphics)
- Approach (database)
- 1-2-3 for Windows (spreadsheet)
- Organizer (personal information manager)

PerfectOffice, by Novell, includes the following programs:

- WordPerfect (word processor)
- Presentations (presentation graphics)
- Quattro Pro (spreadsheet)
- Paradox (database)
- GroupWise (e-mail, calendaring, and scheduling client)
- Envoy (electronic publisher and viewer)

- InfoCentral (personal information manager)

- Visual AppBuilder (visual application development program)

Fig. 24.3

Lotus has built a powerhouse suite around its 1-2-3 and Ami Pro products.

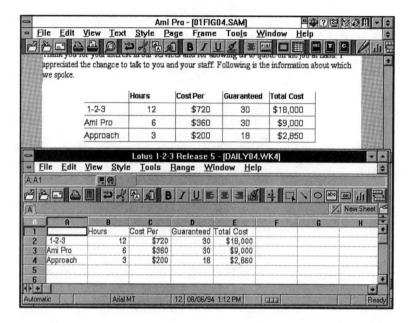

How does a suite work? (skip this if you don't care)

The programs in suites transfer and share information because of a thing called OLE (pronounce it like a cheer at a bullfight). OLE is short for object linking and embedding. Basically, OLE lets you pull chunks of information or a whole file from one Windows program into another.

As nice as OLE sounds, not all Windows programs have it. Although Windows provides the tools to make OLE possible, it's up to each software company to make its software use OLE. Some do, some don't.

Are software suites the same thing as integrated packages?

Nope. Integrated packages and software suites are kind of the same idea, but the products are different. The programs in an integrated package usually don't have as many features as their suite cousins. On the other hand, the integrated package can be a lot cheaper than the suite. Think of it as the difference between buying a Honda Civic and a Honda Accord. Both are reliable transportation. The Accord version (like a suite) offers more bells and whistles. If those features are important to you, you pay more to get them.

An integrated package generally includes software for word processing, spreadsheets, graphics, database management, and/or communications. Popular integrated packages include Microsoft Works, GeoWorks Pro, PFS: First Choice (for DOS), PFS: WindowWorks (for Windows), ClarisWorks, and Enable/OA.

✸ *{Note}*

Software suites are huge compared to integrated software packages, which typically require less than 5M of disk space. For a suite, be prepared to sacrifice up to 80M of hard disk space.

So should I buy a suite or an integrated package?

Integrated software and suites are both an excellent bargain. In fact, suites may turn out to be the software deal of the century. For the price of a stand-alone package, you can own a collection of three or more powerhouse programs, all conveniently supported by the same vendor. Entire suites can often be bought for under $300 through special "competitive upgrade" programs.

✸ *{Note}*

Most suite packages offer two options: a standard suite and a professional version. The professional version includes more software (or more advanced versions of the software) but costs more money. Consult your software dealer to decide which options you need.

Some vendors, such as Lotus, even offer "mini-suites." Instead of combining all five of their top-selling programs, you can buy Lotus 1-2-3 Release 5 and Approach 3.0 for less than $150.

The following sections give you some pros and cons on buying suites versus integrated packages. Both versions have advantages and disadvantages.

Many computer dealers offer an integrated package or a suite as part of the deal for the equipment. Don't let the offer make the decision for you, or you may regret it! Consider this: If all you need is to write a few letters and memos, do a couple of spreadsheets, and maybe draw something once in a while with a graphics package, an integrated package should suit you nicely. If you want to share files with clients, do multicolumn statistical analysis with graphs, or produce presentations and newsletters, a suite is your best bet.

A suite is a good bargain...

With a suite, you own a group of programs that have been designed to work together in the same way. The common design makes you feel at home among multiple, complex programs. You then can work smarter and more efficiently. Better yet, all the software you'll be using is sold by the same vendor. So, you're able to direct all your product questions to one company.

If you opt for the security of Lotus SmartSuite or Microsoft Office, though, your freedom comes at a price. If you buy a software program outside the suite, you do so at an additional cost. Not only do you pay for the extra software, but you'll have to decide how to make all the programs work well together.

For other programs to be compatible with its suite, Microsoft requires these programs to adhere to its designs. Lotus' SmartSuite is designed to connect to more products than Microsoft Office is, including the famous electronic mail program cc:Mail and powerful groupware product Lotus Notes.

 Plain English, please!

Groupware is simply a trendy term that describes applications in which files and information can be shared with other users.

(Tip)

> If you buy a suite, you may also have to invest in more memory. Most suites require at least 8M of memory—since more than one component may have to be open simultaneously. Many businesses and homes still use computers with only 4M.

...but maybe an integrated package is a better choice for you

Integrated software started as a DOS attempt to create the "killer application," a Swiss army knife for all your computing needs. But like a Swiss army knife, integrated software packages may not have the power to perform special functions.

If your needs are modest, you could buy an integrated software program, such as Microsoft Works for Windows 3.0. This inexpensive ($139) program provides word processing, database, spreadsheet, and communications software in one package. It doesn't offer all the features of high-end suites, but Works' components share a common home screen, making it easy to move data among the applications. One-step printing of envelopes and labels is included. For some home users and small-business owners who will be using a computer occasionally, it is an ideal package.

What suites are available?

In the Windows arena, only three major companies offer suites: Microsoft, Lotus Development Corp., and Novell. All of these suites include word processors, databases, spreadsheets, graphics, and electronic mail.

Lotus, however, positions its SmartSuite as a link between desktop and "groupware" applications, with its Lotus Notes providing a connection between its SmartSuite applications and Notes databases. The advantage of a groupware approach is that it's much easier to share files and information with others. A groupware system acts like your local library, letting you "check out" and work with files—documents being used and modified by several people can be better controlled so that your changes don't screw up the work someone else is doing with that same file.

Microsoft Office

Microsoft Office started the suite boom. Since then, Microsoft has stepped up its intensity by incorporating Word, Access, PowerPoint, Excel, and Mail into a competitively priced Microsoft Office suite of programs.

Fig. 24.4

The cool thing about suites is that you can work in one program and use the info from another. In this picture, the user has stuck an Excel spreadsheet into a Word document.

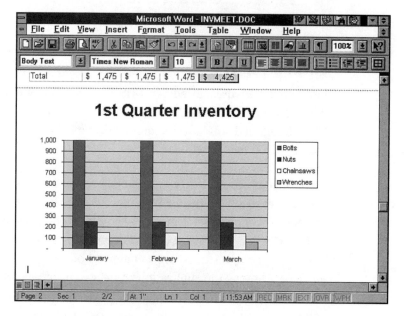

Cool features

One nice feature of this suite is Microsoft's "IntelliSense" technology, which recognizes what you want to accomplish next and adapts to the way you work. Toolbars, menus, dialog boxes, and screen layouts are consistent in all the programs. Most of the menus are identical among Excel, Word, and PowerPoint. Because of this common look, common tasks are faster and easier to complete.

System requirements

This suite requires up to 82M of disk space and can occupy as little as 29M. You'll also need a fair amount of RAM for Office—the recommended amount of memory is 8M of RAM, although it can limp along with 4M.

Lotus SmartSuite

The software programs in Lotus' SmartSuite are almost entirely revamped from earlier versions. With Lotus 1-2-3 and Approach—its two core programs—and the other programs built into SmartSuite, this suite is poised to compete with big-boy Microsoft Office. SmartSuite's strength is that it's great in a client/server environment.

Plain English, please!

Client/server refers to a computing system that splits the workload between PCs and one or more larger computers on a network. It's like a restaurant where the waiter (server) takes your order for a hamburger, goes to the kitchen, and comes back with some raw meat and a bun. You (the client) get to cook the burger at your table and add your favorite condiments. Although it sounds like more work, the service is faster and the food (data) is cooked to your liking. Also, the giant, expensive stove (the mainframe computer) in the kitchen can be replaced by lots of cheap little grills (desktop PCs). Computer geeks refer to this as **distributed processing**.

Fig. 24.5
Lotus Organizer is included with SmartSuite and is a welcome addition for people with busy schedules.

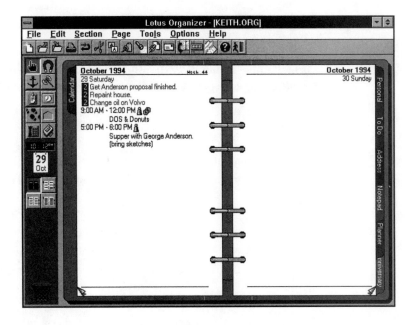

The major improvement in SmartSuite 3.0 is its common design. It is now more consistent with 1-2-3 and Approach, with a convenient SmartCenter icon box for switching among the three. You can just click the icon for the program you want to go to.

Cool features

Online Help Cards help you figure out how to do stuff with more than one of the SmartSuite programs. Bubble help, which debuted in Organizer, now appears in all the SmartSuite applications. Place the pointer on a toolbar icon, and a balloon tells you what the icon does. Sure beats clicking it and maybe sending yourself into limbo!

System requirements

SmartSuite 3.0 requires 70M of disk space for a full installation. Lotus recommends you have 4M of memory for one application and 2M for each additional application or major feature.

Novell PerfectOffice

Novell has come up with the perfect name for its new office suite. The PerfectOffice 3.0 bundle will differ significantly from its predecessor Borland Office, which included WordPerfect, Quattro Pro, and Paradox.

Cool features

All the programs in PerfectOffice look pretty much alike, have the same tools, and use a customizable toolbar for starting and switching among programs.

One very useful part of this suite is PerfectSense Technology, a feature similar to Microsoft's AutoCorrect. PerfectSense understands the meaning and context of words, and can therefore correct your grammar and spelling errors.

Also, QuickTasks automate many simple and complex tasks for you from the desktop. You don't even need to know which programs you need to open.

The Select version of PerfectOffice even includes a CD-ROM containing a wide range of other programs that you can use to build your own customized suite.

System requirements

Depending on which pieces of PerfectOffice you wish to install, you'll need anywhere from 42M to 98M of free disk space. Like Microsoft Office, you'll need a minimum of 4M of RAM, but you'll probably need at least 6M if you want to run a couple of programs simultaneously.

CD-ROM Software, Games, and Family Software

It's little wonder why the CD-ROM is so popular. You can get massive libraries of data on a single disc, as well as vast collections of stereo sound clips, high-color graphics, and full-motion video.

Although you may never access the **information superhighway** via the **Internet** from your computer, you can still have the latest in the information revolution right at your fingertips and use it every day (you learn about the Internet in Chapter 33).

The **CD-ROM drive** provides a way to distribute hundreds of megabytes (about 600M) of information on a small 4 3/4-inch silver disc. That's about equal to 240,000 pages of text. With such storage abilities, owning a CD-ROM drive in the 1990s will soon be as necessary as owning a hard disk was in the 1980s.

Plain English, please!

If you want to impress friends, remember that CD-ROM stands for **compact disc, read-only memory**. 🎵🎵

Although CD-ROMs look remarkably like audio CDs, you can't just hook your audio CD player to your computer. However, you can play your audio CDs on your computer. (Strange, huh? Just don't try to listen to your Microsoft Office CD-ROM in your stereo—unless you enjoy listening to spreadsheets singing!)

The read-only portion of the CD-ROM name means that you can load information from the CD, but you can't save information to the disc (you can make cassettes read-only, too, by knocking out those plastic tabs so you can't record on the tape).

See Chapter 27 for information about selecting and using a CD-ROM drive.

What can I use a CD-ROM for?

Major software programs, especially games, are being provided on CD-ROM, and some programs *only* come in CD-ROM format. Over 8,000 CD-ROM titles are available, with more arriving every day.

It's little wonder why the CD-ROM is so popular. You can get massive libraries of data (or even libraries of hundreds of books!) on a single disc, as well as vast collections of stereo sound clips, high-color graphics, or full-motion video. For example, Corel Corp. provides its popular CorelDRAW! software on CD-ROM. The latest release comes on three CD-ROMs with 825 fonts, 22,000 clip-art images, and 100 high-resolution photos. Without CD-ROM, you would need to get the program on about 1,000 floppy disks!

 **{Note}** Although a CD-ROM is a self-contained disk, its installation program may still place some files on your hard disk. Why? Your hard disk is much faster than a CD-ROM drive. The program would run very slowly if you ran it from your CD-ROM drive.

After you have a CD-ROM drive, what can you do with it? Check out this impressive list:

- Enjoy elaborate games

- Learn more about the world and historical events

- Install software quickly

- Better learn your software through built-in tutorials

- Sample hundreds of software programs before you buy them

- Run your business more smoothly with business leads and facts

Having fun with your CD-ROM

Games, which require both excellent graphics and sounds, are best suited for CD-ROM. Game makers can add more and more detail, sound, and musical scores with little regard to space. Games such as Broderbund Software's Myst, with its hauntingly beautiful graphic images and multi-level strategies, are provided only on CD-ROM.

Many CD-ROM drives and multimedia upgrade kits—that's a CD-ROM drive, sound card, and speakers you buy together—are bundled with some popular games, including Dynamix's Stellar 7, LucasArts' Loom, ChessMaster 3000, and King's Quest VI. About one out of every seven game titles is available on CD-ROM.

Two of the most popular games on CD-ROM are DOOM and DOOM II: Hell on Earth. The DOOM games are perhaps the most realistic, addicting, and frightening games ever. They've been so popular that an entire industry of DOOM add-ins has sprung up. For example, you can add your own levels to the game. While DOOM is virtually a free game—about $7 in the store (but you'll pay an additional $40 for two more levels)—DOOM II: Hell on Earth is a package for which you'll have to pay the full price (see fig. 25.1).

Fig. 25.1
DOOM II: Hell on Earth, one of the more popular games available on CD-ROM, provides an eerie set of corridors and enemies that you must escape from.

⊛ {Note} You can purchase CD-ROMs with sneak peeks of games for as little as $5. Companies such as Electronic Arts, Microsoft, and Software Toolworks have sold hundreds of thousands of CD-ROM "samplers"—inexpensive demos of games that let you "test drive" a game before plunking down $49.95 or more for the full version.

Can I learn from CD-ROM?

In addition to playing games on your CD-ROM, you can also use it for something productive—like sharpening your skills and furthering your education. Many multimedia upgrade kits include several "free" CD-ROM titles. For example, the Reveal Multimedia FX-04 kit includes Mavis Beacon Teaches Typing, *U.S. Atlas and World Atlas*, and Software Toolworks' *Multimedia*

Encyclopedia. Mavis Beacon Teaches Typing, for example, provides a lifelike keyboard, help windows, and timed typing tests. Speed and accuracy meters are provided to show you your improvement as you learn to type.

 **{Note}**

> Often, a manufacturer will have several similar multimedia upgrade kits, with the only difference being the type and quantity of CD-ROMs included. For example, a "family" multimedia upgrade kit may include an encyclopedia and children's games.

Getting educated from CD-ROM

Because it is so large, a single CD-ROM can easily hold the contents of an entire encyclopedia set. For a comprehensive encyclopedia, consider the *New Grolier Multimedia Encyclopedia.* This CD-ROM is based on the 21-volume *Academic American Encyclopedia,* many of whose 2,300 contributors are authorities in their fields. This encyclopedia includes 10 million words, 4,000 photos and illustrations, 53 video clips, and 300 maps.

While an entire encyclopedia of hardback books costs over $1,500, this electronic one costs $149.95. For that price, you can afford to update your encyclopedia every year. Figure 25.2 shows another of the popular CD-ROM encyclopedias.

Fig. 25.2
Another popular encyclopedia is the Software Toolworks Multimedia Encyclopedia. Here you can see a photograph from the Civil War entries.

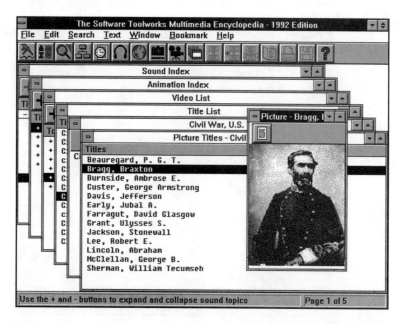

{Note}___ | You might have seen the popular Microsoft Encarta Multimedia Encyclopedia CD-ROM in your local software stores. This encyclopedia offers much more multimedia dazzle but is not as complete.

You can also find many educational programs on CD-ROM. Want your favorite student to succeed at college entrance exams? Your Personal Trainer from Davidson & Associates Inc. includes test-taking drills, strategies, and actual SAT-like printed materials. Version 2.0 of this program has been rewritten to reflect the new Scholastic Aptitude Tests that went into effect in March 1994.

Doing research from CD-ROM

You can also keep current on the computer industry via CD-ROM by subscribing to a service such as Computer Select from computer magazine publisher Ziff-Davis (see fig 25.3). Computer Select includes either the full text or abstracts of articles from over 170 computer magazines and newsletters. Also, Computer Select includes prices and specifications for about 74,000 hardware and software products, two computer dictionaries, and profiles on over 12,000 computer companies. Updated every month, an entire year's worth of articles is on a single disc. However, at $1,250 per year, you would have to use it extensively to make it pay for itself.

Fig. 25.3
Computer Select, a magazine-article-searching program, allows you to narrow your search to find articles on a particular subject or product.

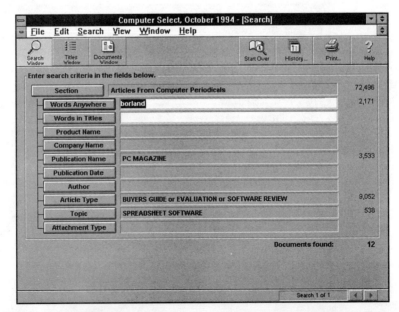

Simpler software installation

Installing large programs from a CD-ROM is a breeze. A single disc provides enough room for an entire software program. You can slip in a CD-ROM and make installation a breeze.

Eventually, you may see your next operating system available only on CD-ROM. In fact, the lowly 5 1/4-inch floppy disk is about to be replaced by the CD-ROM a way to deliver software. Microsoft Windows NT, for example, comes with a few floppy disks and a CD-ROM. Simply load the CD-ROM and answer a few questions. This installation is almost as quick as a full installation of Windows 3.1—and you don't need to keep swapping floppy disks!

Installing CorelDRAW! is simplified by replacing 10 floppy disks with a CD-ROM. In fact, ordering just the CD-ROM version saves the buyer $200 over the CD-ROM/floppy disk combination.

Perhaps CD-ROMs will even save some trees. Lotus 1-2-3 is provided on CD-ROM. No paper documentation or disks are included. The program and documentation, except for a tiny startup booklet, are all on a single CD-ROM. The printed documentation is available for an additional $59.

More and more information at your fingertips

Software makers often use the leftover room on a CD-ROM to add tutorials for the new software program, complete with animation, sound effects, and graphics. A CD-ROM edition of Microsoft Publisher 2.0, for example, provides additional desktop publishing templates, artwork, and a tutorial.

Peachtree Software ships Peachtree Accounting for Windows in a CD-ROM edition, which adds several small-business-oriented software packages onto a single CD-ROM. Besides Peachtree Accounting 2.0 for Windows, you get the following:

- The Multimedia Business Library from Allegro New Media (a collection of 12 books on a variety of business subjects)

- CompuServe's WinCIM (for navigating the CompuServe Information Service)

- SoftNet's FaxWorks 3.0 for fax modem owners

- Avery's LabelPro for Windows, which includes clip art and bar codes

- Individual Software's Professor Windows, which is a Windows tutorial program

- Mastering Computers' Tip-A-Day software

All of this on a single CD-ROM!

Ordering software by phone, thanks to CD-ROM

The latest, and perhaps easiest way to buy software is to receive a CD-ROM from a computer dealer packed with full retail versions of over 100 business applications (and maybe even a game or two).

Fig. 25.4

The On Hand CD-ROM from Softbank allows you to read about and test any of over 100 programs before buying.

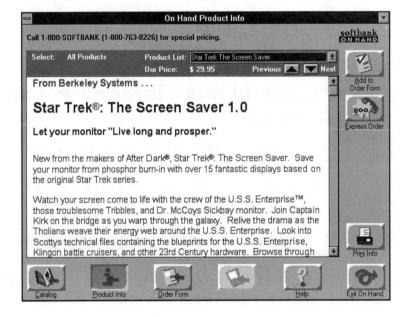

You can browse through detailed descriptions of every program on the disc and install demo versions before you buy the software. Some free programs are often included, too.

To close the deal, simply call your dealer or an 800 number and exchange a credit card number for a secret code. Type in the code, click OK, and install the application right off the CD-ROM. (The printed documentation, if you want it, arrives in the mail a day or two later.)

Graphics and photos on CD-ROM

You can liven up your presentations and newsletters with digitized photos and artwork on CD-ROM. Using a Kodak Photo CD-compatible drive (most CD-ROM drives are), you can place images in any document.

There are two types of photography you can use: **stock photography** and **clip images**. Stock photography requires you to pay fees for using each image. Clip images, on the other hand, are the perfect alternative. Unlike stock photos, which you can only use once, clip images are yours to use however and as often as you'd like. Both types of photography can be found through the same sources—retail software stores or mail-order catalogs.

Clip image libraries, such as Corel's Professional Photos CD-ROM ($49.95 each) and Digital Stock Professional's images ($249 each), are relatively inexpensive sources of high-quality images.

While right now photo CD-ROMs are only useful for retrieving photos, there may even be a day when you can store your family photo album on a single CD-ROM!

Should our office buy a CD-ROM?

While CD-ROMs are a hot topic in the home, can they have an impact on business?

A product such as Microsoft Bookshelf is a welcome reference set for the office. This multimedia reference includes the following:

- Dictionary

- Book of quotations

- Thesaurus

- Chronology of world events

- Encyclopedia

- World atlas

- Almanac

Bookshelf is updated yearly by Microsoft, so you are assured of using the most current references available. Bookshelf's QuickShelf feature puts volumes of data at your fingertips. When you're creating a document in a Windows word processor and you need to flesh out an idea, highlight the word you're stuck on and click the QuickShelf tool on the toolbar. From there, you can access any work in the library for more information about the highlighted word. And since all seven volumes are linked, you can search all of them for citations—any of which may have accompanying photos, sound, or video clips. For all that, Microsoft Bookshelf requires just 2M of hard disk space—slightly more than a single floppy disk contains!

Fig. 25.5

Microsoft Bookshelf is an affordable collection of reference books that work together.

What Microsoft Bookshelf is to the consummate writer, the *Allegro Reference Series Business Library, Vol. 1,* is to entrepreneurs. This collection of 12 books provides answers to questions such as: What are the principles of a successful telemarketing campaign? What's the tax benefit of real-estate trusts? This collection includes superb books on marketing, finance, real estate, international business, selling your product, and promoting your own career.

Need a handy reference on public relations? The *Public Relations Handbook* from Compton's NewMedia is filled with general advice and specific examples that can be adapted easily to your own PR events. The Windows interface makes it simple to get all you need to hold down the fort until the spin doctor arrives.

Another type of CD-ROM package that you might find useful in the office for marketing is one of the many phone directory applications. Pro CD's ProPhone line is such a tool, which provides you with company names, phone numbers, mailing addresses, sizes, and numbers of employees—great for putting together mailing lists. Its $299 SelectPhone is a four-CD-ROM set providing over one million U.S. residential and business listings, along with 2,700 SIC code headings.

 **{Note}**

You could become your own CD-ROM publisher. You can put just about anything on a custom CD-ROM, such as a regularly updated product catalog, up-to-the-minute service manual, or a disc full of digitized forms. Desktop CD-recordable (CD-R) technology allows you to do your own publishing. However, self-publishing is only economical if you intend to make dozens of copies.

26

Printers and Scanners

In this chapter:

- What types of printers are available?

- What's a font?

- What should I look for in a printer?

- What's PostScript?

- I really want to print in color

- Why would I need a scanner?

"Experts" may predict the paperless office, but most offices find that PCs add to the paper blizzard. We can now spew reams of paper at up to 20 pages per minute.

A lthough the information in a computer is electronic, you often need to print that information to paper (thus creating a **printout** or **hard copy**). On the other hand, sometimes you need to get stuff *into* your computer that has already been printed—such as a company logo or the text of a product sheet. This process is called **scanning**. This chapter covers both.

What kinds of printers are available?

PC printers come in several designs. One may print envelopes, while another excels at carbonless forms. One may offer high quality, the other is amazingly fast. There are three basic types of printers:

- **Dot-matrix printers** use a combination of small pins that strike an inked ribbon, like a typewriter.

- **Laser printers** work much like a copier. With these printers, an ink substance called **toner** is "melted" onto the page to leave a permanent, high-quality image.

 **{Note}**

> Some printers are mistakenly called laser printers but actually don't use lasers. Okidata's OkiLaser 400E and 410E, for example, use shutters of light-emitting diodes (LEDs) to create the image. Despite the operating difference, the quality is the same as laser printers.

- **Inkjet printers** are like a "poor man's" laser printer. They use small nozzles that spray fast-drying ink onto the page. The quality is high, but speed is low.

What are fonts, and why should I care?

A **font** is the style of letters (both shape and size) that your printer puts on the paper. Most printers come with a bunch of fonts built-in. These fonts are known as **internal** or **resident fonts**. All you have to do to use these fonts is tell your software what printer you have.

Besides built-in fonts, most laser printers support **downloadable** fonts, sometimes known as **soft fonts**. (Some dot-matrix and most inkjet printers also support downloadable fonts.) These fonts are contained in files on your hard drive and are transferred (downloaded) to the printer as they are needed. To use these fonts, you have to tell your software what kind of printer you have and what soft fonts you have.

Some printers also support **font cartridges**, stored in little boxes that look like an 8-track tape or Nintendo game. They plug directly into the printer and then act like internal fonts.

What kind of fonts are best?

There are distinct advantages and disadvantages to each font type. Internal fonts print faster and generally look better. Soft fonts come in endless varieties from standard Times Roman to "PostCrypt," where the letters look like ghouls and goblins.

When buying a printer, look for one that comes with several internal fonts and supports soft fonts. When buying fonts, make sure they are **scalable**. A font that is scalable can be printed in many sizes. (Many printers have scalable internal fonts.)

> If you have Windows and at least one popular word processor, you probably have more fonts than you can handle. Windows, and most of the word processors, come with a bunch of scalable, downloadable fonts called **TrueType** fonts. Before investing in fonts, check out what fonts are already listed in your word processor's font menu.

How to choose a printer

Picking the right printer is like picking the right vehicle. How many miles will you be driving? How fast do you want to go? Will you be hauling anything heavy? Some questions you should consider:

- What quality does your printing require? Do you need to impress or just show the facts?

- How fast do you need your printing? Can you afford to wait a little for the pages to print, and thus buy a less-expensive printer?

- What type of paper do you have to print on? Do you need a wide printer for 11×17-inch ledger sheets or mailing labels? Do you need to print carbon or carbonless forms? What about envelopes?

- How much printing do you intend to do? Are you just printing occasionally or do you need to print massive numbers of pages?

- How expensive are the **consumables**—that is, the inked ribbons, toner, or ink cartridges the printer uses?

- Does your software support your printer? Some programs, especially non-Windows programs, may work with only a handful of printers.

When to choose a dot-matrix printer

Dot-matrix printers are the cheapest printers available (see fig. 26.1). Compatibility with your software is rarely a problem because most software can print easily to an Epson printer or IBM Pro Printer, and most other brands of dot-matrix printers can act like the Epson or IBM.

Fig. 26.1

A dot-matrix printer is cheap to own and operate.

These printers form text and images by hammering away at several small pins against an inked ribbon. The more pins used, the better the image (and the noisier the printer because more pins are striking the ribbon). Dot-matrix printers typically come in two choices of quality: **9-pin** and **24-pin**. Nine-pin printers are used for inexpensive but fast printing. At best, these printers provide **near-letter-quality** (**NLQ**) printing. That is, they do the job, but you wouldn't want to print your resume on them.

⊛ **{Note}** ___ | The term **letter-quality** used to be common to describe the final product of good printers; that is, good enough to use for your important letters. **Near-letter-quality** is considered to be pretty close (near) to that letter-quality standard. But don't be fooled by a salesperson. Near-letter-quality is just that—close, but no cigar.

The 24-pin dot-matrix printers provide real **letter-quality** (**LQ**) printing. Although typically slower than a 9-pin printer, these printers can be used for important correspondence. They can also be scaled back to **draft mode** so that you can print quickly—the printer just uses a handful of the 24 pins to produce a result that is just legible, not attractive.

Plain English, please!

The term **mode** or **print mode** describes which way you're printing: draft, near-letter-quality, or letter-quality. Often you can specify in your software program how you want something to print. If you just need a quick copy you can show to somebody for corrections or for a meeting, use draft mode. When the document is ready to be finalized, then you want letter-quality, or near-letter-quality if it's not very important.

Fig. 26.2
Don't confuse draft quality with near-letter-quality.

This is 9-pin type.

This is NLQ 9-pin type.

How fast is a fast printer?

The speed of dot-matrix printers is measured in **characters per second**, or **cps**. The speed in a printer ad may be given in draft, near-letter-quality, or letter-quality modes. Advertisers typically print only the draft speed because that's the fastest speed of the printer.

 **{Note}** Dot-matrix printers are sometimes very slow compared to laser printers, which are measured in **pages per minute**, or **ppm**, instead of characters per second.

Here's an example of the difference in speed between one print mode and another. An Okidata 590 is a speedy little printer that can zip along at up to 450 cps in draft mode. In letter-quality mode, it slows down to about 100 cps.

If you'll be printing hundreds of mailing labels or long reports, get a printer with a high cps rating. Also, you may want to get a printer that has a **noise-reduction** feature, so it doesn't interrupt nearby conversations.

A note about print buffers

Computers think a lot faster than printers. Thus, it's common that when you send something to print, the **print job** takes longer to complete than it takes you to walk to the printer. If the print job includes a lot of pages, complicated drawings, and so on, you might be able to get a cup of coffee or go to the hardware store while you're waiting.

To speed up the printing process, many printers include a small amount of memory, up to 64K. This **print buffer** (or just **buffer**) stores the characters that have been sent from the computer until the printer is ready to print that information. Think of it as an assembly line. The data goes from the computer to the printer cable, travels along the cable to the printer, waits in the print buffer, then goes to the print head (the part that prints the characters), and comes out on paper.

Each 5K in the buffer holds about one page of text. The bigger the buffer, the sooner you and your PC can finish that print job and work on something else.

What kind of paper can I use?

Dot-matrix printers use various types of paper: **continuous-feed** or **fanfold paper** (the paper with those pinholes on the sides and perforated edges), mailing labels, forms that create duplicate copies, and even single sheets. Printers that can print on single sheets are often known as **sheet-fed printers**. Some include a gadget called a **sheet feeder** to put the paper into the printer page by page, so you don't have to do it. Some printers can use either kind of paper.

Dot-matrix printers are the only printers covered here that can print on two-, three-, or four-part carbon or carbonless forms. Why? These printers *hit* the page and can make duplicate copies. Almost every business needs such a printer for printing invoices, service orders, and so on.

Some dot-matrix printers come in two **styles**: **narrow carriage** and **wide carriage**. Narrow printers can handle letter-size sheets (8 1/2 inches wide). (These are also called **80-column printers**.) Wider printers can handle 11×17-inch ledger sheets and mailing labels on sheets wide enough to hold three or four labels. (These are also called **136-column printers**.) If you need to print only letter-size sheets, you can save about $100 by choosing a narrow printer.

②Q&A

I need to be able to switch between continuous-feed paper and letterhead. What kind of printer is best for me?

Get a dot-matrix printer with a **paper-parking** feature, which pulls the continuous-feed paper out of the way so you can print on single sheets without having to unload the continuous paper.

Ups and downs of dot-matrix printing

The good features of a dot-matrix printer are

- Prints reports and mailing labels cheaply since the inked ribbons are cheap

- Can print on carbon and carbonless forms

- Relatively inexpensive

The downsides of dot-matrix printers are

- Often slower than other printers

- Generally noisy

- Paper jams may occur if unattended

Maintaining a dot-matrix printer

Simple maintenance can prolong the life of a dot-matrix printer.

- Clean and lubricate the track on which the print head moves. Wipe it periodically with a soft cloth and use a light oil, such as sewing machine oil. Don't use motor oil or synthetic oils, though, because they can ruin the printing mechanisms!

- Use manufacturer-recommended ribbons. A ribbon not only provides ink for printed characters, but contains lubricant to keep the small pins in the print head moving freely (see fig. 26.3). Cheap or re-inked ribbons may skimp on the lubricant.

Fig. 26.3

The correct ribbon lubricates the dot-matrix pins.

- Clean the print head occasionally. A build-up of ink may cause one or more of your printer's pins to stick. A sign of this build-up is a continuous, white, horizontal line through your type or graphics. Use isopropyl alcohol with a foam (not cotton) swab.

- Position the print head according to the thickness of your paper. If you set the print head too close to the surface of the paper, you shorten the life of your print head. Some printers, such as those from Okidata, intelligently sense the thickness of your paper and set the print head accordingly. Check your printer's manual for the correct setting for the paper you use.

- Use the correct paper path. Your printer may be able to accept paper from the front, rear, bottom, and top. Select the best path for the paper being used. Mailing labels, for example, are best used through the front or bottom paper path—not the rear, where they are more likely to jam.

When do I need a laser printer?

For about $500 and up, you can get a high-quality laser printer (see fig. 26.4). These printers use laser beams to burn special toner onto the page for a permanent impression.

The most popular laser printer is the **Hewlett-Packard LaserJet** (it has various models, often just referred to as **HP**s). Most laser printers imitate the LaserJet and many are less expensive alternatives. One HP-compatible printer is the OkiLaser 400E from Okidata.

Fig. 26.4
The laser printer is quiet and fast but more expensive than dot-matrix printers.

Laser printers use a **toner cartridge**, a plastic box that contains enough toner to print about 3,000 pages before being replaced. Toner cartridges are not cheap, costing from $25 to $95 each.

Whereas a dot-matrix printer uses a number of pins to determine its print quality, laser printers use **dots per inch** (**dpi**). Most print at 300 dpi. This is fine for most work, such as correspondence and simple newsletters. **High-resolution laser printers**, such as the HP LaserJet 4 and OkiLaser 410E, print at 600 dpi. High-resolution printers are best for creating in-house ads, material that needs to be "camera-ready," or other documents that need the finest resolution.

The need for speed

Laser printers are fast. Most come in one of three speeds: 4, 8, or 12 pages per minute (ppm). If you print only a few pages per day, you can save money by buying a slower 4-ppm printer. The busy home or small office is best with the 8-ppm models. Businesses that love to crank out paper should choose the 12-ppm (or more) printers.

Don't be too impressed by page-per-minute speeds. These rated speeds are the top speeds at which the printers can print. The complexity of the pages you are printing determines how fast you'll see some output. If you use lots of fonts and have several pictures, for example, you can expect the printer to slow significantly.

The speed of the printer's processor is often more important than page-per-minute speed. Some printers, such as the LaserJet 4 Plus, use a special processor that helps the printer print close to its top speed even with complex documents.

Space and paper requirements can make a difference

As a rule, 4-ppm printers tend to be smaller, requiring little desk space. (The amount of desk space used is called a **footprint**, so you might hear these small printers called **small-footprint** machines.) Some printers, such as the Panasonic KX-P4401 SideWriter, stand vertically and require very little desk space.

If you'll be printing several pages quickly, your printer will need to hold several sheets of paper. Some only hold 50 sheets of paper, requiring frequent reloading. Others may hold 200 to 250 letter-size sheets. Most printers can also print envelopes, one at a time. An optional envelope feeder allows you to print up to 50 before reloading. If you often switch between blank paper and special letterhead, you may want an optional sheet feeder that allows you to specify which paper bin the paper should feed from.

I keep hearing about PostScript—what is it?

Laser printers must use a common language for describing how text and graphics should be placed on a page during printing. This **page description language**, or **PDL**, determines which fonts work with your printer.

Most laser printers understand one of two page description languages that have become standards. The most prevalent is the **Printer Control Language** (**PCL**), developed by Hewlett-Packard for its LaserJet printers. The newer HP LaserJet III and LaserJet 4 use a version called **PCL5**. The other PDL standard, **PostScript**, was developed by Adobe Systems.

Both have their advantages and drawbacks. Most PostScript printers cost more than PCL printers and print more slowly. However, PostScript printers usually have better fonts, produce better gray scales, and are better supported by high-end graphics and design packages. The newer PCL printers have better resolution and incorporate support for special effects (like drop-shadowing).

Almost every laser printer imitates the Hewlett-Packard LaserJet. (This imitation is called an **emulation**.) Other printers may use the PostScript standard. The important point is that your software must be capable of working with whichever standard your printer uses and vice versa. Not all software programs can work with a PostScript printer; on the other hand, some programs require PostScript printing. Some more expensive printers support both printing standards.

When does a laser printer need more memory?

To prepare a page for printing, laser printers require some memory. Most include at least 1M of memory. For simple text, this memory may be adequate. If you intend to print several fonts or graphics, however, you may need more. Otherwise, you may see partially printed pages. If more memory is needed, check to see how much memory your printer can accommodate.

Most laser printers include 14 to 45 fonts. Some, such as the HP LaserJet 4, even include **scalable** fonts. If printing from Microsoft Windows, the number of included fonts may be irrelevant. Windows uses software fonts to create text and sends a "snapshot" of the page to your printer.

Ups and downs of laser printers

The pluses of a laser printer are

- Fast printing

- High quality

- Quiet operation

And the downsides are

- Can't print carbon or carbonless forms

- Per-page cost of printing is expensive

- Can be expensive to buy and to maintain

A couple of other little things may not bother you at all. A laser printer cannot print to the edge of the page. At least one-quarter of an inch around the entire page is unprintable. And you can only print 60 lines of text per sheet of paper, rather than the usual 66 (assuming six lines per inch, like a typewriter).

Maintaining a laser printer

Because of their price, laser printers are worth caring for. If you own a laser printer, follow these tips:

- Clean your printer. Most printer manuals tell you how to clean the printer, and most want you to clean the corona wire and fuser. (The **corona wire** creates the electric charge that attracts the toner to the paper.) If the corona wire gets dirty, it won't be able to apply the proper charge to the paper. If this happens, you'll get light or even blank streaks on your page. The **fuser** is the part that melts the toner onto the page. If it's dirty, the toner may not stick. Clean these parts with a soft cloth and cotton swabs or the built-in cleaning brush. Avoid solvents and liquid cleaners.

- Protect the **printer drum**. Don't touch it or expose it to light for long periods. The laser's drum may be part of the machine or built into the replaceable toner cartridge (such as in the HP LaserJets).

- Keep toner cartridges level. Never tilt or store your toner cartridges on one side. This shifts the toner to one side, causing uneven printing.

- Avoid using recycled or refilled toner cartridges. They may save money, but many leak, use substandard materials, and don't last as long. In general they aren't worth the savings.

> If your laser printer says that the toner is low, remove the cartridge and shake it from side to side. Reinsert it into the printer. The low-toner light may go out and you'll be able to squeeze a few more pages from the cartridge.

- Keep the **print density** (how heavily the toner is placed on the page) as low as possible. Some laser printers have dials for adjusting the print density. For drafts, keep this setting low, conserving toner. For final copies, set the dial to its normal level.

What about inkjet printers?

An **inkjet printer** provides gorgeous print quality that rivals laser printers for a portion of the price. An inkjet printer, such as the Hewlett-Packard DeskJet 520, can provide sharp-looking letters and reports.

Inkjet printers spray a fine quick-drying ink onto the page from several small nozzles. Despite earlier problems with ink smudging and fading, the latest printers are inexpensive and quiet…but not fast. Also, inkjet printers do not provide as crisp printing as laser printers. One other strike against inkjet printers is that their ink cartridges are expensive and do not last long. If you consider the falling prices of laser printers, the inkjet printer doesn't necessarily provide as good a value.

How the printer forms and aims ink drops is only part of the print-quality factor. If you use a porous paper, the drops will tend to bloom as they soak into the paper, leading to a fuzzy appearance.

One niche inkjet printers serve is as portable printers for laptop computers. An inkjet printer such as the Canon BJ-230 is the size of a notebook computer and sells for under $400.

Thermal printers also are used by laptop computers. These printers use heat to print on wax-like paper.

Is color printing ready for prime time?

Not long ago, color printers were priced at a minimum of $3,000. Color inkjet printers could print charts on standard copier paper but produced washed-out colors on transparencies, and they couldn't print plain black-and-white text at all.

Color is still far from the norm in business, mostly because of cost—not only up front for the printer itself but every day, thanks to expensive color printer supplies. But new inkjets offer both text printing at reasonable speeds and impressive color at reasonable costs. The Hewlett-Packard DeskJet 550C provides adequate color quality. Move a notch higher and you can get the HP DeskJet 1200C for about $1350. This inkjet printer can use either copier paper or transparencies.

You could try thermal wax transfer or dye-sublimation (what?)

For serious color, consider **thermal wax transfer** technology. Usually priced at $3,000 to $5,000, thermal wax transfer printers produce rich, full colors on transparencies as well as on specially coated papers. Fargo Electronics offers the Primera, a low-volume thermal wax transfer printer that sells for just $995.

The next step up—with prices near $10,000 despite declines over the past year—is **dye-sublimation** technology. (Last summer, Kodak set a low price point for dye-sublimation printers by pricing its ColorEase PS under $8,000.)

Dye-sublimation printers, sometimes called **thermal dye transfer printers**, are known for producing photographic-like colors. These printers vaporize and merge color dyes, rather than ink or wax.

Color printing prices vary with how you print. Dye-sublimation pages cost about $2 to $5 per page. Thermal wax transfer printers cost about 50 cents to $1.50 per page. Pages from a color inkjet printer cost about 15 cents.

Scanning stuff into your PC

Whereas printers get information *out* of your computer, **scanners** put the information from paper documents and images *into* your PC. Like a photo-copier, a scanner takes a "photograph" of a paper document. Instead of getting a duplicate sheet of paper, though, you get an image stored on your computer (see fig. 26.5).

A scanner can be used two ways:

- To save an artwork image—such as a company logo or a photograph—as a graphics file you can use in a newsletter or on letterhead

- To turn text on the paper document into typed text for your word processor

Two scanner types for different purposes

Scanners come in two types. A **hand scanner** (or **handheld scanner**) allows you to scan small areas of text and graphics, typically about four inches wide (see fig. 26.5). You roll the scanner across the page you want to scan. Don't worry if your page is wider than the scanner; many scanner software pro-grams allow you to "stitch" together multiple scans.

Fig. 26.5
The less expensive handheld scanner allows you to scan portions of a page and is ideal for occasional use.

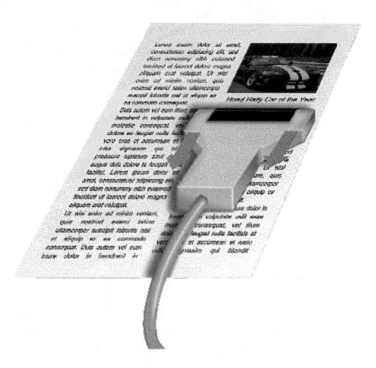

⊛ {Note}

Handheld scanners require a steady hand and a flat surface so that the scanned image is smooth. You often can preview an image and repeat the scan until you get it right.

Flatbed scanners are ideal for scanning entire pages quickly (see fig. 26.6). Like a photocopier, you place the entire page on the glass surface. To speed scanning, optional document feeders can automatically feed subsequent pages into the scanner so you don't have to.

Whichever scanner size you pick, you'll have to add a special card inside your computer. You can't hook a scanner to your PC's printer port.

Fig. 26.6
The flatbed scanner is like a photocopier, with a glass surface on which you place the page to be scanned.

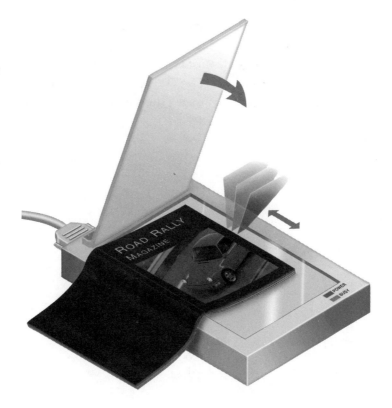

And what about OCR?

While scanning artwork sounds cool, it is most often used by desktop publishers and artists. The truly handy use of scanners is for **optical character recognition**, or **OCR**. With OCR, you can scan and have words on a piece of paper appear quickly and almost error-free in your document. OCR is like having a 200-word-per-minute typist. Software programs such as Caere OmniPage Professional and Calera's WordScan Plus are leaders in the OCR software marketplace.

Packages such as OmniPage Professional and WordScan Plus also have abilities to take fax transmissions and turn them into text files. The fax/communications program WinFax Pro also can turn fax transmissions into text through OCR, but not with the same accuracy.

OCR isn't perfect. The typical OCR accuracy rate is about 98 percent, or one mistake for every 49 characters scanned, so you'll still need to proofread your final document. Most errors come from similar-looking characters, such as "0" and "O" or "c" and "e." This confusion is multiplied if your original page is of bad quality, such as a fax transmission or a copy of a copy.

27

Multimedia Mayhem: CD-ROMs and Sound Cards

The computer industry,
like the rest of the world,
always keeps its priorities
straight. That's why multi-
media was first developed
for computer games!

In this chapter:

- Why all the excitement about multimedia?

- What do I need to use multimedia?

- What features do I look for in a multimedia computer?

Loosely translated, the phrase **multimedia** means "a bunch of communication methods." In a nutshell, it means using sound, images, and data on a computer at the same time. This is kind of like using "Victory at Sea" to help present the end-of-year fiscal data you have assembled.

 Plain English, please!

Multimedia is the blending of video, graphics, text, and sound.

As you can imagine, that opens up endless possibilities. Most of today's multimedia programs are designed for education, entertainment, or reference. Since a CD-ROM can hold as much as 600M (more than 400 floppy disks!), you can stuff volumes of information on a single disc (see fig. 27.1).

What can multimedia do for me?

The multimedia encyclopedia is a perfect mainstream example of what multimedia can do for you. You might begin a search for information about the Watergate scandal. By clicking on the entry for Richard M. Nixon, you can jump to the former president's biography. Click on the movie camera icon and the encyclopedia plays a video of Nixon's farewell address, complete with sound.

When the speech is over, you can look up cross references to H.R. Haldeman, impeachment, Khruschev, and more and jump over to any of them. You might start out at Watergate and end up at the Berlin Wall! The endless avenues you can explore using a multimedia encyclopedia keep your interest, so you learn better.

You can search an encyclopedia on CD–ROM and listen to history.

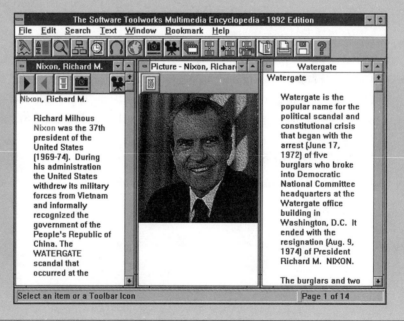

Fig. 27.1
The CD-ROM delivers over 200,000 pages of information on a single disc.

⊛ *{Note}* No, it's not a typo. A CD is a disc (with a "c") and a floppy is a disk (with a "k").

Is multimedia all play and no work?

Sound cards and multimedia aren't just for kids anymore. Business users and educators also have a lot to gain from multimedia. For example, you can

- *Add sound effects to business presentations*. Businesses are discovering that multimedia presentations that combine graphics, animation, and sound are more impressive, and often less expensive, than those tired old slide shows. See Chapter 22 for details.

- *Enhance training programs*. Many software manufacturers already ship special CD-ROM versions of some of their products. These versions include animated on-line help, complete with music.

- *Add voice notes to Windows files.* A business executive could pick up a microphone and place a spoken message into a contract to give her assistant explicit instructions, like in the spreadsheet in figure 27.2. This message is called a **voice annotation**—but think of it as a verbal Post-It note.

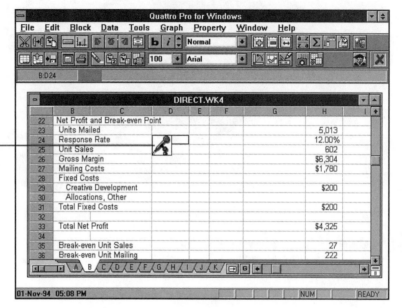

Fig. 27.2
This message might say, "Joan, remember this figure is based on third-quarter sales only."

Click here to play back the message.

- *Give your PC voice commands.* As you learned in Chapter 9, some computers are capable of voice recognition. Imagine giving your PC voice commands from within Windows. "File open. Page down! Left. Enter."

- *Make your computer talk back.* Text-to-speech utilities can read back a list of numbers or text to you. (Kind of like a proofreader you don't have to pay.) Hearing a letter read aloud may reveal forgotten words or awkward phrases. Accountants can double-check spreadsheet numbers, and busy executives can have their e-mail read to them while they are doing paperwork.

What kind of equipment do I need?

To use multimedia programs, you must have at least

- A 25MHz 486SX processor

- 4M of RAM

- 160M hard disk space

- 16-bit digital sound card

- A pair of speakers or headphones

- 300-Kbps (or **double-speed**) CD-ROM drive

 Q&A

My friend's computer meets the specs here, but his multimedia programs run really slow and clunky. What's wrong?

Remember, these specs are the bare minimum. If your computer is on the low end, you can use multimedia, but you can't use it very well. If you think you'll want to use multimedia a lot, get a computer with more power, like a 486DX with 16M of RAM.

Why do I need a CD-ROM drive?

Today's hottest games and reference materials come either optionally on CD-ROM or exclusively on CD-ROM. The sheer capacity of a CD-ROM allows you to get massive libraries of data on a single disc, as well as vast collections of stereo sound clips, high-color graphics, and full-motion video. This makes the CD-ROM ideal for providing

- Encyclopedias

- Technical reference information

- Databases of phone numbers and marketing leads

- Games and educational software

Why do I need a sound card?

Folks who have used computers for years usually don't see the big deal with **sound cards**—until they get one. But that's understandable. If you've always driven a car that doesn't have a radio, then you get one that does, it doesn't take long for you to wonder how you ever remained sane without it.

A sound card is a small piece of hardware (like the one shown in figure 27.3) that goes inside your computer and lets you record and play sounds. You can hook up microphones and speakers to sound cards, giving you all kinds of new toys to play with.

Fig. 27.3
That's funny, it doesn't look like a tape recorder!

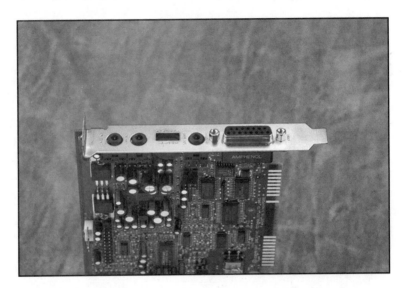

A sound card doesn't work like a tape recorder, though. Instead of going onto a tape or other physical storage place, the sound is **digitized** and stored in a file just like any other data.

Here are just a few of the things you can do with a sound card:

- *Add stereo sound to computer games.* Today's multimedia games often include movie-quality musical scores, recorded human voices, or video clips.

- *Create your own original music, or edit music "entered" from a synthesizer.* **MIDI**, which is short for **Musical Instrument Digital Interface**, is essentially a musical programming language that lets your computer store and edit or play back music—kind of like a tape recorder on steroids. With MIDI, you can compose and edit music, learn about music theory, or turn your PC into a one-stop music mixing studio.

- *Make your Windows programs talk to you.* You can use a sound card to jazz up your everyday computing experience. For example, you might want Windows to play a loud "Ta-da" when it starts or say "Adios, amigo!" when you exit a program.

- *Play your favorite music CDs on your computer.* A good multimedia computer can play Billy Joel in the background while you type away in Word for Windows, without missing a beat.

- *Record your own sounds (called **WAV files**), or get them from other places.* Prepackaged sounds are available from lots of different sources.

⊛ {Note} Although we all want great sound, recorded WAV files eat up a lot of disk space. A sound recorded at CD-audio quality takes as much as 10.5M per minute! At this rate, you could quickly fill your hard disk.

What do I look for in a multimedia system?

Many computers that you purchase now are **multimedia PC (MPC) systems**. This just means that they have at least the minimum requirements needed to meet the MPC standards. Now let's look at the parts of a multimedia PC.

⊛ {Note} A group called the Multimedia PC Marketing Council has set the **Multimedia PC Level 2 standards**, known as the **MPC standards**, for what a multimedia PC should have. Make sure that your CD-ROM and sound card meet the MPC standards.

How to choose a CD-ROM drive

The CD-ROM drive is the heart of your MPC system. To ensure that your computer is compatible with current and upcoming CD-ROM software, keep these things in mind (and ask the salesperson for more information) as you shop for a CD-ROM drive:

- *How fast can this CD-ROM access data?* You will want a CD-ROM drive with an average **seek time** of about 300ms or less. The faster your CD-ROM drive's access speed, the quicker you'll be able to get certain tasks done, especially those that frequently search the CD-ROM drive, such as a CD-ROM encyclopedia or magazine index. Look for a double- or **triple-speed** CD-ROM drive.

 Plain English, please!

> Access speed, usually referred to as **seek time**, is measured in **milliseconds (ms)**, or thousandths of a second. This is the time it takes the drive to find the information. The data transfer rate is measured in **kilobytes transferred per second (Kbps)**. This is how fast the data is transferred once it is found.

- *How fast can this CD-ROM transfer data?* After you find the data, you will then need to use the data. The MPC specs require a drive capable of sustaining a data transfer rate of 150K per second (or single speed), while claiming no more than 40 percent of your computer's attention, *and* a data transfer rate of 300K per second (or double speed) is also required, while claiming no more than 60 percent of your computer's brain power. Why have both rates? NEC Technologies Inc., for example, uses its **MultiSpin** technology on its CD-ROM drives, which doubles the speed of the drive when reading certain kinds of information off the disc.

- *What basic controls do I need?* A CD-ROM drive should have a few controls. Look for an accessible **eject button**. A smooth, motorized load-eject tray is best. External controls for audio CDs, ranging from a thumb wheel for controlling volume to a full set of play, pause, next-track, and previous-track buttons, is handy. This way, you can load, play, stop, eject, and even change CD tracks without having to use software utilities.

Fig. 27.4
Most CD-ROM drives
include the basics, such
as a volume control
and a headphone jack.

- *How much should I spend?* What you spend on a CD-ROM drive
  depends on what you want. Some low-end, single-speed drives are
  currently being sold for under $100. Beware! These drives are very slow
  and limited in capabilities. Stick to a double-speed drive (around $200)
  or higher. The current maximum-speed drives (**quad-speed**, or four
  times as fast) can be found for as low as $350. Shop around for the
  lowest price.

Best features for sound cards

Selecting a sound card is like buying a car. They're all basically the same, but
oh!, the difference a few features can make! Be sure to ask your hardware
dealer these questions and get as many of these features as you can afford:

- *Is my game supported?* There are no official sound card standards, but
  the popular Sound Blaster card is the closest thing yet. Although nearly
  all sound cards claim to be compatible with Sound Blaster, only those
  of two companies are strictly compatible: Creative Labs, the originator
  of the de facto standard, and IBM, which has licensed the technology
  from Creative Labs. If you stick to either of these two cards, you can be
  sure that almost any game will work. At least look for a card that says it
  is 100 percent Sound-Blaster-compatible.

- *MPC ready?* Most sound cards support the Multimedia PC (MPC) Level 2 specifications.

- *Can I add a CD-ROM?* Most stereo sound cards not only provide great sound, but also can control certain types of CD-ROM drives at the same time.

Make sure your CD-ROM drive and sound card are compatible, or that your CD-ROM drive comes with its own controller card. For maximum compatibility, buy a multimedia kit that contains both in one package.

- *DSP included?* One new addition to many sound cards is the **digital signal processor**, or **DSP**. DSPs add intelligence to your sound card, freeing your computer from some tasks, such as filtering noise from recordings or compressing your recorded sounds.

If you're seeking to add both a sound card and a CD-ROM drive, consider a **multimedia upgrade kit**. These kits bundle a sound card, CD-ROM drive, CD-ROM titles, software, and cables in an attractively priced package. A multimedia upgrade kit may save you some money over buying individual components. Plus you'll have the peace of mind that the components will work together.

Don't forget speakers!

Quality sound depends on quality speakers. This applies to all audio systems, from your home theater setup to the radio in your car. Computers are no exception! An expensive sound card may provide better sound to computer speakers, but even a cheap sound card sounds better from a good speaker. Never skimp on the speakers!

Speakers come in several styles and price ranges. A growing number are designed specifically for multimedia and sound cards. Some systems offer individual satellite speakers that can be placed anywhere; others come pre-installed in a cabinet that matches the case of your PC, fitting between it and your monitor.

Fig. 27.5
They might look small, but don't be fooled. These little guys can blow you away!

Here are some tips to remember about the audio end of your multimedia setup:

- Take speaker specifications with a grain of salt. On paper, one product may seem superior to another. You can't listen to paper; audition a sound card or speaker before you buy.

- You'll get even better results if you plug your sound card into powered speakers, that is, speakers with built-in amplifiers. (Another alternative is to patch your sound card into your stereo system for greatly amplified sound.)

- Although most computer speakers are magnetically shielded (make sure that the ones you buy are!), do not leave recorded tapes, watches, personal credit cards, or floppy disks near the speakers.

- If you are short on cash, consider buying a pair of headphones. The sound can be just as good as a pair of speakers and provides privacy.

28

Hooking Up to the Information Superhighway with a Modem

In this chapter:

- What is the information superhighway?
- What is a modem?
- Why do I need a modem?
- What modem is right for me?
- How do I set up my modem?

The information super-highway is a giant com-puter network connected through telephone lines, and your modem is your entrance ramp.

You've probably already been pelted by the phrase *information superhighway*; it's being thrown at us constantly by the media these days! Although the exact definition of the term is open for debate, one fact is clear: To access the information superhighway and the multitude of re-sources and information it provides, you need to hook your PC up to your phone line.

The information superhighway is nothing more than a massive bunch of computers—millions of them—all connected together in a worldwide network. How is this giant network connected? Through telephone lines.

✱ {Note} Although it's possible that the information superhighway in the future might be connected via cable television wire, fiber-optic cable, cellular transmissions, or satellite transmissions, for the time being it's connected with normal phone lines.

So, to merge onto the information superhighway, you need to connect your PC to your phone line. And once you have it connected, you need to get it to do something. This is where your modem comes in.

Your modem: The phone inside your PC

A modem is nothing more than a little telephone that's specially designed to work with a PC. That means it doesn't have a handset (because your computer doesn't have an ear or a mouth), although it does have a basic dialing apparatus. And, since a modem has to "talk" to your computer, a modem can also issue and receive commands to and from your PC.

A modem starts to work when it receives a specific command from your computer. (This command is most often generated by a communication software program, without direct intervention from you.) How does it work? Well, pretty much the same way you do when you want to use the phone: It picks up your telephone line and gets a dial tone, then dials a number specified by you, and waits for the call to connect. If the modem receives a busy signal, it hangs up, and might try again in a few seconds (or a few minutes, depending how you've told it to behave).

Fig. 28.1
At its most basic form, this is how the information superhighway works. Your PC sends a signal to your modem, which sends a signal over normal phone lines to another modem, which talks to that PC.

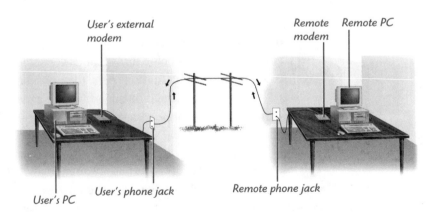

User's external modem

Remote modem   Remote PC

User's PC   User's phone jack

Remote phone jack

When a modem on the other end of the line answers, it issues a brief spurt of noise, a "hello, I'm a modem" signal. Your modem recognizes this noise and begins to "handshake" (negotiate the fine points of how the two will talk to one another). Once the two modems are connected, they begin "talking" to each other. That is, they start sending bits and bytes of data back and forth; this data can be commands, or output from your keyboard, or even a computer file. Whatever it is, it's sent from one modem to another modem over your phone line.

 Q&A

I only have one phone line. Can I still hook up a modem to my PC?

You bet! All modems allow a regular telephone signal to "pass through" without interruption when the modem isn't in use. Although a second, modem-only phone line is nice, it certainly isn't necessary.

When you're done with a **session**, the other modem issues a command to your modem to disconnect, which hangs up the phone line.

 Plain English, please!

A **session** (or **on-line session**) is the time you spend and the activities you do when connected to another machine or service via modem. Each session lasts from when the two modems first connect until when you hang up, ending the connection.

What can you do with a modem?

Now that you know how a modem works, you might be asking, "Yeah, but what can it do for me?" That's a fair question, and here are some answers:

- It can dial up other users to let you transfer information or just chat.
- It can **download** (copy) files from another computer or on-line service to your PC.

- It can let you exchange electronic mail with other computer users all over the world.

- It may be able to send and receive faxes, depending on the type of modem you have.

- It can help you chit-chat with a physicist from North Carolina about the benefits of cold fusion (or a favorite egg salad recipe).

- It can let you crush several "live" opponents while playing interactive multi-player PC games with other on-line users.

- It can help you get information about activities for active or retired military personnel by visiting Desert Nights, a bulletin board system based in Camp Pendleton, CA.

- It can connect to national commercial on-line services, such as CompuServe and America Online (see Chapter 32).

- It can connect to the Internet (see Chapter 33).

In short, your modem connects your computer (and therefore you) to the outside world. It enables you to communicate with other users, both individually and through large on-line services. It enables you to find and down-

Commanding your modem

Your modem doesn't just work by itself. It requires the proper communication software (discussed in Chapter 31, "Communications Packages") to tell it what to do.

Your communication software issues a series of **commands** to your modem, such as "dial this number, talk to the other modem like this," and so on. Most communication programs let you see these commands in their main windows as they are being executed.

You normally shouldn't have to worry about modem commands; your communication software does all the work for you. However, you may stumble across some on-line services that require you to add special commands to your normal command strings. When this happens, most communication programs make it easy to edit your command strings to insert new commands.

load files of all types and sizes. It even enables you to search giant electronic libraries of information and retrieve the data that best fits your needs.

Without a modem, you can't do any of this. So, unless you want to be a recluse cut off from the information superhighway, you need a modem.

Getting the right kind of modem

Once you decide to add a modem to your personal computer system, you're faced with a variety of choices. What kind of modem should you buy?

Inside or outside?

The first choice is simple—do you want an **internal** or **external** modem?

An internal modem (see fig. 28.2) has to be installed inside your PC. It looks like any other board inside your PC and slides into any empty slot inside the PC case. It's a little difficult to install, but—unlike an external modem—it doesn't take up any extra space on your desktop. Also, it doesn't use up any valuable connections on the back of your PC.

How to download a file

Downloading a file means you're copying it from another computer to your computer. **Uploading** a file means you're copying a file from your computer to another computer.

Today's communication programs (like ProComm Plus and WinComm Pro) make it easy to download files. In most cases, all you have to do is click a button or pull down a menu and your software automatically downloads the file.

To properly download a file, however, both your computer and the **host** computer (the one you're sending the file to) must be talking the same language, or **protocol**. There are several protocols for downloading files; they have names like Kermit, XMODEM, YMODEM, and ZMODEM. The protocol for downloading files on the Internet is called File Transfer Protocol (FTP).

Fig. 28.2

An internal modem, which hooks up *inside* your PC.

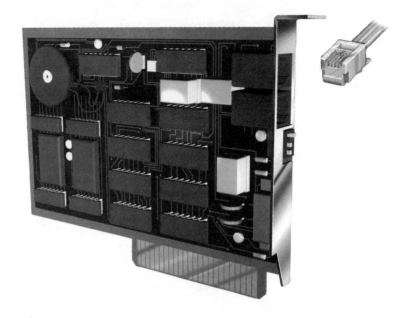

An external modem (see fig. 28.3) hooks up to the back of your PC. It's easy to install (just hook it up to an open connector on the back of your computer), but it has to be plugged into a separate power outlet and it takes up valuable desk space.

Which type of modem should you buy? Take a gander at the following table:

Table 28.1   Do I Need an Internal or External Modem?

Your computing needs	The modem you need
You don't want to mess around inside your PC.	External
You don't have an empty port (connector) on the back of your PC.	Internal
You need to move the modem from one PC to another.	External
You want to save a few bucks.	Internal
You like to look at little lights that tell you it's working.	External
You don't have extra room on your desk.	Internal

Fig. 28.3
An external modem, which hooks up to the back of your PC.

To fax or not to fax

Not only can you use a modem to communicate with other PCs, you can also use special **fax/modems** to send faxes to regular old fax machines. These modems work just like regular modems for normal communications, but also function as fax machines when you want to send or receive faxes.

Should you buy a fax/modem instead of a normal modem? Well, these days just about every modem on the market has fax capabilities. So as long as you're not paying extra for it, why not get a fax/modem? You never know when you might need to do some faxing—and using your PC is a pretty handy way to do it!

To use your fax/modem for faxing, you'll need specific fax software or regular communication software that includes fax capabilities. Most fax/modems come with software that will work just fine, or you can buy a program like WinFax Pro from your local computer store.

How fast can you go?

The speed of your modem determines how much time you'll spend on-line; a faster modem transmits data faster, which cuts down the time you spend on-line (which can save you money if you are being charged for the call or the connection). Think of it like a garden hose. The hose is always the same diameter, but if you increase the water flow you send more water through the hose.

Increasing modem speed is just like increasing water flow. The size of the hose (your telephone line) remains the same, but you pump more water (data) through the hose—which means you can water your lawn (e.g., move data to your hard disk) in less time!

Modem speed is measured in **bits per second**, or **bps**. This describes the number of data bits that your modem can transmit in a single second. Obviously, the higher the bps, the faster the modem.

In addition to simple modem speed, you'll see some modems described with "V" numbers, which is an optional way to describe performance. For example, a V.32 modem communicates at 9600 bps, and a V.FAST modem communicates at 28,800 bps. You don't need to worry too much about "V" numbers, however, because bps speed is almost always listed, too.

The only thing stopping you from buying the fastest modem available is the simple fact that *faster modems are more expensive!* So you probably want to balance speed with price, as shown in the following table:

Table 28.2   The Benefits of Different Modem Speeds

Speed	How good is it?
300 bps	Old and slow; not used anymore.
1200 bps	Still old, still slow; pretty much obsolete.
2400 bps	Slow but tolerable; still used by some older BBSs.
9600 bps	Moderate performance at a moderate price.
14,400 bps	Pretty zippy, but slightly more costly; necessary if you want to communicate with the Internet; pretty much the standard speed today.
28,800 bps	Today's best performance, but only found on the newest, most expensive modems; wait for the price to come down before you buy.

Which is the right speed for you? I recommend at least a 9600 bps modem; anything less just won't cut it if you do a lot of downloading or if you often visit highly graphical on-line services. If possible, spend a few extra bucks and go for a 14,400 bps model; in fact, if you're on the Internet, this is the bare minimum for acceptable performance. As for the new 28,000 bps modems, you probably want to wait until the price comes down a tad, especially since many BBSs and on-line services don't even operate at this speed yet.

Hooking it all up

When you get a new modem, you have to figure out how to hook it up and how to configure your system for the new modem.

The first part is pretty easy, especially if you have an external modem. See Chapter 3, "The First Day at Home: How to Hook It All Up," for detailed connection instructions. If you have an internal modem, you'll need to take the top off your CPU and follow the directions included with the modem (it's generally as easy as sliding the modem board into an empty slot).

Once your modem is in place, you need to install a communication software program. This program enables you to control your modem and get on-line. Popular programs (discussed in Chapter 31, "Communications Packages") include ProComm Plus and WinComm Pro.

Once you have it all hooked up, it's time to get on-line! See Chapter 32, "Going On-Line with Bulletin Boards and On-Line Services," for help on finding and connecting to BBSs and other on-line services.

❓ Q&A

When I dial a number, my modem won't connect.

This problem is usually caused by an incorrect configuration, which occurs when you select the wrong port or IRQ. You'll probably need to reconfigure either your modem or your communication software.

Techie talk about ports and IRQs

Before you can use your modem, you have to configure it and your system for proper operation. Although many modems come with their own configuration software programs, there is one important point you need to keep in mind.

For your modem to work properly, it has to be assigned to a particular **port** and **IRQ**. If you do this wrong, it won't work and it may cause other parts of your system to quit working, too!

The average PCs can have four ports, labeled COM1, COM2, COM3, and COM4, but most only have COM1 and COM2. Only one piece of equipment can be assigned to each port; so if you have your mouse hooked up to COM1, you'll need to connect your modem to another port, probably COM2.

Describing what an IRQ (interrupt **request**) does is more technical than we need to get into. If your trouble is with the IRQ, get a guru to help you out.

?Q&A

My modem disconnects in the middle of a call.

This can happen for a number of reasons. Most common is a noisy telephone line; your modem can't understand garbage in the line and hangs up. If you're using the Internet, you can also be disconnected if traffic gets too heavy at a particular site. In addition, picking up your telephone while your modem is working (or getting a call via Call Waiting) usually disconnects your modem. In any case, about the only cure for a disconnected modem is to reconnect!

?Q&A

When I use my modem I'm getting nothing but weird characters on my screen.

Garbage on your screen can be caused when your communication program isn't configured properly for the service you're dialing. Check the instructions for your on-line service and set up your software accordingly. (This problem can also be caused by noisy phone lines; you may need to manually disconnect and retry another connection.)

?Q&A

When I try to download a file, parts of it are missing.

This can happen if your on-line session is prematurely interrupted or if you're plagued by a noisy phone line. You'll probably have to attempt the download again.

29

Networks: Getting Connected

Networks make it possible to quickly share ideas, information, gossip, and the location of the doughnuts from this morning's management seminar.

In this chapter:

- What are networks and how do they help me?

- What makes up a network?

- What is a server-based network?

- What is a peer-to-peer network?

Networks turn a bunch of individual computers into a team of computers working cooperatively. Sports teams are more successful when the players work together and divide the responsibilities according to each player's skills. The more cohesive and organized the players are—and the better they communicate—the more successful the team becomes. Working together as a team brings the same benefits to a business organization, and a computer network makes sure that everyone in the office is on the same page of the "playbook."

Why would I use a network?

There are two primary reasons for using a network. The first is for easily sharing information with everyone on the network. The second is that networks allow each person on the network to access expensive, specialized hardware and software that they couldn't afford to purchase just for themselves.

Sharing information

Networks make it easy to keep co-workers updated on important company information. For example, with a network you could centrally store product specification sheets so that any updates are instantly available to everyone on the network. Or you may keep price lists on the network so that everyone is working with the same information. That way, no outdated information is mistakenly sent to a customer.

What makes up a network?

There are three necessary components to any network: a network operating system, network interface cards, and network cables.

Getting all the computers to work together as a team requires a special operating system (see Chapter 2 for info on what an operating system is). A **network operating system** (**NOS**) can organize and control all the different computers attached to the network—think of this operating system as the network equivalent of a sports team's coach. They just don't throw chairs.

The next necessary item is the **network interface card** (**NIC**). An NIC is a device that is installed inside your PC and allows your PC to see, hear, and talk with other computers on the network. Just as a New York Knick might yell to other players on his team, "I'm open. Pass me the ball," your PC's NIC can yell to other computers on the network, "I'm ready. Pass me some data." The NIC lets your PC coordinate its efforts with other computers on the network.

The final necessary piece of the network team is the **network cable**. The NICs are only able to communicate across the network cable. Your computers, once networked, are basically on a very busy conference phone call, with every computer either receiving or yelling out instructions across the network cable.

Passing notes to each other

Networks also allow co-workers to send memos and computer files to each other through popular **e-mail** systems (see Chapter 30, "What Is E-Mail?"). E-mail systems accelerate the distribution of important company information (like where we're all meeting after work!) and provide a means of tracking the receipt of each memo. No more "I didn't get that memo" or "No one told me about that" excuses—your e-mail system can prove that the information arrived and that it was even read! Unfortunately, it works in reverse as well, and you can't use lame excuses anymore, either.

All together now...

Everybody using the same software at the same time is no problem for a network. Network operating systems allow companies to run **multiuser software**, which is software that lets more than one person work with the same application simultaneously.

66 *Plain English, please!*

Multiuser systems let a whole bunch of people access the same data at the same time, a capability that used to be available only with a mainframe. 99

The most common multiuser programs are accounting programs. The data stored in accounting programs is usually divided into several files: customer, inventory, orders, accounts receivable, and accounts payable. These files are continually accessed by many different people. For example, order entry may be checking inventory to make sure they can fill a customer's order, while at the very same time someone in accounting is performing a credit check on that customer. The network makes certain everyone gets the information they need and that all conflicting requests for information are handled in an orderly fashion.

Sharing the good stuff

The ability to share resources allows a company to let each computer, printer, modem, or other piece of equipment do what it does best—just as a coach decides which players play best at certain positions.

Within an organization, there are many different types of computers. Some are very large and can store lots of information; others are better at graphics, and still others are speed demons that process information very quickly. All of these qualities are seldom found in one computer.

Networks make sure that everyone in the office utilizes the maximum amount of available resources.

I don't care about the other guy—how does sharing help me?

A great example might involve three different employees with three different computers and a printer. Suppose Bob's computer is relatively slow, but it has a large amount of disk space. Your computer is fast and great at graphics but has limited disk storage. Lori's computer is used mostly for printing color transparencies and is attached to a very fast, color laser printer.

Before being networked, you could only create smaller, less impressive graphics because you couldn't store the big files necessary for larger, more impressive graphics. You also had to carry your disk down to Lori's computer and wait for her to get out of your way so you could get printouts of your graphics.

If your company installed a network, you could "borrow" disk space from Bob's computer and you could also print to Lori's printer without carrying a disk to the other side of the office. By combining resources and playing off of each computer's strengths, a network results in a more flexible and productive team.

Making the techie's job easier

Another benefit of a network is that it makes it easier for a company to keep its software updated and trouble-free. From one location, the technical staff can update and manage the distribution of software across the entire network. These updates are like a football team's huddle—everyone gets updated at the same time by the same person.

What is a server-based network?

Server-based networks are built around specialized computers, called **servers**, that run a network operating system (refer to the earlier text box, "What makes up a network?"). Servers contain information or computing resources that need to be shared.

Once the servers are set up, the **workstations**, running normal PC operating systems, access either information stored on the server or resources attached to the server. A server's resources may include disk space, shared files, printers, modems, or other specialized hardware. In a server-based network, all the workstations can share the resources of the server.

Do I need a server-based network?

What is so great about a server-based network? These networks are typically faster, more secure, and better suited for use with multiuser applications. What's not so hot? They aren't quite as flexible as peer-to-peer networks (discussed later in this chapter) and may be overkill for smaller organizations.

What's with all this "client/server" talk?

A client (also called a workstation) is any computer accessing the services of another computer, which is called (you guessed it) a server.

With some network operating systems, a computer can be both a server and a client! That is, the computer shares some of its resources and stored information with other computers but can simultaneously use resources and information stored on other computers.

The coolest server-based products

The two leading server-based network products are Novell NetWare and...well, Novell NetWare. A competing product from Microsoft, LAN Manager, has gotten better with each new release but has made very little headway into a market largely dominated by Novell. Microsoft needn't feel bad, though, because no other network software manufacturer has made much of dent in Novell's market dominance, either.

NetWare, produced by Novell, Inc., is the industry's leading network operating system (NOS, remember?) software by a large margin. NetWare is supported by thousands of dealers and specially trained personnel worldwide.

NetWare is available in many different flavors and for many different-sized networks. Here is a partial list:

- *Personal NetWare.* This is a peer-to-peer product (see the next section) that is great for smaller networks.

- *NetWare 3.x.* Currently version 3.12, this is the most popular NOS. This product is great for medium-to-large networks.

- *NetWare 4.x.* This NOS is designed for very large networks, and includes special tools for organizing and managing the resources of a very large, or multi-location, network.

What is a peer-to-peer network?

Peer-to-peer networks aren't based around servers with specialized NOS software. With a peer-to-peer network, all the computers run some type of NOS and have the ability to share their information and resources (usually printers and disk space) with other computers on the network.

What's so great about peer-to-peer networks?

The great thing about peer-to-peer networks is their flexibility. Each user can make any part of his system available to other users on the network. If one day you suddenly feel like sharing your printer, you can set it so that everyone else can print to your printer. If it gets a little too noisy in your office, you can "disconnect" your printer from the network and have it all to yourself again. The same is true for any resource or data file on your system.

What's not so great about peer-to-peer networks?

The downside of peer-to-peer networks is that they are tougher to manage and control because the resources are spread out and not centralized on one server. Also, they typically don't perform as quickly as server-based networks. This is especially true if your computer is being used heavily by others on the network.

The coolest peer-to-peer products

The top two peer-to-peer networks are Windows for Workgroups by Microsoft and LANtastic from Artisoft, Inc. Both products can either work entirely on their own, or they can co-exist with other server-based networks like NetWare.

Windows for Workgroups

Microsoft Windows for Workgroups is the networking version of the incredibly popular Microsoft Windows program. Microsoft Windows for Workgroups lets you share any of your local resources (disk space, printers, modems—you get the picture by now) with your co-workers. It even communicates with today's more complex and capable fax machines and photocopiers. Talk about connected!

Windows for Workgroups comes with built-in group scheduling software and a set of network-management tools that make managing the network easier. All the features of Windows for Workgroups are expected to be standard features in the next release of Windows, which will be called Windows 95.

LANtastic

LANtastic (the current version is 6.0) is the other popular peer-to-peer network. Its main claim to fame is that it requires very little of your computer's memory to run.

LANtastic has a full suite of Windows and DOS applications that make managing the network easier. Artisoft also makes a full range of hardware designed to work with LANtastic, but LANtastic will work with hardware built by other companies.

30

What Is E-Mail?

In this chapter:

- Why all the excitement about e-mail?

- I want to send a message to the guy in marketing

- What the heck does <g> mean?

- I have so many messages in my mailbox, I can't find anything!

- I've heard you can send messages to the other side of the world in the blink of an eye. How?

E-mail is like a fax machine without the paper. Green Peace rejoice!

These days it seems like everybody's talking about "e-mail" and "the Net" and "on-line" and other such buzz. Why? Because it's changing the face of the world. Electronic mail and other computer-based communication methods are changing the way we work, the way we communicate, and even the way we socialize.

There are two basic types of e-mail: the kind you use on a regular network (like the one you probably have at work), and the kind you can send to people who aren't connected to your network (via "on-line" mail services). This chapter covers office e-mail. You'll learn about the other kind (such as CompuServe and America Online) in Chapter 32, "Going On-Line with Bulletin Boards and On-Line Services."

The quest for the paperless office

Most people are familiar with fax machines. You compose and print out your message, put it on your machine, dial a phone number, wait a few minutes, and poof! The same message comes out on another fax machine, miles and miles away.

Electronic mail programs, fondly (or not so fondly) referred to as **e-mail**, function similarly. Like a fax machine, you can send messages, receive them, forward them to others, and more. There's one big difference, however: No paper! It's all done electronically through your office's computer network or over regular phone lines.

Another important difference is that e-mail is lightning-quick! Certainly much faster than U.S. Mail (often called "snail mail" by e-mail users) or your interoffice mail system. Your message is delivered as fast as the network can deliver it (which is usually *really* fast).

Is an electronic mailbox the same as a regular mailbox?

When you start an office e-mail program, like Microsoft Mail or cc:Mail, you usually have to enter your username and a password, just like you do for any other network function. Your username usually works as your e-mail **address.** Like your mailbox at home, you usually have an electronic **mailbox**, or **Inbox**, where your mail is delivered and stays until you're done with it. If your office uses a program called cc:Mail, your screen will look a little like figure 30.1.

Fig. 30.1
So how much of this is
junk mail, and how
much is important???

Double-click here
to see what's in
your mailbox

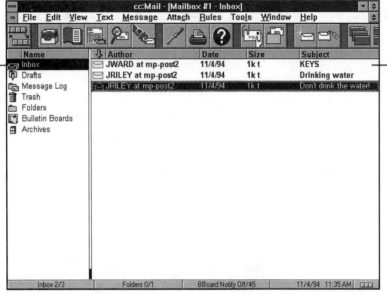

Here's all
your mail,
read and
unread

 Q&A | ***I forgot my password. What do I do?***

The person in charge of your company's network (the **system administrator**)
sets up the addresses and passwords for all e-mail users. That person can help
you find out what your password is and even help you change it to something
that's easier to remember.

How do I keep someone else from figuring out my password?

Be careful in choosing a password. Don't choose a number or phrase that's
publicly available, such as your phone extension, your employee number, or
your spouse's name. Choose something private like the name of the stray cat
you adopted when you were 10.

Let's play post office: Sending and receiving mail

All e-mail programs work differently, but the concept is the same no matter which package you have. And generally, they're pretty easy to use, as least for simple messages. For example, sending a message involves three basic steps:

1 Start a new message and address it. You can usually address a message to several people at once, or address it to a specific person and "cc" others.

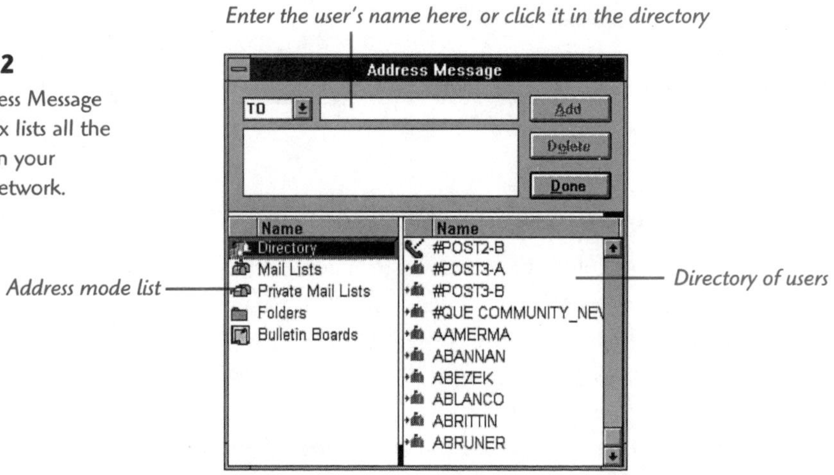

Enter the user's name here, or click it in the directory

Fig. 30.2

The Address Message dialog box lists all the people on your cc:Mail network.

Address mode list

Directory of users

2 Type the text of your message. Most e-mail programs let you just type a message as you would in a word processor, edit the message, and even spell check to find mistakes.

3 Send the message. Your message is sent to each recipient's mailbox, no stamps required!

Can I send a report or a spreadsheet as a message?

You can send just about any kind of document through the mail as long as it's in an envelope: checks, your resume, newspaper clippings from your aunt Selma's wedding, or a catalog (and don't we all get enough of those?!?). Similarly, you can attach almost any file(s) to almost any message and send it along with the message, like we're doing in figure 30.3. Sending the file as an attachment to an e-mail message doesn't alter the file at all; it arrives in its recipient's mailbox completely intact.

Fig. 30.3
Sending files through e-mail is a lot easier than copying them to a disk and carrying them up six flights of stairs!

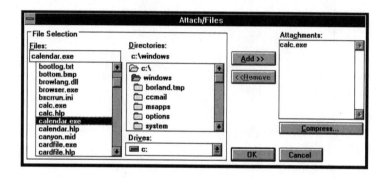

> *(Tip)*
>
> When you get a message that has an attachment and open the message to read it, you should use the Save As command from the File menu to save it to your hard drive.

File this, trash that, let that one sit there so I don't forget about it

When you want to read a message, you usually just have to click on it and it opens up. Once you've read a message, you can discard it or file it to view or use later.

Most e-mail packages let you create **file folders**, or **filing cabinets**, to store and organize messages you've received.

Fig. 30.4

Create the folder, then just drag a message into the folder where you want to store it.

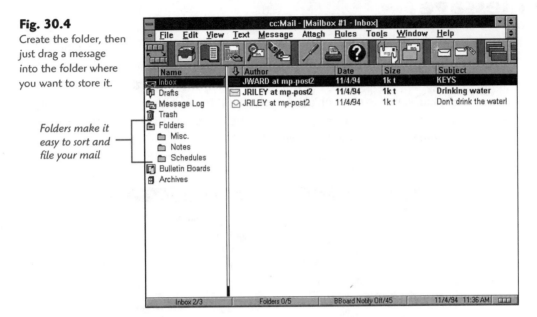

Folders make it easy to sort and file your mail

When you want to review a message you've filed in a folder, simply double-click on the folder to display its contents, then double-click on the message you want to read again.

Is this some kind of secret code or what?

Electronic messages can't convey the dynamics of vocal and visual cues normally expressed in your voice and face. Over time, an "electronic language" has developed among e-mail users to make up for the lacking human factor. Here are a few examples:

- To emphasize a particular word or add a particular inflection to your "voice," put asterisks around it, like *this*.

- If you're angry or want to really stress an important point, WRITE IT IN ALL CAPS! Don't use all caps all the time, however; it's considered the equivalent of shouting, which is very rude.

- Many common phrases have been boiled down to acronyms, like IMHO (In My Humble Opinion) and ROTFL (Rolling On The Floor Laughing).

- Some e-mail users like to actually write the intended emotion along with their text:

    Hey, congratulations on your promotion! Does that mean you're buying lunch?<grin>

    or

    The boss just announced mandatory overtime this weekend.<groan>

- One of the cleverest parts of this new language are **emoticons**, or **smileys**. If you tilt your head to the left, they resemble a face, and they convey what you're feeling. (Okay, so you have to use your imagination a little.) Here are some smiley examples:

: -)	I'm smiling or happy; that's a joke.
: 0	I'm yawning; that's boring.
; -)	I'm winking at you or what you just said.
: - (	I'm sad or sorry about that.
> : - (	I'm angry or annoyed.
=8 -)	I'm wearing glasses and a flat-top.

So which program should I use?

Generally, when you're working on a network, you have to use the e-mail program that's installed on that network. You really don't have a choice. Having all the users on one package ensures that the communications will work smoothly. It's also a lot less confusing!

Here's a description of the most common e-mail programs, as well as a mention of some other e-mail packages that are available.

cc:Mail

cc:Mail is the leading e-mail package for networks. It's made by Lotus Development Corp. (you know, as in Lotus 1-2-3?). The screen pictures shown so far in this chapter are from cc:Mail.

cc:Mail is available for both DOS and Windows. The Windows version offers easy-to-use SmartIcons, which give you that familiar Windows point-and-click capability that you're growing to know and love.

Microsoft Mail

Also available for Windows or DOS is Microsoft Mail from Microsoft Corp. (Bet you couldn't have guessed that.) Like cc:Mail, Microsoft Mail offers all the features described in this chapter, including simple buttons you can point at and click to create and send messages, and folders for storing messages.

Fig. 30.5

Microsoft Mail also offers an Outbox you can use to store messages before you send them.

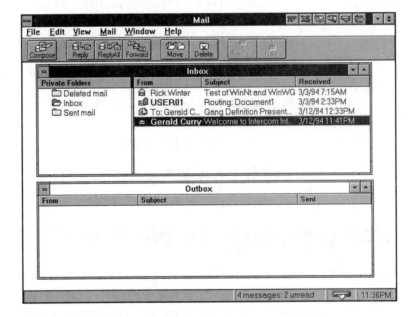

How can I send e-mail to my clients (or cousins) in Timbuktu?

If interoffice e-mail isn't enough for you, there are special **on-line services** you can join specifically for e-mail. If you have a client or friend you communicate with a lot, you should try one of these services. Sending e-mail is a thousand times faster than conventional mail and *much* less expensive than overnight services. Examples of this service include MCIMail and SprintNet, but there are numerous other services out there.

Usually, you pay a flat fee per month and you're allowed to send a certain number of messages. If you exceed that number of messages, you're then charged per message. If you're familiar with "measured" telephone service, you'll understand what this is all about.

To use one of these services, you need a modem (you'll remember these clever devices from Chapter 28). This exception aside, they work about the same as network e-mail: create the message, address it, and send it (over the modem through the service).

 E-mail can be habit-forming. Don't spend so much time using e-mail that you forget to do your work!

31
Communications Packages

In this chapter:

Without communications software, about all you can do with your modem is dial; you can't send messages or download or do anything to promote world peace.

In this chapter:

- Do I really need a communications package?
- What does communications software do?
- But is there a communications software relevant to what I do?
- What's an on-line session like?

Back in Chapter 28, "Hooking Up to the Information Superhighway with a Modem," you learned all about modems and how they connect your computer to the outside world through normal telephone lines. The modem serves as your passport to the wonderful world of on-line communication, but the passport isn't the trip, is it? You see, your modem only connects you to other computers—it doesn't help you do anything once you get connected.

To do anything on-line, you need special **communications software**. Communications software gives the directions that your modem needs to properly connect to other computers.

(Tip)

With the right software, you can use your modem to send faxes to and receive faxes from other computers and fax machines.

What does communications software do?

Communications software issues strings of commands to your modem. These commands instruct your modem to do various things at various times. Basic communications programs do at least these things:

- Pick up the phone line and get a dial tone

- Dial the number

- Connect when it hears a tone from the other computer

- Display a screen of information from the other computer

- Relay signals and instructions from your computer to the other computer

- Download files from the other computer to your computer

- Send and retrieve messages and e-mail between the two computers

 Plain English, please!

When you copy a file from another computer to your personal computer, that's called **downloading** the file to your PC. When you send a file, on the other hand, it's called **uploading**.

More advanced communications software allows you to save electronic "address books" with frequently dialed phone numbers. With some software, you even can automatically log on to other computers through "scripts" that contain the necessary commands.

 When you download program files (files with EXE or COM extensions) from other computers, you run the risk of infecting your computer with a **computer virus**. See Chapter 34, "Taking Care of Your Disks and Files," for details on how to stay safe.

How to choose the right communications software

There are a variety of communications programs on the market. They all pretty much do what you need them to do—some just pay more attention to certain types of tasks. To make things simple, let's just take a look at three core programs.

Simple (and free): Windows Terminal

Windows Terminal is the communications package included with Microsoft Windows (it's in the Accessories group—see fig. 31.1). It's a fairly easy program to use, in part because it doesn't have a lot of advanced features.

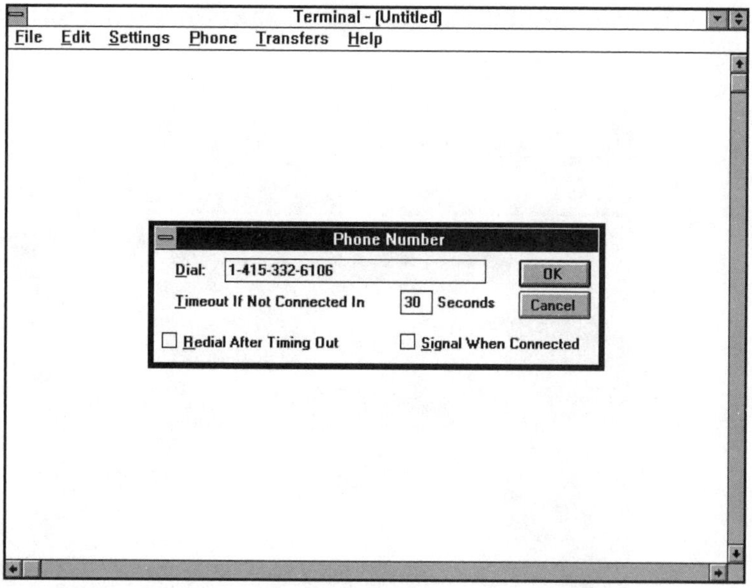

Fig. 31.1

Simple communications software you already own—Windows Terminal.

If you don't do a lot of on-line communicating, you can probably get by with Windows Terminal. Terminal isn't a very robust package, but the price is right! If you plan to participate in on-line cruising more than once a week, however, you probably want to invest in a more fully-featured program.

An all-around performer: ProComm Plus for Windows

ProComm Plus is a program that's been around a long, long time. Consequently, the program has evolved into what may be the best all-around communications program available. Just look at what you get with the latest version of ProComm Plus:

- Basic on-line communications

- Automated logon scripts

- Multiple dialing directories (address books)

- Basic fax operation

ProComm Plus is a good program to use for most basic on-line communications (see fig. 31.2). It's easy to use, yet powerful when you need advanced features.

Fig. 31.2

Good software for computer communications—ProComm Plus for Windows.

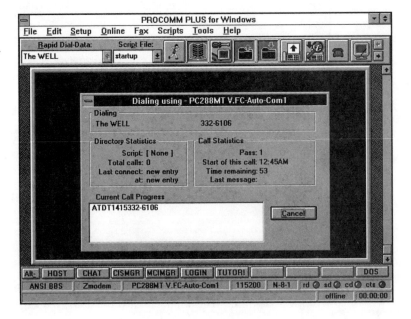

When you need the fax: WinFax Pro for Windows and the Delrina Communications Suite

WinFax Pro is a program specifically designed for sending and receiving faxes with your personal computer (sure, ProComm Plus does faxing, but WinFax Pro does it better). WinFax Pro includes numerous predesigned fax cover sheets and can automatically receive faxes when you're away from your computer. You can also program it to "broadcast" a single fax to hundreds of different recipients.

But what if you need to do faxing *and* normal PC communications? Then turn to a combination of products called the Delrina Communications Suite. This product includes WinFax Pro and its sister product, WinComm Pro (see fig. 31.3). WinComm Pro does most of what ProComm Plus does but has the added benefit of working alongside WinFax Pro.

Fig. 31.3
The best software for faxing from your PC—WinFax Pro for Windows.

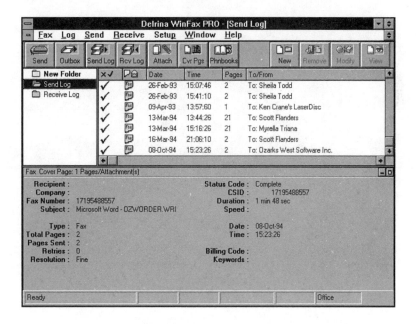

Which software is right for me?

Perhaps the best thing to do at this point is to list some common communications needs and then match them up with the right programs. And to help speed you through this process, table 31.1 provides a brief roadmap to help choose the right software for your needs.

 **{Note}**

How frequently you use bulletin board systems will have an impact on what kind of software you need. See Chapter 32, "Going On-Line with Bulletin Boards and On-Line Services," for more details on BBSs.

Table 31.1   Finding the Right Communications Software for Your Needs

Your needs:	The right software:	Looks like this in Windows:
Occasional BBS use, no faxing	Windows Terminal	
Occasional or regular faxing, no BBS use	WinFax Pro	
Regular BBS use, occasional or no faxing	ProComm Plus	
Regular faxing, occasional or regular BBS use	Delrina Communications Suite (WinFax Pro & WinComm Pro)	

Once I get the modem and the communications program, how do I get on-line?

An on-line session is really quite simple. And the process is pretty much the same no matter what service you're connecting to.

The following steps walk you through a typical on-line session:

1 Start your communications software.

2 Tell your software where you want to connect to (what phone number). If you work in an office that requires you to dial 9 first for outside calls, make sure you add a 9 and a comma (so it looks like 9,) to the beginning of the number. The comma is a special character that tells the modem to wait a bit for a dial tone before dialing the rest of the number.

⊛ {Note}
Most software lets you keep frequently dialed numbers in an electronic address book (you know, that speed-dial concept). Otherwise, you have to enter the phone number manually.

3 Tell your software to start the connection process. Most software will display some strange-looking commands on-screen (see fig. 31.4). These commands tell your modem to get ready, make sure you have a dial tone on your phone line, and then dial the number you entered.

This line dials the number
This line confirms the reset
This line resets your modem

Fig. 31.4

These weird command lines indicate the commands your software is sending to your modem.

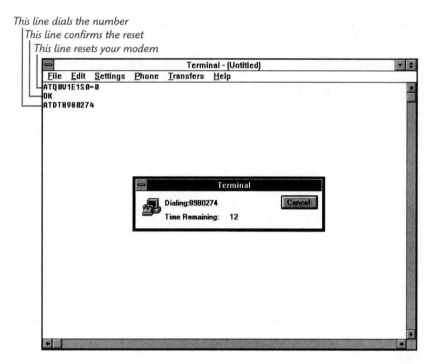

4 You'll hear a dial tone from your modem, and then the sound of your modem dialing the phone number. When the modem at the other end of the line answers, you'll hear a loud static-like noise, the same kind of sound you hear when your fax machine is working. When your modem hears this noise, it knows to finalize the connection to the other system.

5 When the connection is finalized, you'll see the service you dialed appear on your computer monitor (see fig. 31.5).

Fig. 31.5

Your modem dialed and your communications software kicked in, and next thing you know—you're on-line!

```
┌─────────────────────── Terminal - [Untitled] ──────────────────── ▼ ◆ ┐
│ File  Edit  Settings  Phone  Transfers  Help                           │
│ Main menu:                                                          ▲   │
│                                                                    ▒    │
│ [M].............Message menu          [F].................File menu      │
│ [C]....Comments to the sysop          [B].............Bulletin menu     │
│ [P]............Page the sysop         [I]...Initial welcome screen      │
│ [Q]............Questionnaire          [S].......System statistics       │
│ [D]...................Doors           [N]...............Newsletter      │
│ [G].......Goodbye & Logoff            [H]..............Help level       │
│ [?]...........Command help            [J].........Join conference       │
│ [K].....New Caller Verifier           [T]............... Wildchat       │
│ [A]......Local Weather Report                                          │
│                                                                        │
│ ConF: "[0] - Mail Boxes (Private)", time on 4, with 5 remaining.       │
│                                                                        │
│ Main menu: [M F C B P I Q S D N G H ? J K T A] ? █                      │
│                                                                        │
│                                                                        │
│                                                                    ▼    │
│ ◄ ►                                                                ► │  │
└────────────────────────────────────────────────────────────────────────┘
```

It's really that easy—enter the number and tell the software to go. Everything else is completely automated!

⑦ Q&A

> ### Why won't my communications program dial?
>
> If your software won't dial, there are several things to check. Is your modem properly installed and configured? Is your modem connected to your phone line? Is your communications software properly configured for your modem?

32
Going On-Line with Bulletin Boards and On-Line Services

Once you get started on-line, you'll find it hard to quit. After you're hooked, you might talk yourself into paying any price for the satisfaction of dialing up!

In this chapter:

- What is a BBS?
- What do on-line services really offer?
- How much does an on-line service cost?
- How do I sign up for an on-line service?
- What are the leading commercial services?
- Which type of service is best for me?
- Is the Internet an on-line service?

Now that you have your modem up and running and you've learned how to operate your communication program, it's time to log onto an on-line service.

Browsing through an on-line service is kind of like walking through your hometown. You pass the post office, the newsstand, the video arcade, the library, and all sorts of small shops, stopping to chat with other passersby once in a while. When you connect to an on-line service, you find pretty much the same activities—only electronically.

Playing postman with electronic mail

One of the prime uses of any on-line service is the ability for users to exchange electronic mail (discussed in Chapter 30, "What Is E-Mail?"). E-mail is nothing more than a message sent electronically. No paper, no envelope, no stamp—just words and an address. Unlike regular mail, e-mail arrives where it's meant to, almost instantaneously.

Getting the latest scoop

Most on-line services provide some sort of news service. This may range from a simple "top of the news" bulletin on a local **BBS** (**bulletin board system**), to a full Associated Press newsfeed on CompuServe or America Online. In any case, on-line is a great place to get up-to-the-minute news, weather, and sports information.

Chewing the fat

If you've never done it, you might find it difficult to believe. But it's possible—and popular—to "talk" to other users of an on-line service. That is, you can use your computer keyboard to send **real-time messages** back and forth in what are called on-line **chat** sessions. Most services allow private (one-on-one) chats, as well as multiple-user conversations, often called **conferences**. Really, it's a great way to meet new people—even if you never get to look them in the face!

 Plain English, please!

A real-time conversation is like the kind you have on the phone: you and the person on the other end of the line communicate back and forth with no delay. Contrast this with, say, playing "phone tag," where you and someone else are forced to leave detailed messages on each other's answering machines. E-mail messages are sort of "phone tag" on the information superhighway.

Playing games

If you like to play games—either by yourself or with a partner—you can't do better than a good on-line service. On-line, you can find lots of single-player games, as well as (on some services) the ability to engage other users in multiplayer action and adventure games. (It beats playing checkers at the barber shop!)

Bringing home interesting files

One of the most popular parts of any on-line service is the file library area. This is where you can find files—pictures, lists, software programs, you name it—that you can download directly to your computer. It's like having a giant software giveaway at the end of your phone line!

Shopping, shopping, shopping!

In addition to all the free files you can download, many on-line services (particularly the commercial ones) provide on-line electronic shopping areas. From these services you can browse through and order all sorts of merchandise. It's like peeking inside your PC and finding the Home Shopping Network, complete with cubic zirconia!

Browsing through electronic libraries

When you need to do some information research, you can head to your handy encyclopedia or down to your local library—or you can jump on-line. You see, commercial on-line services provide massive electronic libraries of information of just about any sort you can imagine. Want to check a company's performance? Look up incidence of repair for a particular make of toaster oven? Search through some old magazine articles? You can do all this—and more—on-line.

Getting technical support

And if all that isn't enough, you can also use on-line services to find answers to any computer problems you might have. Most major software and hardware companies maintain a significant presence on the commercial on-line services. You can go on-line and talk directly to technical specialists who can help you solve software and hardware problems.

How much does it cost and how do I sign up?

Okay, you're sold. You want to join an on-line service. But what's involved?

It costs *how much?*

First, you need to decide which service (or services) to join. Depending on your needs, you may be satisfied with a local BBS, or you may need to subscribe to a large, national, commercial service. Either way, it'll probably cost you money.

While some local BBSs are still free, many are now charging for access. Typically, you send them a check (or give them your credit card number), and you get "x" number of hours of access. However, local BBSs are probably the biggest on-line bargains; you can get by for $10 or less a month with most systems.

Commercial services, however, aren't nearly as low-priced. While CompuServe, Prodigy, and America Online all offer a variety of pricing plans, you'll probably end up spending at least $30 a month—more if you want to access some of their more exclusive services.

Is it worth it? That's up to you. But I'll tell you this—once you get started on-line, you'll find it hard to quit. After you're hooked, you might talk yourself into paying any price for the satisfaction of dialing up!

All right, where do I sign?

With local BBSs, joining is normally as simple as having your modem dial the phone number of the BBS, and then typing the answers to a few questions. You normally have to pick an on-line nickname for yourself, as well as a secret password. (This is so no one else can log on using your name—and your bank account!)

With the commercial services, you can buy an official membership kit. These kits, available at most software retailers, cost around $20-$30, and give you everything you need for instant on-line access—including special connection software. In addition, most of the services offset the cost of the kit with an equal amount of free on-line time. So to join CompuServe or other on-line services, it's as easy as installing a new piece of software and following some on-screen instructions.

 Q&A

> **I've changed my mind—I don't want to use an on-line service anymore. Is it hard to quit?**
>
> No, not really. Although it varies from service to service, you shouldn't have any problem canceling your subscription. In fact, several services offer 30-day trial memberships where you get to try them out before making a commitment. Even if the service you joined doesn't offer a trial membership period, it probably either offers a way to cancel your subscription on-line or via a quick phone call.

The smallest services: Bulletin board systems

Remember when I said cruising an on-line service was like walking through your hometown? Well, a BBS is more like a *small* town—not a lot of variety and with modest offerings of local interest only.

What you'll find on a typical BBS

Most local BBSs offer the following features:

- Bulletin boards for notices of local events
- E-mail and messaging
- File libraries for downloading
- Games

In addition, many local BBSs also offer connections to larger national networks. Some BBSs are even providing access to the **Internet** (see Chapter 33 for more information about the Internet)! BBSs that offer these features enable their users to connect with users across the nation.

In general, though, most BBSs stay local in their focus. If you want a more national or global perspective, you need to join one of the commercial services or get on the Internet.

On the plus side, however, the best place to meet local users and find out items of local interest is on your local BBS. I find myself logging onto several local BBSs (see fig. 32.1), even though I subscribe to the national services— for the same reason I read both my local newspaper and the *Wall Street Journal*. I need local *and* national news.

Fig. 32.1

The opening screen of Sight & Sound BBS (617-894-5990), a large BBS specializing in laser discs.

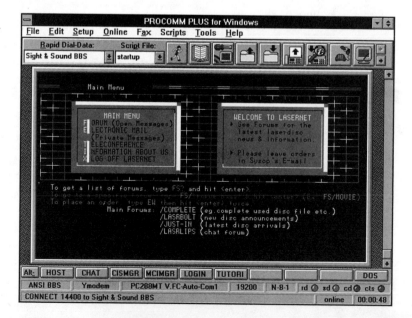

Finding the best BBSs

There are literally tens of thousands of BBSs in the United States. How do you find the one that has the features you need? One of the best sources of information about different BBSs is *Que's BBS Directory*. Here's a short list of some of the country's best BBSs:

Table 32.1   A Sampler of the Top BBSs in the U.S.

BBS	Location	Number	Comments
Burn This Flag	San Jose, CA	408-363-9766	Devoted to controversial subjects.
CT Adult Connections	Farmington, CT	203-889-0735	Lots of adult pictures and chat.
CD-ROM Specialty	Thousand Oaks, CA	805-373-2965	Tens of thousands of shareware, freeware, and public domain programs via CD-ROM.
Desert Nights	Camp Pendleton, CA	619-430-7734	Information and files of interest to military personnel.
Dissociation Network	Albany, NY	518-462-6134	Devoted to social work, mental health, mutual support, and the medical profession.
GIFt Shop	Concord, CA	510-689-4686	Lots and lots of graphics files (in the GIF format), including adult graphic images.
Japanese Network	Brooklyn, NY	718-833-5949	Specializing in Asian issues—it even has an option for Japanese language text!
Public Brand	Indianapolis, IN	317-856-2087	The premier source for shareware software.
Sports Club	Pasadena, CA	818-792-4752	Devoted to sports fans of all types.
The WELL	San Francisco, CA	415-332-6106	One of the nation's oldest and most impressive BBSs. Always worth checking out.

Plain English, please!

The files and programs you'll find on-line are either **shareware** or **freeware**. Shareware authors ask that you pay them a modest registration fee if you decide to keep and use their programs. By paying this fee, you'll usually receive documentation and information on future versions of the program. Since shareware registration payments are based solely on "the honor system," it's up to you to make sure you pay for any shareware you find useful. Freeware authors, on the other hand, don't ask for any fees for use of their programs.

To find a BBS near you, dial the User Group Locator at 914-876-6678 (using your voice phone).

The big services: Commercial systems

If cruising a BBS is like walking the streets of a small town, joining a commercial on-line service is like moving to the big city. All of a sudden you have access to *thousands* of shops and services, and you can run into an incredible variety of people on the street. The newspapers are bigger and more comprehensive, the libraries have much more to offer, and so on.

Get on-line for free with community FreeNets

In addition to traditional BBSs (most of which have some sort of use fee) and commercial on-line systems (all of which cost money), there is one other way to get connected—and this way is free. **FreeNets** are community-based BBSs that provide a way for citizens to get on-line at no charge.

Communities provide FreeNet access to their citizens as a community service; it's like an electronic town hall. FreeNets are normally nonprofit organizations, funded by government sources and corporate donations.

Most FreeNets assemble information of specific interest to their communities. You might find local news items, community calendars, lists of public-service organizations, and other such information. In addition, many FreeNets now feature free access to the Internet.

Starting simple with Prodigy

The easiest commercial service to use is Prodigy. Prodigy was formed as a joint venture between IBM and Sears and designed to be accessible by all levels of computer users.

Prodigy features a very simple interface (see fig. 32.2), with large type and big navigation buttons. Among Prodigy's features are

- News, weather, and sports coverage

- Business and finance information

- Entertainment news

- E-mail and messages

- On-line shopping

- On-line travel reservations

In addition, Prodigy has recently added access to the Internet newsgroups (sort of an electronic messaging and discussion center arranged by topic), as well as the ability to send and receive messages to and from the Internet.

Fig. 32.2

It's easy to find your way around Prodigy.

I find Prodigy to be kind of like an on-line service with training wheels. That is, it's easy to get up and going with Prodigy, but you really can't go too far or too fast. Specifically, Prodigy doesn't offer the breadth or depth of services offered by competitors like CompuServe or America Online. It's a good way to learn about the world of on-line services, but you might find yourself yearning for a bigger on-line service soon.

Expanding your horizons with America Online

America Online (AOL) is the fastest-growing on-line service today. With more than one million users, AOL provides a variety of services to the average computer user. AOL looks and feels a bit more sophisticated than Prodigy, but it's really just as easy to use (see fig. 32.3). Almost everything is done by clicking a button or selecting a menu item, which is pretty easy.

America Online offers the following types of services to users:

- News, weather, and sports
- A large selection of national newspapers and magazines in electronic format
- Stock market and financial services
- On-line shopping
- E-mail and messages
- A variety of **departments**, or on-line neighborhoods, for special interests
- Live on-line chat

In addition, AOL has recently added several types of Internet access, including newsgroups, e-mail, and **Gopher**, an Internet searching tool.

Even though AOL isn't my primary service, I do like it. It's probably the best place to get packaged information, especially periodicals. In addition, many companies are hooking up with AOL for exclusive services, including MTV, DC Comics, NBC, and the *New York Times*. It's definitely worth a look.

Fig. 32.3
Lots of options are
available on America
Online.

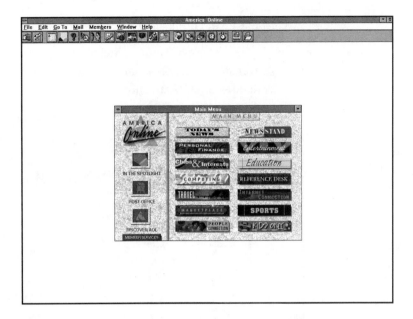

Going global with CompuServe

CompuServe is the world's largest commercial on-line service and is truly global. (You can get versions of the CompuServe operating software in German and French!) While CompuServe isn't hard to use, it does require a little more skill than Prodigy or America Online (see fig. 32.4). But you'll be rewarded for your work by the largest selection of different services of any on-line service.

Here's what CompuServe offers:

- The largest number of special-interest forums of any commercial service

- News, weather, and sports

- Stock market and financial services

- A vast repository of information in searchable electronic databases

- On-line shopping

- E-mail and messages

- Live on-line chat

- Several of the Internet features, including newsgroups, e-mail, and **FTP** (for *file transfer protocol*—a fancy term for a tool that lets you transfer files from one computer to another).

Fig. 32.4
CompuServe, the on-line service for professionals (and dedicated amateurs).

For the slightly more experienced computer user, CompuServe could be the service of choice. The variety is much greater here, and the user traffic is livelier. In addition, CompuServe better serves research needs, while offering all the amenities of the other services.

The biggest service: The Internet

In the next chapter we'll talk about the Internet. I'm mentioning it here only because some people confuse it with BBSs and commercial services. The truth is, the Internet isn't local and isn't commercial. It's a conglomeration of individual computers and computer networks, joined together in a giant web that spans the globe. So you'll find individual services (of various sorts) on the Internet, even though the Internet itself isn't a service. The Internet offers more on-line resources than any one of the commercial providers alone do. Got that? If not (or even if you do but want to know more), turn to Chapter 33 for more information.

Which service is for you?

Let's wrap this up with a table that will hopefully direct you to the type of service best suited to your needs.

Table 32.2   Choosing the Right Service for You!

Your computing needs	Type of service
Adult interests	Local BBS (specializing in adult graphics and chat)
E-mail	America Online, CompuServe
Entertainment news	America Online, Prodigy, CompuServe
Family use	Prodigy
Games	Local BBS (specializing in games), CompuServe
Graphics files	Local BBS (specializing in graphics), CompuServe
Learning the on-line ropes	Prodigy
Local interests	Local BBS
Minimal Internet access	America Online, CompuServe
On-line chat (not limited to local)	America Online, CompuServe
On-line chat (with local users)	Local BBS
On-line news and magazines	America Online
On-line research	CompuServe
On-line shopping	Prodigy, America Online, CompuServe
Software files	Local BBS (specializing in shareware), CompuServe
Special interest forums	America Online, CompuServe
Stock market & financial services	America Online, CompuServe
Technical support	CompuServe
Travel reservations	CompuServe, America Online, Prodigy

33 The Internet

In this chapter:

- Why is everyone talking about the Internet?

- What can the Internet do for me?

Unless you live in a cave, you have already heard or read about the Internet.

Did you know that Internet users are part of a revolution? That may seem like a strong statement, but the Internet *is* a revolution, or at least part of one. It's the Communication Revolution. An age in which a large percentage of our daily activities (entertainment, education, news, financial transactions, shopping, and communication) occur via electronic communications.

⊛ {Note}

The Internet is a many-tentacled beast whose workings are much too complex to cover in this space. The information in this chapter will enable you to speak with some authority on what the Internet is and some of the stuff available on it. To actually *use* the Internet, however, you'll need more information. Many books are available on the subject of the Internet; one we highly recommend is Que's *Using the Internet.*

Everybody's talking about the Internet

One clear sign of a revolution is when all forms of mass media, including the popular press, cover the events of the revolution. That has surely happened with the Internet. In fact, unless you live in a cave, you have already heard or read about the Internet. Consider this:

- Each weekend a National Public Radio announcer asks listeners to send comments about the show to an Internet mail address (**wesun@npr.org**).

- The Canadian Broadcasting Corporation (CBC) maintains an Internet Web site (**http://debra.dgbt.doc.ca/cbc/cbc.html**) where you can download actual radio shows to your personal computer.

 **{Note}**

Don't be alarmed by all these bold letters and symbols. They're all different types of Internet addresses, and as you become familiar with the Internet you'll understand Internet addressing as well as you understand how to address and mail a letter to Aunt Harriet.

- Is print your medium of choice? *Time, Newsweek, The Wall Street Journal*, and *USA Today* have all had stories about the Internet.

- Perhaps you'd like to read news stories on-line. The Electronic Newsstand (**gopher.enews.com:70/11**) offers Internet access to articles in publications as diverse as *Business Week, Inc. Magazine, Computerworld, Canoe & Kayak*, and *Federal Employees News Digest.*

- Let's not forget television. When you get onto the Internet, you'll find newsgroups devoted to discussion of just about every TV program you can imagine, including some—like *Twin Peaks* (**alt.tv.twin-peaks**)— you thought had disappeared.

What can the Internet do for me?

The saying goes "if we were all the same, the world would be a very dull place." Well, the Internet is anything but dull. No matter what your profession, weekend pastime, or personal hobby, you can find valuable (and fun!) resources and people who share your interests. For example:

- *You need some more software programs for your computer.*

  Connect with computers at the University of Michigan, Washington University, and University of Iowa—all have programs that you can bring to your computer.

- *You'd like to see photographs of distant planets.*

  Visit one of NASA's Internet computers (see fig. 33.1). You can even view a collection of images from the Hubble Space Telescope.

Fig. 33.1
NASA has several computers connected to the Internet. This shows an interactive map where you click on a section of the country to go to a specific NASA site. NCSA Mosaic is the software program that is shown.

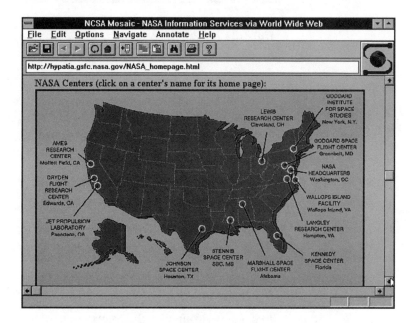

- *You are interested in the rights and welfare of children.*

  Try the UNICEF Internet Gopher computer, where you can browse through newsletters, press releases, legislative issues, and speeches that deal with the rights and conditions of children around the world (see fig. 33.2).

Fig. 33.2
UNICEF maintains an Internet computer that has a variety of information devoted to improving the welfare of children. WinGopher is the software program.

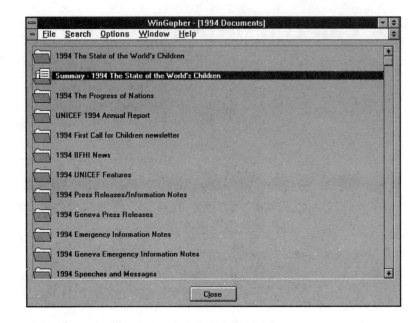

- *Your son or daughter wants to know exactly how tall a Tyrannosaurus Rex really was.*

  Try an interactive museum of dinosaurs located on a computer at the Honolulu Community College in Hawaii (**http://www.hcc.hawaii.edu/dinos/dinos.1.html**). View drawings of dinos and photos of fossils of these prehistoric creatures—oh, and you'll learn that old T. Rex stood 13 feet tall (check out fig. 33.3).

- *You always wanted a hot, red sports car.*

  Subscribe to the exotic cars mail list (**exotic-cars-request@sol.asl.hitachi.com**) to get into regular discussions about exotic and rare automobiles, including maintenance and what it's like to drive these cars.

- *You need to know what's going on in the world.*

  Join a newsgroup like **clari.news.urgent**—you'll get the major news stories of the day, as shown in figure 33.4.

Fig. 33.3

Come face-to-face with T. Rex at this interactive multimedia display about dinosaurs that is on a computer in Hawaii.

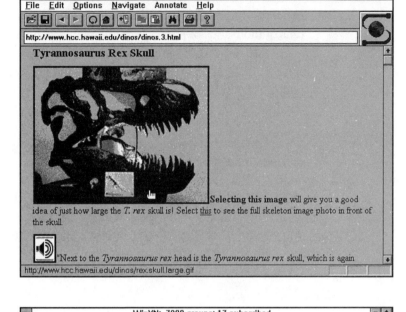

Fig. 33.4

All the hottest, late-breaking news stories can be found in the **clari.news.urgent** newsgroup. WinVN is the newsgroup software program shown.

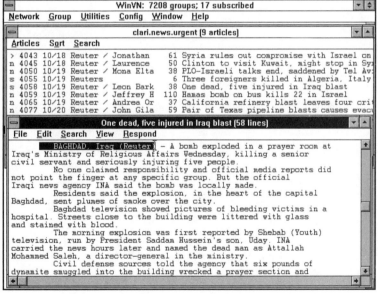

This diversity of information is partially due to the fact that no single person, company, or government owns the Internet. The Internet is an affiliation of tens of thousands of private, commercial, academic, and government-supported networks that exist in more than 80 countries around the world. It is a collaboration among many different computer systems and millions of people. The Internet has been called a "network of networks," and that's just what it is. (For more information on networks, see Chapter 29.)

When you connect your personal computer with the Internet, you can share data and information with all the millions of other people who are connected.

This chapter has merely whetted your appetite, hasn't it? Now that you know all the possibilities of life on the Internet, you know you're dying to try it. And you should! It's a big old world out there, and the Internet can bring it all home to you.

34

Taking Care of Your Disks and Files

Keeping your computer running right requires a bit of regular housekeeping—some file neatening here, some memory cleaning there, and more.

A friend's slightly mad great Aunt Helen filled up her cavernous house with nearly 80 years of leather-bound books, back issues of *Life* and *National Geographic*, stacks of newspapers dating back to Prohibition, etc.

The packrat system is fine if you're filling up a house. But when you are a *computer* packrat, you fill up valuable hard disk space if you don't clean up old files.

How to start cleaning up the mess

Your files can be sorted into several categories:

- *Files that you currently need.* This category includes any files that you access frequently, including programs on your hard drive and files for current projects.

- *Files that you may need again.* Files in this category include old documents, letters, and work that you've finished with for the time being but may want to refer to later.

- *Files that you'll never need again.* This category includes things like duplicate files, temporary files, backups of files you've already deleted, or any other files that you're absolutely sure you'll never refer to again.

There are a couple of things you can do to rearrange files to free up hard disk space. First, you can delete any files that you're sure you'll never need again. Second, you can move files you may need again onto floppy disks. You can also **compress** files on your hard drive, as described later in this chapter, to free up space. And you should make sure that the files you need are protected by backing them up, described later in this chapter.

Delete those temporary files

Many programs create **temporary files** on your hard disk. Normally, such programs delete the temporary files when you exit the program, but sometimes temporary files get left behind (such as when your system crashes before you exit the program). Often, these temporary files have the file extension TMP. When you're at the DOS prompt, you can delete any files with the TMP extension. Use the DOS DIR command, as described in Chapter 11, to find any TMP files.

 **<Caution>** When scanning your hard drive for files you no longer need, you may run across files whose names you don't recognize. There are many files on your hard drive that you may not use directly but which are required for programs to run properly. Never delete a file unless you know exactly what that file is!

Make backup copies of files you need

The most obvious thing to say about files you need is that you shouldn't delete them from your hard drive! You should, however, keep a full **backup** of every important file, a task that you can perform in a couple of ways.

One way to protect key files is to make sure you save every important file to both your hard disk and to a floppy disk. This way, if you have a hard drive problem or accidentally delete a file from your hard disk, you can copy the file back to the hard disk.

The trouble with this method is that it's difficult to manage. You can forget to make a copy of every file. Worse, you can't always know exactly what files are important to what program. A database program, for example, may actually create several files every time you save your work. Are you sure you know which ones to save to a floppy?

When working with a particular program for an extended period of time, make sure you save your work every five minutes or so. Now and then, copy the file you're working with to a floppy drive, just in case. It's better to lose an hour's work than a whole day's worth!

Take a "snapshot" of your hard drive daily

Another way to preserve key files is to back up your hard drive once a week. This involves running a special backup program that reads every file on your hard disk and then transfers those files (in a special format) to floppy disks. It's like taking a snapshot of everything on your hard disk at that moment in time.

DOS comes with a program called MS Backup that you can use to back up the data from your hard disk to floppy disks. This program comes in both DOS and Windows versions, so no matter which operating system you use, you can be sure that your valuable data is safe.

Squeeze the fat out of files with disk compression

The best way to deal with files you may need in the future, but don't need now, is to **compress** them with a program called PKZIP and then store the compressed files on a floppy disk.

PKZIP is a special utility program that takes a file and squeezes it down to its smallest possible size. You then can store the file on a disk without it taking up as much room as the full file would. When you want to use the file again, you use a program called PKUNZIP to bring the file back to its normal size (**decompress** it).

PKZIP and PKUNZIP are exclusively DOS programs. There are no Windows versions. However, there is a clever Windows program called WinZip that lets you use PKZIP and PKUNZIP from Windows. Moreover, WinZip makes using the ZIP programs as easy as clicking a couple of buttons.

Can I *really* double the space on my hard disk?

When you need more hard disk space, especially if you have a laptop, the cheapest and easiest solution is to use a program sometimes referred to as a **disk doubler**. The name comes from the fact that these programs can painlessly and invisibly double (or nearly double) the amount of data your hard disk can hold.

Doubling your disk space is like packing for a trip. You start out with clothes spread all over the bed. When you neatly fold them and arrange the clothes, you can cram an awful lot of them into your suitcase. A disk doubler program "folds and arranges" your files so more of them can fit in a given disk space.

There are two leading disk doubler programs:

- Microsoft's **DriveSpace**, formerly known as **DoubleSpace**. If you have DOS 6.x, you already have DoubleSpace or DriveSpace.

- Stac Electronics' **Stacker**. You may want to consider Stacker even if you already have DriveSpace or DoubleSpace because Stacker is currently the only product that can actually *more* than double your disk space.

⊛ {Note}———| Some files are more easily compressed than others. For example, a program file (one with an EXE extension) may compress only 20 percent, whereas a text file usually compresses around 50 percent. To really put a twist on the average compression, some graphics files can be compressed by over 90 percent! As you can see, how much space you end up with on your drive depends on the types of files you have stored on the drive.

How disk doublers work

Disk compression files such as PKZIP make files smaller. But your programs probably can't use a compressed file. To use the file again, you have to return the file to its regular size.

The folks who make disk doubling programs thought it would be cool if your computer could automatically compress and uncompress files as necessary. You wouldn't have to do the work, and your hard disk drive would seem to have a lot more space because everything was compressed most of the time.

⊗<Caution>—| The process of compressing a hard drive may take quite a while—maybe *hours*.

⊛ {Note}———| To work, disk doubling programs must automatically load a special program into your computer's memory when you start your computer. Just like any program, the disk doubler takes up room in memory. Programs that require as much free memory as possible (usually games) may not run when you're using a disk doubler.

Freeing up more memory

If you've been bumping into a lot of programs that won't run due to a lack of memory, a little organizing of how your computer uses its memory may save the day. Although this sounds like a highly technical task, users of DOS 6.x have a wonderful little program called MEMMAKER that can handle this chore automatically. When you run MEMMAKER, it determines the best way to load the various programs and drivers you need to have in memory at start-up time, leaving you with as much free memory as possible.

After MEMMAKER finishes shuffling things around on your system, you'll probably have a lot more free memory than before. You may even find that programs that wouldn't run before now load up without a hitch.

(!) (Tip)

> You can rerun MEMMAKER any time you like. You might want to rerun MEMMAKER, for example, after you've added something like a mouse, CD-ROM drive, or sound card to your computer. This is because these devices need driver programs loaded at start-up time. MEMMAKER can shuffle the drivers around in memory so that you have the cleanest system possible.

Tidying up your hard disk

Hard-disk space, just like memory, is often at a premium. You want as much of it as you can get, and you want it to be as fast as it can be. Unfortunately, hard-disk drives don't always operate perfectly. Over time, small areas of the drive can get "lost" and become unavailable to the system. Also over time, information on a hard drive gets more and more scattered, making the system work harder to find that information. This causes the hard disk to run more slowly. Luckily, recent versions of DOS come with two programs that fix these two problems.

Recovering lost clusters

Those little areas of the hard drive that get lost are called **lost clusters**. The more lost clusters you have on your hard drive, the less space you have for your data. To remedy this situation, DOS comes with a handy program called ScanDisk (an earlier version was called CHKDSK, short for "check disk") that can scan your hard drive, finding and recovering those lost clusters.

Both programs are pretty simple to use but do have some special details that you should know about. For more information, consult your DOS documentation or use the DOS Help system in Version 6.x.

Defragmenting your hard drive

It takes longer to get out the door for your morning run if your shorts are in the wash, your windbreaker is in the basement, and your shoes are in the garage. Your hard drive sometimes slows down for much the same reason—everything is scattered all over. This problem's called **fragmenting** because, rather than files always being stored all in one place on the hard disk, different pieces of files are stored in different places on the disk. Loading a fragmented file takes more time, and so it slows down the system.

A **defragmenting program** fixes your hard drive. Such a program scans your drive looking for all the little, scattered pieces of files and bringing them back together in one place. DOS 6.x comes with a program called DEFRAG (see fig. 34.1).

Fig. 34.1
This is DOS's DEFRAG program. Other defragmentation utilities are also available as part of The Norton Utilities and PC Tools.

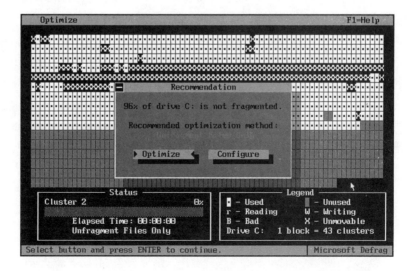

My computer's been acting funny, and someone said it might have a virus

A computer **virus** is a prank or sabotage program that attaches itself to files that you copy to your hard disk, usually from a floppy disk. Once a virus infects your computer in this way, it performs operations that are annoying or damaging. For example, a virus can delete valuable program files, corrupt existing data files, or copy itself hundreds of times to fill up your hard disk.

Removing a virus from a computer system is often a difficult task. For example, a virus that controls the computer's operating system can intercept commands you issue to the computer. If you try to remove the virus, the virus may protect itself by not allowing the computer to respond to the command.

Luckily, the current anti-virus programs (such as those that come with DOS 6.x, The Norton Utilities, and PC Tools) are pretty good at searching out and destroying these destructive mini-programs.

You can drastically reduce your chances of computer virus infection by following a few simple rules:

- Avoid booting your system from a floppy. If, for some reason, you must boot from a floppy, boot from a floppy that you've checked for viruses.

- Download programs only from reputable BBSs or commercial on-line services. All downloaded software should be treated with suspicion, but if you run a program you obtained from a pirate BBS, you significantly increase your chances of a virus infection.

- Do not run pirated software. Use commercial products purchased at a reputable store that are still in their shrink-wrapped packages. Pirated versions of commercial software are infamous for carrying viruses.

- Be sure to run the contents of any floppies through an antivirus program before installing files to your hard disk.

{ Index }

PLUG YOURSELF INTO...

The MCP Internet Site

Free information and vast computer resources from the world's leading computer book publisher—online!

Find the books that are right for you!

A complete online catalog, plus sample chapters and tables of contents give you an in-depth look at *all* our books. The best way to shop or browse!

✦ **Stay informed** with the latest computer industry news through discussion groups, an online newsletter, and customized subscription news.

✦ **Get fast answers** to your questions about MCP books and software.

✦ **Visit** our online bookstore for the latest information and editions!

✦ **Communicate** with our expert authors through e-mail and conferences.

✦ **Play** in the BradyGame Room with info, demos, shareware, and more!

✦ **Download software** from the immense MCP library:
   - Source code and files from MCP books
   - The best shareware, freeware, and demos

✦ **Discover hot spots** on other parts of the Internet.

✦ **Win books** in ongoing contests and giveaways!

Drop by the new Internet site of Macmillan Computer Publishing!

To plug into MCP:

World Wide Web: http://www.mcp.com/
Gopher: gopher.mcp.com **FTP:** ftp.mcp.com

GOING ONLINE DECEMBER 1994!